YOUR MOST COMPREHENSIVE AND REVEALING INDIVIDUAL FORECAST

SUPER HOROSCOPE

CANCER

19 98

June 21 - July 20

B

BERKLEY BOOKS, NEW YORK

The publishers regret that they cannot answer
individual letters requesting personal horoscope information.

1998 SUPER HOROSCOPE CANCER

PRINTING HISTORY
BERKLEY TRADE EDITION / AUGUST 1997

The Putnam Berkley World Wide Web address is
http://www.berkley.com

ISBN: 0-425-15889-6

CONTENTS

THE CUSP-BORN CANCER

Are you *really* a Cancer? If your birthday falls during the fourth week of June, at the beginning of Cancer, will you still retain the traits of Gemini, the sign of the Zodiac before Cancer? And what if you were born late in July—are you more Leo than Cancer? Many people born at the edge, or cusp, of a sign have difficulty determining exactly what sign they are. If you are one of these people, here's how you can figure it out, once and for all.

Consult the cusp table on the facing page, then locate the year of your birth. The table will tell you the precise days on which the Sun entered and left your sign for the year of your birth. In that way you can determine if you are a true Cancer—or whether you are a Gemini or Leo—according to the variations in cusp dates from year to year (see also page 17).

If you were born at the beginning or end of Cancer, yours is a lifetime reflecting a process of subtle transformation. Your life on Earth will symbolize a significant change in consciousness, for you are either about to enter a whole new way of living or are leaving one behind.

If you were born during the fourth week of June, you may want to read the Gemini book as well as Cancer. Because Gemini holds the keys to the more hidden sides of your personality, many of your dilemmas and uncertainties about the world and people around you can be revealed. You can tune in to your secret wishes, and your potential for cosmic unfoldment.

Although you feel you have a lot to say, you will often withdraw and remain silent. Sometimes, the more you say the more confused a situation can get. Talking can drain you, and you are vulnerable to gossip. You feel secure surrounded by intimates you can trust, but sometimes the neighbors—even your own relatives— seem to be talking behind your back and you sense a vague plot in the air.

You symbolize the birth of feeling, the silent but rich condition of a fertilized seed growing full with life. The family is always an issue. At best you are a "feeling" type whose power of sensing things remains a force behind everything you think and do.

If you were born the fourth week of July, you may want to read the horoscope book for Leo as well as Cancer, for Leo could be your greatest asset. You need a warm embrace, the comfort and safety of being cared for, protected, fed. You need strong ties to the past, to the family. Attachments are natural for you. You want

4

to be your own person, yet you often find ties and attachments prohibiting you from the rebirth you are anticipating. You may find it hard to separate yourself from dependencies without being drawn backward again and again.

You symbolize the fullness of growth, the condition of being nearly ripe, the new life about to emerge from the shadows into the sunshine.

THE CUSPS OF CANCER

DATES SUN ENTERS CANCER (LEAVES GEMINI)

June 21 every year from 1900 to 2000, except for the following:

June 20	June 22		
1988	1902	1915	1931
92	03	18	35
96	06	19	39
	07	22	43
	10	23	47
	11	26	51
	14	27	55

DATES SUN LEAVES CANCER (ENTERS LEO)

July 23 every year from 1900 to 2000, except for the following:

July 22				
1928	1953	1968	1981	1992
32	56	69	84	93
36	57	72	85	94
40	60	73	86	96
44	61	76	88	97
48	64	77	89	98
52	65	80	90	

THE ASCENDANT: CANCER RISING

Could you be a "double" Cancer? That is, could you have Cancer as your Rising sign as well as your Sun sign? The tables on pages 8–9 will tell you Cancer people what your Rising sign happens to be. Just find the hour of your birth, then find the day of your birth, and you will see which sign of the Zodiac is your Ascendant, as the Rising sign is called. The Ascendant is called that because it is the sign rising on the eastern horizon at the time of your birth. For a more detailed discussion of the Rising sign and the twelve houses of the Zodiac, see pages 17–20.

The Ascendant, or Rising sign, is placed on the 1st house in a horoscope, of which there are twelve houses. The 1st house represents your response to the environment—your unique response. Call it identity, personality, ego, self-image, facade, come-on, body-mind-spirit—whatever term best conveys to you the meaning of the you that acts and reacts in the world. It is a you that is always changing, discovering a new you. Your identity started with birth and early environment, over which you had little conscious control, and continues to experience, to adjust, to express itself. The 1st house also represents how others see you. Has anyone ever guessed your sign to be your Rising sign? People may respond to that personality, that facade, that body type governed by your Rising sign.

Your Ascendant, or Rising sign, modifies your basic Sun sign personality, and it affects the way you act out the daily predictions for your Sun sign. If your Rising sign indeed is Cancer, what follows is a description of its effect on your horoscope. If your Rising sign is not Cancer, but some other sign of the Zodiac, you may wish to read the horoscope book for that sign as well.

With Cancer on the Ascendant, that is, in the 1st house, the ruling planet of the 1st house is the Moon. The Moon here gives you an especially keen ability to sense patterns and changes in the environment. The Moon in this position makes you more than just receptive; it makes you reactive and adaptive. You can integrate the most fleeting, irrational impressions received from the environment. There is, however, the danger that such sensory overload, so to speak, could inhibit your ability to act appropriately in a given situation.

Cancer in the 1st house accentuates your ambitiousness. Tenac-

6

ity, a strong Cancer trait, is translated here into a highly developed power of focus. You can focus your energy on several levels at once—social, emotional, even psychic—in order to realize your aims. But always the scene of struggle and realization is personal rather than public, concrete rather than abstract. Your three basic loves—food, home, money—are all personal ones. Power is not a burning issue for you, but on the other hand, concepts of right and wrong are. You may also hide behind your concepts, posing as a more intellectual person than you really feel, whenever you become too timid to express your strongly emotional nature.

Sympathy and sensitivity are basic personality traits for Cancer Rising. That combination may lead to a subjective view of the world, one which has little in common with the views of other people. For that reason, you may appear to be shy, when in fact you are merely retiring from a possible occasion of misunderstanding or conflict. You prefer to protect yourself and those you love from any pain or suffering. You want to provide a comfortable haven for all the hurt creatures of the world. You can, therefore, be labeled a homebody or a mothering type.

Although the concept of home is central in your life, you are not a stick-in-the-mud; indeed, you do not necessarily like to be rooted in one place. You would like a family, to nurture and protect it, to develop and instill pervasive attitudes of right conduct. If you don't have a natural family, you will be happy serving a community cause, even if that service takes you far and wide and results in reversals of fortune along the way. There may be many travels and voyages in the lifetimes of those of you with Cancer Rising. Home is where your heart is. Possessions, too, have little meaning for you unless they are connected with a special person or intimate situation.

Supportiveness to others continually wars with inner insecurity, making you doubt the value and extent of your attachment. You need to feel appreciated by everyone in your immediate environment. Emotional satisfaction may be more compelling than honor and success. You could enter secret love affairs or alliances just for the personal gratification they provide, and despite the dangers they pose. There may be an aura of mystery surrounding you, inspired partly by your fondness for secrets, partly by your hidden, inaccessible, unsteady emotionality, partly by your success in isolation; some of you may engender enemies and long-standing rivals as a result.

Intuition and imagination are the key words for Cancer Rising. You can put them to use in the service of a fruitful lifestyle, or you can squander them in complaints. You are at your best when you are building something.

RISING SIGNS FOR CANCER

Hour of Birth*	Day of Birth		
	June 20–25	June 26–30	July 1–5
Midnight	Pisces; Aries 6/22	Aries	Aries
1 AM	Aries	Taurus	Taurus
2 AM	Taurus	Taurus	Taurus
3 AM	Gemini	Gemini	Gemini
4 AM	Gemini	Gemini	Gemini; Cancer 7/3
5 AM	Cancer	Cancer	Cancer
6 AM	Cancer	Cancer	Cancer
7 AM	Cancer; Leo 6/23	Leo	Leo
8 AM	Leo	Leo	Leo
9 AM	Leo	Leo; Virgo 6/30	Virgo
10 AM	Virgo	Virgo	Virgo
11 AM	Virgo	Virgo	Virgo
Noon	Virgo; Libra 6/24	Libra	Libra
1 PM	Libra	Libra	Libra
2 PM	Libra	Libra; Scorpio 6/29	Scorpio
3 PM	Scorpio	Scorpio	Scorpio
4 PM	Scorpio	Scorpio	Scorpio
5 PM	Scorpio; Sagittarius 6/23	Sagittarius	Sagittarius
6 PM	Sagittarius	Sagittarius	Sagittarius
7 PM	Sagittarius	Sagittarius; Capricorn 6/27	Capricorn
8 PM	Capricorn	Capricorn	Capricorn
9 PM	Capricorn	Aquarius	Aquarius
10 PM	Aquarius	Aquarius	Aquarius
11 PM	Pisces	Pisces	Pisces

*Hour of birth given here is for Standard Time in any time zone. If your hour of birth was recorded in Daylight Saving Time, subtract one hour from it and consult that hour in the table above. For example, if you were born at 9 AM D.S.T., see 8 AM above.

Hour of Birth*	Day of Birth		
	July 6–10	July 11–17	July 18–23
Midnight	Aries	Taurus	Taurus
1 AM	Taurus	Taurus	Taurus; Gemini 7/19
2 AM	Gemini	Gemini	Gemini
3 AM	Gemini	Gemini	Gemini
4 AM	Cancer	Cancer	Cancer
5 AM	Cancer	Cancer	Cancer; Leo 7/23
6 AM	Leo	Leo	Leo
7 AM	Leo	Leo	Leo
8 AM	Leo	Leo; Virgo 7/15	Virgo
9 AM	Virgo	Virgo	Virgo
10 AM	Virgo	Virgo	Virgo; Libra 7/23
11 AM	Libra	Libra	Libra
Noon	Libra	Libra	Libra
1 PM	Libra	Libra; Scorpio 7/15	Scorpio
2 PM	Scorpio	Scorpio	Scorpio
3 PM	Scorpio	Scorpio	Scorpio; Sagittarius 7/23
4 PM	Scorpio; Sagittarius 7/7	Sagittarius	Sagittarius
5 PM	Sagittarius	Sagittarius	Sagittarius
6 PM	Sagittarius	Capricorn	Capricorn
7 PM	Capricorn	Capricorn	Capricorn
8 PM	Capricorn	Aquarius	Aquarius
9 PM	Aquarius	Aquarius	Pisces
10 PM	Pisces	Pisces	Pisces; Aries 7/22
11 PM	Pisces; Aries 7/7	Aries	Aries

*See note on facing page.

THE PLACE OF ASTROLOGY IN TODAY'S WORLD

Does astrology have a place in the fast-moving, ultra-scientific world we live in today? Can it be justified in a sophisticated society whose outriders are already preparing to step off the moon into the deep space of the planets themselves? Or is it just a hangover of ancient superstition, a psychological dummy for neurotics and dreamers of every historical age?

These are the kind of questions that any inquiring person can be expected to ask when they approach a subject like astrology which goes beyond, but never excludes, the materialistic side of life.

The simple, single answer is that astrology works. It works for many millions of people in the western world alone. In the United States there are 10 million followers and in Europe, an estimated 25 million. America has more than 4000 practicing astrologers, Europe nearly three times as many. Even down-under Australia has its hundreds of thousands of adherents. In the eastern countries, astrology has enormous followings, again, because it has been proved to work. In India, for example, brides and grooms for centuries have been chosen on the basis of their astrological compatibility.

Astrology today is more vital than ever before, more practicable because all over the world the media devotes much space and time to it, more valid because science itself is confirming the precepts of astrological knowledge with every new exciting step. The ordinary person who daily applies astrology intelligently does not have to wonder whether it is true nor believe in it blindly. He can see it working for himself. And, if he can use it—and this book is designed to help the reader to do just that—he can make living a far richer experience, and become a more developed personality and a better person.

Astrology and Relationships

Astrology is the science of relationships. It is not just a study of planetary influences on man and his environment. It is the study of man himself.

We are at the center of our personal universe, of all our relationships. And our happiness or sadness depends on how we act, how we relate to the people and things that surround us. The emotions that we generate have a distinct effect—for better or worse—on the world around us. Our friends and our enemies will confirm this. Just look in the mirror the next time you are angry. In other words, each of us is a kind of sun or planet or star radiating our feelings on the environment around us. Our influence on our personal universe, whether loving, helpful, or destructive, varies with our changing moods, expressed through our individual character.

Our personal "radiations" are potent in the way they affect our moods and our ability to control them. But we usually are able to throw off our emotion in some sort of action—we have a good cry, walk it off, or tell someone our troubles—before it can build up too far and make us physically ill. Astrology helps us to understand the universal forces working on us, and through this understanding, we can become more properly adjusted to our surroundings so that we find ourselves coping where others may flounder.

The Challenge of Love

The challenge of love lies in recognizing the difference between infatuation, emotion, sex, and, sometimes, the intentional deceit of the other person. Mankind, with its record of broken marriages, despair, and disillusionment, is obviously not very good at making these distinctions.

Can astrology help?

Yes. In the same way that advance knowledge can usually help in any human situation. And there is probably no situation as human, as poignant, as pathetic and universal, as the failure of man's love.

Love, of course, is not just between man and woman. It involves love of children, parents, home, and friends. But the big problems usually involve the choice of partner.

Astrology has established degrees of compatibility that exist between people born under the various signs of the Zodiac. Because people are individuals, there are numerous variations and modifications. So the astrologer, when approached on mate and marriage matters, makes allowances for them. But the fact remains that some groups of people are suited for each other and some are not, and astrology has expressed this in terms of characteristics we all can study and use as a personal guide.

No matter how much enjoyment and pleasure we find in the different aspects of each other's character, if it is not an overall compatibility, the chances of our finding fulfillment or enduring happiness in each other are pretty hopeless. And astrology can help us to find someone compatible.

Astrology and Science

Closely related to our emotions is the "other side" of our personal universe, our physical welfare. Our body, of course, is largely influenced by things around us over which we have very little control. The phone rings, we hear it. The train runs late. We snag our stocking or cut our face shaving. Our body is under a constant bombardment of events that influence our daily lives to varying degrees.

The question that arises from all this is, what makes each of us act so that we have to involve other people and keep the ball of activity and evolution rolling? This is the question that both science and astrology are involved with. The scientists have attacked it from different angles: anthropology, the study of human evolution as body, mind and response to environment; anatomy, the study of bodily structure; psychology, the science of the human mind; and so on. These studies have produced very impressive classifications and valuable information, but because the approach to the problem is fragmented, so is the result. They remain "branches" of science. Science generally studies effects. It keeps turning up wonderful answers but no lasting solutions. Astrology, on the other hand, approaches the question from the broader viewpoint. Astrology began its inquiry with the totality of human experience and saw it as an effect. It then looked to find the cause, or at least the prime movers, and during thousands of years of observation of man and his *universal* environment came up with the extraordinary principle of planetary influence—or astrology, which, from the Greek, means the science of the stars.

Modern science, as we shall see, has confirmed much of astrology's foundations—most of it unintentionally, some of it reluctantly, but still, indisputably.

It is not difficult to imagine that there must be a connection between outer space and Earth. Even today, scientists are not too sure how our Earth was created, but it is generally agreed that it is only a tiny part of the universe. And as a part of the universe, people on Earth see and feel the influence of heavenly bodies in almost every aspect of our existence. There is no doubt that the Sun has the greatest influence on life on this planet. Without it there would be no life, for without it there would be no warmth, no division into day and night, no cycles of time or season at all. This is clear and easy to see. The influence of the Moon, on the other hand, is more subtle, though no less definite.

There are many ways in which the influence of the Moon manifests itself here on Earth, both on human and animal life. It is a well-known fact, for instance, that the large movements of water on our planet—that is the ebb and flow of the tides—are caused by the Moon's gravitational pull. Since this is so, it follows that these water movements do not occur only in the oceans, but that all bodies of water are affected, even down to the tiniest puddle.

The human body, too, which consists of about 70 percent water, falls within the scope of this lunar influence. For example the menstrual cycle of most women corresponds to the 28-day lunar month; the period of pregnancy in humans is 273 days, or equal to nine lunar months. Similarly, many illnesses reach a crisis at the change of the Moon, and statistics in many countries have shown that the crime rate is highest at the time of the Full Moon. Even human sexual desire has been associated with the phases of the Moon. But it is in the movement of the tides that we get the clearest demonstration of planetary influence, which leads to the irresistible correspondence between the so-called metaphysical and the physical.

Tide tables are prepared years in advance by calculating the future positions of the Moon. Science has known for a long time that the Moon is the main cause of tidal action. But only in the last few years has it begun to realize the possible extent of this influence on mankind. To begin with, the ocean tides do not rise and fall as we might imagine from our personal observations of them. The Moon as it orbits around Earth sets up a circular wave of attraction which pulls the oceans of the world after it, broadly in an east to west direction. This influence is like a phantom wave crest, a loop of power stretching from pole to pole which passes over and around the Earth like an invisible shadow. It travels with equal effect across the land masses and, as scientists were recently amazed to observe, caused oysters placed in the dark in the middle of the United States where there is no sea to open their shells to receive the nonexistent tide. If the land-locked oysters react to this invisible signal, what effect does it have on us who not so long ago in evolutionary time came out of the sea and still have its salt in our blood and sweat?

Less well known is the fact that the Moon is also the primary force behind the circulation of blood in human beings and animals, and the movement of sap in trees and plants. Agriculturists have established that the Moon has a distinct influence on crops, which explains why for centuries people have planted according to Moon cycles. The habits of many animals, too, are directed by the movement of the Moon. Migratory birds, for instance, depart only at or near the time of the Full Moon. And certain sea creatures, eels in particular, move only in accordance with certain phases of the Moon.

Know Thyself—Why?

In today's fast-changing world, everyone still longs to know what the future holds. It is the one thing that everyone has in common: rich and poor, famous and infamous, all are deeply concerned about tomorrow.

But the key to the future, as every historian knows, lies in the past. This is as true of individual people as it is of nations. You cannot understand your future without first understanding your past, which is simply another way of saying that you must first of all know yourself.

The motto "know thyself" seems obvious enough nowadays, but it was originally put forward as the foundation of wisdom by the ancient Greek philosophers. It was then adopted by the "mystery religions" of the ancient Middle East, Greece, Rome, and is still used in all genuine schools of mind training or mystical discipline, both in those of the East, based on yoga, and those of the West. So it is universally accepted now, and has been through the ages.

But how do you go about discovering what sort of person you are? The first step is usually classification into some sort of system of types. Astrology did this long before the birth of Christ. Psychology has also done it. So has modern medicine, in its way.

One system classifies people according to the source of the impulses they respond to most readily: the muscles, leading to direct bodily action; the digestive organs, resulting in emotion; or the brain and nerves, giving rise to thinking. Another such system says that character is determined by the endocrine glands, and gives us such labels as "pituitary," "thyroid," and "hyperthyroid" types. These different systems are neither contradictory nor mutually exclusive. In fact, they are very often different ways of saying the same thing.

Very popular, useful classifications were devised by Carl Jung, the eminent disciple of Freud. Jung observed among the different faculties of the mind, four which have a predominant influence on character. These four faculties exist in all of us without exception, but not in perfect balance. So when we say, for instance, that someone is a "thinking type," it means that in any situation he or she tries to be rational. Emotion, which may be the opposite of thinking, will be his or her weakest function. This thinking type can be sensible and reasonable, or calculating and unsympathetic. The emotional type, on the other hand, can often be recognized by exaggerated language—everything is either marvelous or terrible—and in extreme cases they even invent dramas and quarrels out of nothing just to make life more interesting.

The other two faculties are intuition and physical sensation. The sensation type does not only care for food and drink, nice clothes and furniture; he or she is also interested in all forms of physical experience. Many scientists are sensation types as are athletes and nature-lovers. Like sensation, intuition is a form of perception and we all possess it. But it works through that part of the mind which is not under conscious control—consequently it sees meanings and connections which are not obvious to thought or emotion. Inventors and original thinkers are always intuitive, but so, too, are superstitious people who see meanings where none exist.

Thus, sensation tells us what is going on in the world, feeling (that is, emotion) tells us how important it is to ourselves, thinking enables us to interpret it and work out what we should do about it, and intuition tells us what it means to ourselves and others. All four faculties are essential, and all are present in every one of us. But some people are guided chiefly by one, others by another. In addition, Jung also observed a division of the human personality into the extrovert and the introvert, which cuts across these four types.

A disadvantage of all these systems of classification is that one cannot tell very easily where to place oneself. Some people are reluctant to admit that they act to please their emotions. So they deceive themselves for years by trying to belong to whichever type they think is the "best." Of course, there is no best; each has its faults and each has its good points.

The advantage of the signs of the Zodiac is that they simplify classification. Not only that, but your date of birth is personal— it is unarguably yours. What better way to know yourself than by going back as far as possible to the very moment of your birth? And this is precisely what your horoscope is all about, as we shall see in the next section.

WHAT IS A HOROSCOPE?

If you had been able to take a picture of the skies at the moment of your birth, that photograph would be your horoscope. Lacking such a snapshot, it is still possible to recreate the picture—and this is at the basis of the astrologer's art. In other words, your horoscope is a representation of the skies with the planets in the exact positions they occupied at the time you were born.

The year of birth tells an astrologer the positions of the distant, slow-moving planets Jupiter, Saturn, Uranus, Neptune, and Pluto. The month of birth indicates the Sun sign, or birth sign as it is commonly called, as well as indicating the positions of the rapidly moving planets Venus, Mercury, and Mars. The day and time of birth will locate the position of our Moon. And the moment—the exact hour and minute—of birth determines the houses through what is called the Ascendant, or Rising sign.

With this information the astrologer consults various tables to calculate the specific positions of the Sun, Moon, and other planets relative to your birthplace at the moment you were born. Then he or she locates them by means of the Zodiac.

The Zodiac

The Zodiac is a band of stars (constellations) in the skies, centered on the Sun's apparent path around the Earth, and is divided into twelve equal segments, or signs. What we are actually dividing up is the Earth's path around the Sun. But from our point of view here on Earth, it seems as if the Sun is making a great circle around our planet in the sky, so we say it is the Sun's apparent path. This twelvefold division, the Zodiac, is a reference system for the astrologer. At any given moment the planets—and in astrology both the Sun and Moon are considered to be planets—can all be located at a specific point along this path.

Now where in all this are you, the subject of the horoscope? Your character is largely determined by the sign the Sun is in. So that is where the astrologer looks first in your horoscope, at your Sun sign.

The Sun Sign and the Cusp

There are twelve signs in the Zodiac, and the Sun spends approximately one month in each sign. But because of the motion of the Earth around the Sun—the Sun's apparent motion—the dates when the Sun enters and leaves each sign may change from year to year. Some people born near the cusp, or edge, of a sign have difficulty determining which is their Sun sign. But in this book a Table of Cusps is provided for the years 1900 to 2000 (page 5) so you can find out what your true Sun sign is.

Here are the twelve signs of the Zodiac, their ancient zodiacal symbol, and the dates when the Sun enters and leaves each sign for the year 1998. Remember, these dates may change from year to year.

ARIES	Ram	March 20–April 20
TAURUS	Bull	April 20–May 21
GEMINI	Twins	May 21–June 21
CANCER	Crab	June 21–July 22
LEO	Lion	July 22–August 23
VIRGO	Virgin	August 23–September 23
LIBRA	Scales	September 23–October 23
SCORPIO	Scorpion	October 23–November 22
SAGITTARIUS	Archer	November 22–December 21
CAPRICORN	Sea Goat	December 21–January 20
AQUARIUS	Water Bearer	January 20–February 18
PISCES	Fish	February 18–March 20

It is possible to draw significant conclusions and make meaningful predictions based simply on the Sun sign of a person. There are many people who have been amazed at the accuracy of the description of their own character based only on the Sun sign. But an astrologer needs more information than just your Sun sign to interpret the photograph that is your horoscope.

The Rising Sign and the Zodiacal Houses

An astrologer needs the exact time and place of your birth in order to construct and interpret your horoscope. The illustration on the next page shows the flat chart, or natural wheel, an astrologer uses. Note the inner circle of the wheel labeled 1 through 12. These 12 divisions are known as the houses of the Zodiac.

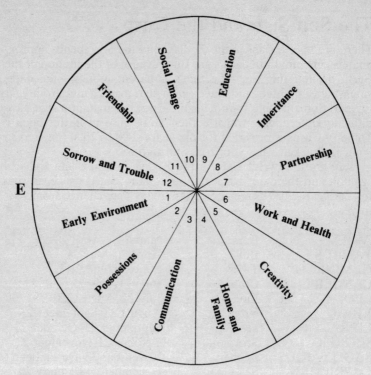

The 1st house always starts from the position marked E, which corresponds to the eastern horizon. The rest of the houses 2 through 12 follow around in a "counterclockwise" direction. The point where each house starts is known as a cusp, or edge.

The cusp, or edge, of the 1st house (point E) is where an astrologer would place your Rising sign, the Ascendant. And, as already noted, the exact time of your birth determines your Rising sign. Let's see how this works.

As the Earth rotates on its axis once every 24 hours, each one of the twelve signs of the Zodiac appears to be "rising" on the horizon, with a new one appearing about every 2 hours. Actually it is the turning of the Earth that exposes each sign to view, but in our astrological work we are discussing apparent motion. This Rising sign marks the Ascendant, and it colors the whole orientation of a horoscope. It indicates the sign governing the 1st house of the chart, and will thus determine which signs will govern all the other houses.

To visualize this idea, imagine two color wheels with twelve divisions superimposed upon each other. For just as the Zodiac is divided into twelve constellations that we identify as the signs, another twelvefold division is used to denote the houses. Now imagine one wheel (the signs) moving slowly while the other wheel (the houses) remains still. This analogy may help you see how the signs keep shifting the "color" of the houses as the Rising sign continues to change every two hours. To simplify things, a Table of Rising Signs has been provided (pages 8–9) for your specific Sun sign.

Once your Rising sign has been placed on the cusp of the 1st house, the signs that govern the rest of the 11 houses can be placed on the chart. In any individual's horoscope the signs do not necessarily correspond with the houses. For example, it could be that a sign covers part of two adjacent houses. It is the interpretation of such variations in an individual's horoscope that marks the professional astrologer.

But to gain a workable understanding of astrology, it is not necessary to go into great detail. In fact, we just need a description of the houses and their meanings, as is shown in the illustration above and in the table below.

THE 12 HOUSES OF THE ZODIAC

1st	Individuality, body appearance, general outlook on life	Personality house
2nd	Finance, possessions, ethical principles, gain or loss	Money house
3rd	Relatives, communication, short journeys, writing, education	Relatives house
4th	Family and home, parental ties, land and property, security	Home house
5th	Pleasure, children, creativity, entertainment, risk	Pleasure house
6th	Health, harvest, hygiene, work and service, employees	Health house
7th	Marriage and divorce, the law, partnerships and alliances	Marriage house
8th	Inheritance, secret deals, sex, death, regeneration	Inheritance house
9th	Travel, sports, study, philosophy and religion	Travel house
10th	Career, social standing, success and honor	Business house
11th	Friendship, social life, hopes and wishes	Friends house
12th	Troubles, illness, secret enemies, hidden agendas	Trouble house

The Planets in the Houses

An astrologer, knowing the exact time and place of your birth, will use tables of planetary motion in order to locate the planets in your horoscope chart. He or she will determine which planet or planets are in which sign and in which house. It is not uncommon, in an individual's horoscope, for there to be two or more planets in the same sign and in the same house.

The characteristics of the planets modify the influence of the Sun according to their natures and strengths.

Sun: Source of life. Basic temperament according to the Sun sign. The conscious will. Human potential.

Moon: Emotions. Moods. Customs. Habits. Changeable. Adaptive. Nurturing.

Mercury: Communication. Intellect. Reasoning power. Curiosity. Short travels.

Venus: Love. Delight. Charm. Harmony. Balance. Art. Beautiful possessions.

Mars: Energy. Initiative. War. Anger. Adventure. Courage. Daring. Impulse.

Jupiter: Luck. Optimism. Generous. Expansive. Opportunities. Protection.

Saturn: Pessimism. Privation. Obstacles. Delay. Hard work. Research. Lasting rewards after long struggle.

Uranus: Fashion. Electricity. Revolution. Independence. Freedom. Sudden changes. Modern science.

Neptune: Sensationalism. Theater. Dreams. Inspiration. Illusion. Deception.

Pluto: Creation and destruction. Total transformation. Lust for power. Strong obsessions.

Superimpose the characteristics of the planets on the functions of the house in which they appear. Express the result through the character of the Sun sign, and you will get the basic idea.

Of course, many other considerations have been taken into account in producing the carefully worked out predictions in this book: the aspects of the planets to each other; their strength according to position and sign; whether they are in a house of exaltation or decline; whether they are natural enemies or not; whether a planet occupies its own sign; the position of a planet in relation to its own house or sign; whether the sign is male or female; whether the sign is a fire, earth, water, or air sign. These are only a few of the colors on the astrologer's pallet which he or she must mix with the inspiration of the artist and the accuracy of the mathematician.

How To Use These Predictions

A person reading the predictions in this book should understand that they are produced from the daily position of the planets for a group of people and are not, of course, individually specialized. To get the full benefit of them our readers should relate the predictions to their own character and circumstances, coordinate them, and draw their own conclusions from them.

If you are a serious observer of your own life, you should find a definite pattern emerging that will be a helpful and reliable guide.

The point is that we always retain our free will. The stars indicate certain directional tendencies but we are not compelled to follow. We can do or not do, and wisdom must make the choice.

We all have our good and bad days. Sometimes they extend into cycles of weeks. It is therefore advisable to study daily predictions in a span ranging from the day before to several days ahead.

Daily predictions should be taken very generally. The word "difficult" does not necessarily indicate a whole day of obstruction or inconvenience. It is a warning to you to be cautious. Your caution will often see you around the difficulty before you are involved. This is the correct use of astrology.

In another section (pages 78–84), detailed information is given about the influence of the Moon as it passes through each of the twelve signs of the Zodiac. There are instructions on how to use the Moon Tables (pages 85–92), which provide Moon Sign Dates throughout the year as well as the Moon's role in health and daily affairs. This information should be used in conjunction with the daily forecasts to give a fuller picture of the astrological trends.

HISTORY OF ASTROLOGY

The origins of astrology have been lost far back in history, but we do know that reference is made to it as far back as the first written records of the human race. It is not hard to see why. Even in primitive times, people must have looked for an explanation for the various happenings in their lives. They must have wanted to know why people were different from one another. And in their search they turned to the regular movements of the Sun, Moon, and stars to see if they could provide an answer.

It is interesting to note that as soon as man learned to use his tools in any type of design, or his mind in any kind of calculation, he turned his attention to the heavens. Ancient cave dwellings reveal dim crescents and circles representative of the Sun and Moon, rulers of day and night. Mesopotamia and the civilization of Chaldea, in itself the foundation of those of Babylonia and Assyria, show a complete picture of astronomical observation and well-developed astrological interpretation.

Humanity has a natural instinct for order. The study of anthropology reveals that primitive people—even as far back as prehistoric times—were striving to achieve a certain order in their lives. They tried to organize the apparent chaos of the universe. They had the desire to attach meaning to things. This demand for order has persisted throughout the history of man. So that observing the regularity of the heavenly bodies made it logical that primitive peoples should turn heavenward in their search for an understanding of the world in which they found themselves so random and alone.

And they did find a significance in the movements of the stars. Shepherds tending their flocks, for instance, observed that when the cluster of stars now known as the constellation Aries was in sight, it was the time of fertility and they associated it with the Ram. And they noticed that the growth of plants and plant life corresponded with different phases of the Moon, so that certain times were favorable for the planting of crops, and other times were not. In this way, there grew up a tradition of seasons and causes connected with the passage of the Sun through the twelve signs of the Zodiac.

Astrology was valued so highly that the king was kept informed of the daily and monthly changes in the heavenly bodies, and the results of astrological studies regarding events of the future. Head astrologers were clearly men of great rank and position, and the office was said to be a hereditary one.

Omens were taken, not only from eclipses and conjunctions of the Moon or Sun with one of the planets, but also from storms and earthquakes. In the eastern civilizations, particularly, the reverence inspired by astrology appears to have remained unbroken since the very earliest days. In ancient China, astrology, astronomy, and religion went hand in hand. The astrologer, who was also an astronomer, was part of the official government service and had his own corner in the Imperial Palace. The duties of the Imperial astrologer, whose office was one of the most important in the land, were clearly defined, as this extract from early records shows:

> This exalted gentleman must concern himself with the stars in the heavens, keeping a record of the changes and movements of the Planets, the Sun and the Moon, in order to examine the movements of the terrestrial world with the object of prognosticating good and bad fortune. He divides the territories of the nine regions of the empire in accordance with their dependence on particular celestial bodies. All the fiefs and principalities are connected with the stars and from this their prosperity or misfortune should be ascertained. He makes prognostications according to the twelve years of the Jupiter cycle of good and evil of the terrestrial world. From the colors of the five kinds of clouds, he determines the coming of floods or droughts, abundance or famine. From the twelve winds, he draws conclusions about the state of harmony of heaven and earth, and takes note of good and bad signs that result from their accord or disaccord. In general, he concerns himself with five kinds of phenomena so as to warn the Emperor to come to the aid of the government and to allow for variations in the ceremonies according to their circumstances.

The Chinese were also keen observers of the fixed stars, giving them such unusual names as Ghost Vehicle, Sun of Imperial Concubine, Imperial Prince, Pivot of Heaven, Twinkling Brilliance, Weaving Girl. But, great astrologers though they may have been, the Chinese lacked one aspect of mathematics that the Greeks applied to astrology—deductive geometry. Deductive geometry was the basis of much classical astrology in and after the time of the Greeks, and this explains the different methods of prognostication used in the East and West.

Down through the ages the astrologer's art has depended, not so much on the uncovering of new facts, though this is important, as on the interpretation of the facts already known. This is the essence of the astrologer's skill.

But why should the signs of the Zodiac have any effect at all on the formation of human character? It is easy to see why people thought they did, and even now we constantly use astrological expressions in our everyday speech. The thoughts of "lucky star," "ill-fated," "star-crossed," "mooning around," are interwoven into the very structure of our language.

Wherever the concept of the Zodiac is understood and used, it could well appear to have an influence on the human character. Does this mean, then, that the human race, in whose civilization the idea of the twelve signs of the Zodiac has long been embedded, is divided into only twelve types? Can we honestly believe that it is really as simple as that? If so, there must be pretty wide ranges of variation within each type. And if, to explain the variation, we call in heredity and environment, experiences in early childhood, the thyroid and other glands, and also the four functions of the mind together with extroversion and introversion, then one begins to wonder if the original classification was worth making at all. No sensible person believes that his favorite system explains everything. But even so, he will not find the system much use at all if it does not even save him the trouble of bothering with the others.

In the same way, if we were to put every person under only one sign of the Zodiac, the system becomes too rigid and unlike life. Besides, it was never intended to be used like that. It may be convenient to have only twelve types, but we know that in practice there is every possible gradation between aggressiveness and timidity, or between conscientiousness and laziness. How, then, do we account for this?

A person born under any given Sun sign can be mainly influenced by one or two of the other signs that appear in their individual horoscope. For instance, famous persons born under the sign of Gemini include Henry VIII, whom nothing and no one could have induced to abdicate, and Edward VIII, who did just that. Obviously, then, the sign Gemini does not fully explain the complete character of either of them.

Again, under the opposite sign, Sagittarius, were both Stalin, who was totally consumed with the notion of power, and Charles V, who freely gave up an empire because he preferred to go into a monastery. And we find under Scorpio many uncompromising characters such as Luther, de Gaulle, Indira Gandhi, and Montgomery, but also Petain, a successful commander whose name later became synonymous with collaboration.

A single sign is therefore obviously inadequate to explain the differences between people; it can only explain resemblances, such as the combativeness of the Scorpio group, or the far-reaching devotion of Charles V and Stalin to their respective ideals—the Christian heaven and the Communist utopia.

But very few people have only one sign in their horoscope chart. In addition to the month of birth, the day and, even more, the hour to the nearest minute if possible, ought to be considered. Without this, it is impossible to have an actual horoscope, for the word horoscope literally means "a consideration of the hour."

The month of birth tells you only which sign of the Zodiac was occupied by the Sun. The day and hour tell you what sign was occupied by the Moon. And the minute tells you which sign was rising on the eastern horizon. This is called the Ascendant, and, as some astrologers believe, it is supposed to be the most important thing in the whole horoscope.

The Sun is said to signify one's heart, that is to say, one's deepest desires and inmost nature. This is quite different from the Moon, which signifies one's superficial way of behaving. When the ancient Romans referred to the Emperor Augustus as a Capricorn, they meant that he had the Moon in Capricorn. Or, to take another example, a modern astrologer would call Disraeli a Scorpion because he had Scorpio Rising, but most people would call him Sagittarius because he had the Sun there. The Romans would have called him Leo because his Moon was in Leo.

So if one does not seem to fit one's birth month, it is always worthwhile reading the other signs, for one may have been born at a time when any of them were rising or occupied by the Moon. It also seems to be the case that the influence of the Sun develops as life goes on, so that the month of birth is easier to guess in people over the age of forty. The young are supposed to be influenced mainly by their Ascendant, the Rising sign, which characterizes the body and physical personality as a whole.

It is nonsense to assume that all people born at a certain time will exhibit the same characteristics, or that they will even behave in the same manner. It is quite obvious that, from the very moment of its birth, a child is subject to the effects of its environment, and that this in turn will influence its character and heritage to a decisive extent. Also to be taken into account are education and economic conditions, which play a very important part in the formation of one's character as well.

People have, in general, certain character traits and qualities which, according to their environment, develop in either a positive or a negative manner. Therefore, selfishness (inherent selfishness, that is) might emerge as unselfishness; kindness and consideration as cruelty and lack of consideration toward others. In the same way, a naturally constructive person may, through frustration, become destructive, and so on. The latent characteristics with which people are born can, therefore, through environment and good or bad training, become something that would appear to be its opposite, and so give the lie to the astrologer's description of their character. But this is not the case. The true character is still there, but it is buried deep beneath these external superficialities.

Careful study of the character traits of various signs of the Zodiac are of immeasurable help, and can render beneficial service to the intelligent person. Undoubtedly, the reader will already have discovered that, while he is able to get on very well with some people, he just "cannot stand" others. The causes sometimes seem inexplicable. At times there is intense dislike, at other times immediate sympathy. And there is, too, the phenomenon of love at first sight, which is also apparently inexplicable. People appear to be either sympathetic or unsympathetic toward each other for no apparent reason.

Now if we look at this in the light of the Zodiac, we find that people born under different signs are either compatible or incompatible with each other. In other words, there are good and bad interrelating factors among the various signs. This does not, of course, mean that humanity can be divided into groups of hostile camps. It would be quite wrong to be hostile or indifferent toward people who happen to be born under an incompatible sign. There is no reason why everybody should not, or cannot, learn to control and adjust their feelings and actions, especially after they are aware of the positive qualities of other people by studying their character analyses, among other things.

Every person born under a certain sign has both positive and negative qualities, which are developed more or less according to our free will. Nobody is entirely good or entirely bad, and it is up to each of us to learn to control ourselves on the one hand and at the same time to endeavor to learn about ourselves and others.

It cannot be emphasized often enough that it is free will that determines whether we will make really good use of our talents and abilities. Using our free will, we can either overcome our failings or allow them to rule us. Our free will enables us to exert sufficient willpower to control our failings so that they do not harm ourselves or others.

Astrology can reveal our inclinations and tendencies. Astrology can tell us about ourselves so that we are able to use our free will to overcome our shortcomings. In this way astrology helps us do our best to become needed and valuable members of society as well as helpmates to our family and our friends. Astrology also can save us a great deal of unhappiness and remorse.

Yet it may seem absurd that an ancient philosophy could be a prop to modern men and women. But below the materialistic surface of modern life, there are hidden streams of feeling and thought. Symbology is reappearing as a study worthy of the scholar; the psychosomatic factor in illness has passed from the writings of the crank to those of the specialist; spiritual healing in all its forms is no longer a pious hope but an accepted phenomenon. And it is into this context that we consider astrology, in the sense that it is an analysis of human types.

Astrology and medicine had a long journey together, and only parted company a couple of centuries ago. There still remain in medical language such astrological terms as "saturnine," "choleric," and "mercurial," used in the diagnosis of physical tendencies. The herbalist, for long the handyman of the medical profession, has been dominated by astrology since the days of the Greeks. Certain herbs traditionally respond to certain planetary influences, and diseases must therefore be treated to ensure harmony between the medicine and the disease.

But the stars are expected to foretell and not only to diagnose.

Astrological forecasting has been remarkably accurate, but often it is wide of the mark. The brave person who cares to predict world events takes dangerous chances. Individual forecasting is less clear cut; it can be a help or a disillusionment. Then we come to the nagging question: if it is possible to foreknow, is it right to foretell? This is a point of ethics on which it is hard to pronounce judgment. The doctor faces the same dilemma if he finds that symptoms of a mortal disease are present in his patient and that he can only prognosticate a steady decline. How much to tell an individual in a crisis is a problem that has perplexed many distinguished scholars. Honest and conscientious astrologers in this modern world, where so many people are seeking guidance, face the same problem.

Five hundred years ago it was customary to call in a learned man who was an astrologer who was probably also a doctor and a philosopher. By his knowledge of astrology, his study of planetary influences, he felt himself qualified to guide those in distress. The world has moved forward at a fantastic rate since then, and yet people are still uncertain of themselves. At first sight it seems fantastic in the light of modern thinking that they turn to the most ancient of all studies, and get someone to calculate a horoscope for them. But is it *really* so fantastic if you take a second look? For astrology is concerned with tomorrow, with survival. And in a world such as ours, tomorrow and survival are the keywords for the twenty-first century.

ASTROLOGICAL BRIDGE TO THE 21st CENTURY

As the last decade of the twentieth century comes to a close, planetary aspects for its final years connect you with the future. Major changes completed in 1995 and 1996 give rise to new planetary cycles that form the bridge to the twenty-first century and new horizons. The years 1996 through 1999 and into the year 2000 reveal hidden paths and personal hints for achieving your potential, for making the most of your message from the planets.

All the major planets begin new cycles in the late 1990s. Jupiter, planet of good fortune, transits four zodiacal signs from 1996 through 1999 and goes through a complete cycle in each of the elements earth, air, fire, and water. Jupiter is in Capricorn, then in Aquarius, next in Pisces, and finally in Aries as the century turns. With the dawning of the twenty-first century, each new yearly Jupiter cycle follows the natural progression of the Zodiac, from Aries in 2000, then Taurus in 2001, next Gemini in 2002, and so on through Pisces in 2011. The beneficent planet Jupiter promotes your professional and educational goals while urging informed choice and deliberation. Jupiter sharpens your focus and hones your skills. And while safeguarding good luck, Jupiter can turn unusual risks into achievable aims.

Saturn, planet of reason and responsibility, has begun a new cycle in the spring of 1996 when it entered fiery Aries. Saturn in Aries through March 1999 heightens a longing for independence. Your movements are freed from everyday restrictions, allowing you to travel, to explore, to act on a variety of choices. With Saturn in Aries you get set to blaze a new trail. Saturn enters earthy Taurus in March 1999 for a three-year stay over the turn of the century into the year 2002. Saturn in Taurus inspires industry and affection. Practicality, perseverance, and planning can reverse setbacks and minimize risk. Saturn in Taurus lends beauty, order, and structure to your life. In order to take advantage of opportunity through responsibility, to persevere against adversity, look to beautiful planet Saturn.

Uranus, planet of innovation and surprise, started an important new cycle in January of 1996. At that time Uranus entered its natural home in airy Aquarius. Uranus in Aquarius into the year 2003 has a profound effect on your personality and the lens through which you see the world. A basic change in the way you project yourself is just one impact of Uranus in Aquarius. More significantly, a whole new consciousness is evolving. Winds of change blowing your way emphasize movement and freedom. Uranus in Aquarius poses involvement in the larger community beyond self, family, friends, lovers, associates. Radical ideas and progressive thought signal a journey of liberation. As the century turns, follow Uranus on the path of humanitarianism. While you carve a prestigious niche in public life, while you preach social reform and justice, you will be striving to make the world a better place for all people.

Neptune, planet of vision and mystery, is in earthy Capricorn until late 1998. Neptune in Capricorn excites creativity while restraining fanciful thinking. Wise use of resources helps you build persona and prestige. Then Neptune enters airy Aquarius during November 1998 and is there into the year 2011. Neptune in Aquarius, the sign of the Water Bearer, represents two sides of the coin of wisdom: inspiration and reason. Here Neptune stirs powerful currents bearing a rich and varied harvest, the fertile breeding ground for idealistic aims and practical considerations. Neptune's fine intuition tunes in to your dreams, your imagination, your spirituality. You can never turn your back on the mysteries of life. Uranus and Neptune, the planets of enlightenment and renewed idealism both in the sign of Aquarius, give you glimpses into the future, letting you peek through secret doorways into the twenty-first century.

Pluto, planet of beginnings and endings, has completed one cycle of growth November 1995 in the sign of Scorpio. Pluto in Scorpio marked a long period of experimentation and rejuvenation. Then Pluto entered the fiery sign of Sagittarius on November 10, 1995 and is there into the year 2007. Pluto in Sagittarius during its long stay of twelve years can create significant change. The great power of Pluto in Sagittarius may already be starting its transformation of your character and lifestyle. Pluto in Sagittarius takes you on a new journey of exploration and learning. The awakening you experience on intellectual and artistic levels heralds a new cycle of growth. Uncompromising Pluto, seeker of truth, challenges your identity, persona, and self-expression. Uncovering the real you, Pluto holds the key to understanding and meaningful communication. Pluto in Sagittarius can be the guiding light illuminating the first decade of the twenty-first century. Good luck is riding on the waves of change.

THE SIGNS OF THE ZODIAC

Dominant Characteristics

Aries: March 21–April 20

The Positive Side of Aries

The Aries has many positive points to his character. People born under this first sign of the Zodiac are often quite strong and enthusiastic. On the whole, they are forward-looking people who are not easily discouraged by temporary setbacks. They know what they want out of life and they go out after it. Their personalities are strong. Others are usually quite impressed by the Ram's way of doing things. Quite often they are sources of inspiration for others traveling the same route. Aries men and women have a special zest for life that can be contagious; for others, they are a fine example of how life should be lived.

The Aries person usually has a quick and active mind. He is imaginative and inventive. He enjoys keeping busy and active. He generally gets along well with all kinds of people. He is interested in mankind, as a whole. He likes to be challenged. Some would say he thrives on opposition, for it is when he is set against that he often does his best. Getting over or around obstacles is a challenge he generally enjoys. All in all, Aries is quite positive and young-thinking. He likes to keep abreast of new things that are happening in the world. Aries are often fond of speed. They like things to be done quickly, and this sometimes aggravates their slower colleagues and associates.

The Aries man or woman always seems to remain young. Their whole approach to life is youthful and optimistic. They never say die, no matter what the odds. They may have an occasional setback, but it is not long before they are back on their feet again.

The Negative Side of Aries

Everybody has his less positive qualities—and Aries is no exception. Sometimes the Aries man or woman is not very tactful in communicating with others; in his hurry to get things done he is apt to be a little callous or inconsiderate. Sensitive people are likely to find him somewhat sharp-tongued in some situations. Often in his eagerness to get the show on the road, he misses the mark altogether and cannot achieve his aims.

At times Aries can be too impulsive. He can occasionally be stubborn and refuse to listen to reason. If things do not move quickly enough to suit the Aries man or woman, he or she is apt to become rather nervous or irritable. The uncultivated Aries is not unfamiliar with moments of doubt and fear. He is capable of being destructive if he does not get his way. He can overcome some of his emotional problems by steadily trying to express himself as he really is, but this requires effort.

Taurus: April 21–May 20

The Positive Side of Taurus

The Taurus person is known for his ability to concentrate and for his tenacity. These are perhaps his strongest qualities. The Taurus man or woman generally has very little trouble in getting along with others; it's his nature to be helpful toward people in need. He can always be depended on by his friends, especially those in trouble.

Taurus generally achieves what he wants through his ability to persevere. He never leaves anything unfinished but works on something until it has been completed. People can usually take him at his word; he is honest and forthright in most of his dealings. The Taurus person has a good chance to make a success of his life because of his many positive qualities. The Taurus who aims high seldom falls short of his mark. He learns well by experience. He is thorough and does not believe in shortcuts of any kind. The Bull's thoroughness pays off in the end, for through his deliberateness he learns how to rely on himself and what he has learned. The Taurus person tries to get along with others, as a rule. He is not overly critical and likes people to be themselves. He is a tolerant person and enjoys peace and harmony—especially in his home life.

Taurus is usually cautious in all that he does. He is not a person who believes in taking unnecessary risks. Before adopting any one line of action, he will weigh all of the pros and cons. The Taurus person is steadfast. Once his mind is made up it seldom changes. The person born under this sign usually is a good family person—reliable and loving.

The Negative Side of Taurus

Sometimes the Taurus man or woman is a bit too stubborn. He won't listen to other points of view if his mind is set on something. To others, this can be quite annoying. Taurus also does not like to be told what to do. He becomes rather angry if others think him not too bright. He does not like to be told he is wrong, even when he is. He dislikes being contradicted.

Some people who are born under this sign are very suspicious of others—even of those persons close to them. They find it difficult to trust people fully. They are often afraid of being deceived or taken advantage of. The Bull often finds it difficult to forget or forgive. His love of material things sometimes makes him rather avaricious and petty.

Gemini: May 21–June 20

The Positive Side of Gemini

The person born under this sign of the Heavenly Twins is usually quite bright and quick-witted. Some of them are capable of doing many different things. The Gemini person very often has many different interests. He keeps an open mind and is always anxious to learn new things.

Gemini is often an analytical person. He is a person who enjoys making use of his intellect. He is governed more by his mind than by his emotions. He is a person who is not confined to one view; he can often understand both sides to a problem or question. He knows how to reason, how to make rapid decisions if need be.

He is an adaptable person and can make himself at home almost anywhere. There are all kinds of situations he can adapt to. He is a person who seldom doubts himself; he is sure of his talents and his ability to think and reason. Gemini is generally most satisfied

when he is in a situation where he can make use of his intellect. Never short of imagination, he often has strong talents for invention. He is rather a modern person when it comes to life; Gemini almost always moves along with the times—perhaps that is why he remains so youthful throughout most of his life.

Literature and art appeal to the person born under this sign. Creativity in almost any form will interest and intrigue the Gemini man or woman.

The Gemini is often quite charming. A good talker, he often is the center of attraction at any gathering. People find it easy to like a person born under this sign because he can appear easygoing and usually has a good sense of humor.

The Negative Side of Gemini

Sometimes the Gemini person tries to do too many things at one time—and as a result, winds up finishing nothing. Some Twins are easily distracted and find it rather difficult to concentrate on one thing for too long a time. Sometimes they give in to trifling fancies and find it rather boring to become too serious about any one thing. Some of them are never dependable, no matter what they promise.

Although the Gemini man or woman often appears to be well-versed on many subjects, this is sometimes just a veneer. His knowledge may be only superficial, but because he speaks so well he gives people the impression of erudition. Some Geminis are sharp-tongued and inconsiderate; they think only of themselves and their own pleasure.

Cancer: June 21–July 20

The Positive Side of Cancer

The Moon Child's most positive point is his understanding nature. On the whole, he is a loving and sympathetic person. He would never go out of his way to hurt anyone. The Cancer man or woman is often very kind and tender; they give what they can to others. They hate to see others suffering and will do what they can to help someone in less fortunate circumstances than themselves. They are often very concerned about the world. Their interest in people generally goes beyond that of just their own families and close friends; they have a deep sense of community and respect humanitarian values. The Moon Child means what he says, as a rule; he is honest about his feelings.

The Cancer man or woman is a person who knows the art of patience. When something seems difficult, he is willing to wait until the situation becomes manageable again. He is a person who knows how to bide his time. Cancer knows how to concentrate on one thing at a time. When he has made his mind up he generally sticks with what he does, seeing it through to the end.

Cancer is a person who loves his home. He enjoys being surrounded by familiar things and the people he loves. Of all the signs, Cancer is the most maternal. Even the men born under this sign often have a motherly or protective quality about them. They like to take care of people in their family—to see that they are well loved and well provided for. They are usually loyal and faithful. Family ties mean a lot to the Cancer man or woman. Parents and in-laws are respected and loved. Young Cancer responds very well to adults who show faith in him. The Moon Child has a strong sense of tradition. He is very sensitive to the moods of others.

The Negative Side of Cancer

Sometimes Cancer finds it rather hard to face life. It becomes too much for him. He can be a little timid and retiring, when things don't go too well. When unfortunate things happen, he is apt to just shrug and say, "Whatever will be will be." He can be fatalistic to a fault. The uncultivated Cancer is a bit lazy. He doesn't have very much ambition. Anything that seems a bit difficult he'll gladly leave to others. He may be lacking in initiative. Too sensitive, when he feels he's been injured, he'll crawl back into his shell and nurse his imaginary wounds. The immature Moon Child often is given to crying when the smallest thing goes wrong.

Some Cancers find it difficult to enjoy themselves in environments outside their homes. They make heavy demands on others, and need to be constantly reassured that they are loved. Lacking such reassurance, they may resort to sulking in silence.

Leo: July 21–August 21

The Positive Side of Leo

Often Leos make good leaders. They seem to be good organizers and administrators. Usually they are quite popular with others. Whatever group it is that they belong to, the Leo man or woman is almost sure to be or become the leader. Loyalty, one of the Lion's noblest traits, enables him or her to maintain this leadership position.

Leo is generous most of the time. It is his best characteristic. He or she likes to give gifts and presents. In making others happy, the Leo person becomes happy himself. He likes to splurge when spending money on others. In some instances it may seem that the Lion's generosity knows no boundaries. A hospitable person, the Leo man or woman is very fond of welcoming people to his house and entertaining them. He is never short of company.

Leo has plenty of energy and drive. He enjoys working toward some specific goal. When he applies himself correctly, he gets what he wants most often. The Leo person is almost never unsure of himself. He has plenty of confidence and aplomb. He is a person who is direct in almost everything he does. He has a quick mind and can make a decision in a very short time.

He usually sets a good example for others because of his ambitious manner and positive ways. He knows how to stick to something once he's started. Although Leo may be good at making a joke, he is not superficial or glib. He is a loving person, kind and thoughtful.

There is generally nothing small or petty about the Leo man or woman. He does what he can for those who are deserving. He is a person others can rely upon at all times. He means what he says. An honest person, generally speaking, he is a friend who is valued and sought out.

The Negative Side of Leo

Leo, however, does have his faults. At times, he can be just a bit too arrogant. He thinks that no one deserves a leadership position except him. Only he is capable of doing things well. His opinion of himself is often much too high. Because of his conceit, he is

sometimes rather unpopular with a good many people. Some Leos are too materialistic; they can only think in terms of money and profit.

Some Leos enjoy lording it over others—at home or at their place of business. What is more, they feel they have the right to. Egocentric to an impossible degree, this sort of Leo cares little about how others think or feel. He can be rude and cutting.

Virgo: August 22–September 22

The Positive Side of Virgo

The person born under the sign of Virgo is generally a busy person. He knows how to arrange and organize things. He is a good planner. Above all, he is practical and is not afraid of hard work.

Often called the sign of the Harvester, Virgo knows how to attain what he desires. He sticks with something until it is finished. He never shirks his duties, and can always be depended upon. The Virgo person can be thoroughly trusted at all times.

The man or woman born under this sign tries to do everything to perfection. He doesn't believe in doing anything halfway. He always aims for the top. He is the sort of a person who is always learning and constantly striving to better himself—not because he wants more money or glory, but because it gives him a feeling of accomplishment.

The Virgo man or woman is a very observant person. He is sensitive to how others feel, and can see things below the surface of a situation. He usually puts this talent to constructive use.

It is not difficult for the Virgo to be open and earnest. He believes in putting his cards on the table. He is never secretive or underhanded. He's as good as his word. The Virgo person is generally plainspoken and down to earth. He has no trouble in expressing himself.

The Virgo person likes to keep up to date on new developments in his particular field. Well-informed, generally, he sometimes has a keen interest in the arts or literature. What he knows, he knows well. His ability to use his critical faculties is well-developed and sometimes startles others because of its accuracy.

Virgos adhere to a moderate way of life; they avoid excesses. Virgo is a responsible person and enjoys being of service.

The Negative Side of Virgo

Sometimes a Virgo person is too critical. He thinks that only he can do something the way it should be done. Whatever anyone else does is inferior. He can be rather annoying in the way he quibbles over insignificant details. In telling others how things should be done, he can be rather tactless and mean.

Some Virgos seem rather emotionless and cool. They feel emotional involvement is beneath them. They are sometimes too tidy, too neat. With money they can be rather miserly. Some Virgos try to force their opinions and ideas on others.

Libra: September 23–October 22

The Positive Side of Libra

Libras love harmony. It is one of their most outstanding character traits. They are interested in achieving balance; they admire beauty and grace in things as well as in people. Generally speaking, they are kind and considerate people. Libras are usually very sympathetic. They go out of their way not to hurt another person's feelings. They are outgoing and do what they can to help those in need.

People born under the sign of Libra almost always make good friends. They are loyal and amiable. They enjoy the company of others. Many of them are rather moderate in their views; they believe in keeping an open mind, however, and weighing both sides of an issue fairly before making a decision.

Alert and intelligent, Libra, often known as the Lawgiver, is always fair-minded and tries to put himself in the position of the other person. They are against injustice; quite often they take up for the underdog. In most of their social dealings, they try to be tactful and kind. They dislike discord and bickering, and most Libras strive for peace and harmony in all their relationships.

The Libra man or woman has a keen sense of beauty. They appreciate handsome furnishings and clothes. Many of them are artistically inclined. Their taste is usually impeccable. They know how to use color. Their homes are almost always attractively arranged and inviting. They enjoy entertaining people and see to it that their guests always feel at home and welcome.

Libra gets along with almost everyone. He is well-liked and socially much in demand.

The Negative Side of Libra

Some people born under this sign tend to be rather insincere. So eager are they to achieve harmony in all relationships that they will even go so far as to lie. Many of them are escapists. They find facing the truth an ordeal and prefer living in a world of make-believe.

In a serious argument, some Libras give in rather easily even when they know they are right. Arguing, even about something they believe in, is too unsettling for some of them.

Libras sometimes care too much for material things. They enjoy possessions and luxuries. Some are vain and tend to be jealous.

Scorpio: October 23–November 22

The Positive Side of Scorpio

The Scorpio man or woman generally knows what he or she wants out of life. He is a determined person. He sees something through to the end. Scorpio is quite sincere, and seldom says anything he doesn't mean. When he sets a goal for himself he tries to go about achieving it in a very direct way.

The Scorpion is brave and courageous. They are not afraid of hard work. Obstacles do not frighten them. They forge ahead until they achieve what they set out for. The Scorpio man or woman has a strong will.

Although Scorpio may seem rather fixed and determined, inside he is often quite tender and loving. He can care very much for others. He believes in sincerity in all relationships. His feelings about someone tend to last; they are profound and not superficial.

The Scorpio person is someone who adheres to his principles no matter what happens. He will not be deterred from a path he believes to be right.

Because of his many positive strengths, the Scorpion can often achieve happiness for himself and for those that he loves.

He is a constructive person by nature. He often has a deep understanding of people and of life, in general. He is perceptive and unafraid. Obstacles often seem to spur him on. He is a positive person who enjoys winning. He has many strengths and re-sources; challenge of any sort often brings out the best in him.

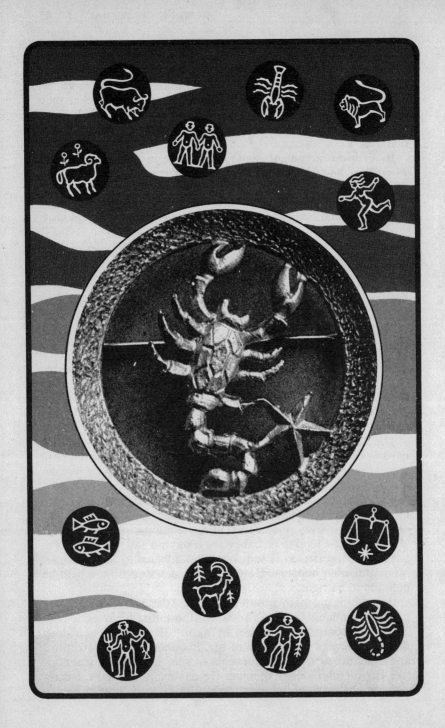

The Negative Side of Scorpio

The Scorpio person is sometimes hypersensitive. Often he imagines injury when there is none. He feels that others do not bother to recognize him for his true worth. Sometimes he is given to excessive boasting in order to compensate for what he feels is neglect.

Scorpio can be proud, arrogant, and competitive. They can be sly when they put their minds to it and they enjoy outwitting persons or institutions noted for their cleverness.

Their tactics for getting what they want are sometimes devious and ruthless. They don't care too much about what others may think. If they feel others have done them an injustice, they will do their best to seek revenge. The Scorpion often has a sudden, violent temper; and this person's interest in sex is sometimes quite unbalanced or excessive.

Sagittarius: November 23–December 20

The Positive Side of Sagittarius

People born under this sign are honest and forthright. Their approach to life is earnest and open. Sagittarius is often quite adult in his way of seeing things. They are broad-minded and tolerant people. When dealing with others the person born under the sign of the Archer is almost always open and forthright. He doesn't believe in deceit or pretension. His standards are high. People who associate with Sagittarius generally admire and respect his tolerant viewpoint.

The Archer trusts others easily and expects them to trust him. He is never suspicious or envious and almost always thinks well of others. People always enjoy his company because he is so friendly and easygoing. The Sagittarius man or woman is often good-humored. He can always be depended upon by his friends, family, and co-workers.

The person born under this sign of the Zodiac likes a good joke every now and then. Sagittarius is eager for fun and laughs, which makes him very popular with others.

A lively person, he enjoys sports and outdoor life. The Archer is fond of animals. Intelligent and interesting, he can begin an

animated conversation with ease. He likes exchanging ideas and discussing various views.

He is not selfish or proud. If someone proposes an idea or plan that is better than his, he will immediately adopt it. Imaginative yet practical, he knows how to put ideas into practice.

The Archer enjoys sport and games, and it doesn't matter if he wins or loses. He is a forgiving person, and never sulks over something that has not worked out in his favor.

He is seldom critical, and is almost always generous.

The Negative Side of Sagittarius

Some Sagittarius are restless. They take foolish risks and seldom learn from the mistakes they make. They don't have heads for money and are often mismanaging their finances. Some of them devote much of their time to gambling.

Some are too outspoken and tactless, always putting their feet in their mouths. They hurt others carelessly by being honest at the wrong time. Sometimes they make promises which they don't keep. They don't stick close enough to their plans and go from one failure to another. They are undisciplined and waste a lot of energy.

Capricorn: December 21–January 19

The Positive Side of Capricorn

The person born under the sign of Capricorn, known variously as the Mountain Goat or Sea Goat, is usually very stable and patient. He sticks to whatever tasks he has and sees them through. He can always be relied upon and he is not averse to work.

An honest person, Capricorn is generally serious about whatever he does. He does not take his duties lightly. He is a practical person and believes in keeping his feet on the ground.

Quite often the person born under this sign is ambitious and knows how to get what he wants out of life. The Goat forges ahead and never gives up his goal. When he is determined about something, he almost always wins. He is a good worker—a hard worker. Although things may not come easy to him, he will not complain, but continue working until his chores are finished.

He is usually good at business matters and knows the value of money. He is not a spendthrift and knows how to put something away for a rainy day; he dislikes waste and unnecessary loss.

Capricorn knows how to make use of his self-control. He can apply himself to almost anything once he puts his mind to it. His ability to concentrate sometimes astounds others. He is diligent and does well when involved in detail work.

The Capricorn man or woman is charitable, generally speaking, and will do what is possible to help others less fortunate. As a friend, he is loyal and trustworthy. He never shirks his duties or responsibilities. He is self-reliant and never expects too much of the other fellow. He does what he can on his own. If someone does him a good turn, then he will do his best to return the favor.

The Negative Side of Capricorn

Like everyone, Capricorn, too, has faults. At times, the Goat can be overcritical of others. He expects others to live up to his own high standards. He thinks highly of himself and tends to look down on others.

His interest in material things may be exaggerated. The Capricorn man or woman thinks too much about getting on in the world and having something to show for it. He may even be a little greedy.

He sometimes thinks he knows what's best for everyone. He is too bossy. He is always trying to organize and correct others. He may be a little narrow in his thinking.

Aquarius: January 20–February 18

The Positive Side of Aquarius

The Aquarius man or woman is usually very honest and forthright. These are his two greatest qualities. His standards for himself are generally very high. He can always be relied upon by others. His word is his bond.

Aquarius is perhaps the most tolerant of all the Zodiac personalities. He respects other people's beliefs and feels that everyone is entitled to his own approach to life.

He would never do anything to injure another's feelings. He is never unkind or cruel. Always considerate of others, the Water

Bearer is always willing to help a person in need. He feels a very strong tie between himself and all the other members of mankind.

The person born under this sign, called the Water Bearer, is almost always an individualist. He does not believe in teaming up with the masses, but prefers going his own way. His ideas about life and mankind are often quite advanced. There is a saying to the effect that the average Aquarius is fifty years ahead of his time.

Aquarius is community-minded. The problems of the world concern him greatly. He is interested in helping others no matter what part of the globe they live in. He is truly a humanitarian sort. He likes to be of service to others.

Giving, considerate, and without prejudice, Aquarius have no trouble getting along with others.

The Negative Side of Aquarius

Aquarius may be too much of a dreamer. He makes plans but seldom carries them out. He is rather unrealistic. His imagination has a tendency to run away with him. Because many of his plans are impractical, he is always in some sort of a dither.

Others may not approve of him at all times because of his unconventional behavior. He may be a bit eccentric. Sometimes he is so busy with his own thoughts that he loses touch with the realities of existence.

Some Aquarius feel they are more clever and intelligent than others. They seldom admit to their own faults, even when they are quite apparent. Some become rather fanatic in their views. Their criticism of others is sometimes destructive and negative.

Pisces: February 19–March 20

The Positive Side of Pisces

Known as the sign of the Fishes, Pisces has a sympathetic nature. Kindly, he is often dedicated in the way he goes about helping others. The sick and the troubled often turn to him for advice and assistance. Possessing keen intuition, Pisces can easily understand people's deepest problems.

He is very broad-minded and does not criticize others for their faults. He knows how to accept people for what they are. On the whole, he is a trustworthy and earnest person. He is loyal to his friends and will do what he can to help them in time of need. Generous and good-natured, he is a lover of peace; he is often willing to help others solve their differences. People who have taken a wrong turn in life often interest him and he will do what he can to persuade them to rehabilitate themselves.

He has a strong intuitive sense and most of the time he knows how to make it work for him. Pisces is unusually perceptive and often knows what is bothering someone before that person, himself, is aware of it. The Pisces man or woman is an idealistic person, basically, and is interested in making the world a better place in which to live. Pisces believes that everyone should help each other. He is willing to do more than his share in order to achieve cooperation with others.

The person born under this sign often is talented in music or art. He is a receptive person; he is able to take the ups and downs of life with philosophic calm.

The Negative Side of Pisces

Some Pisces are often depressed; their outlook on life is rather glum. They may feel that they have been given a bad deal in life and that others are always taking unfair advantage of them. Pisces sometimes feel that the world is a cold and cruel place. The Fishes can be easily discouraged. The Pisces man or woman may even withdraw from the harshness of reality into a secret shell of his own where he dreams and idles away a good deal of his time.

Pisces can be lazy. He lets things happen without giving the least bit of resistance. He drifts along, whether on the high road or on the low. He can be lacking in willpower.

Some Pisces people seek escape through drugs or alcohol. When temptation comes along they find it hard to resist. In matters of sex, they can be rather permissive.

Sun Sign Personalities

ARIES: Hans Christian Andersen, Pearl Bailey, Marlon Brando, Wernher Von Braun, Charlie Chaplin, Joan Crawford, Da Vinci, Bette Davis, Doris Day, W. C. Fields, Alec Guinness, Adolf Hitler, William Holden, Thomas Jefferson, Nikita Khrushchev, Elton John, Arturo Toscanini, J. P. Morgan, Paul Robeson, Gloria Steinem, Sarah Vaughn, Vincent van Gogh, Tennessee Williams

TAURUS: Fred Astaire, Charlote Brontë, Carol Burnett, Irving Berlin, Bing Crosby, Salvador Dali, Tchaikovsky, Queen Elizabeth II, Duke Ellington, Ella Fitzgerald, Henry Fonda, Sigmund Freud, Orson Welles, Joe Louis, Lenin, Karl Marx, Golda Meir, Eva Peron, Bertrand Russell, Shakespeare, Kate Smith, Benjamin Spock, Barbra Streisand, Shirley Temple, Harry Truman

GEMINI: Mikhail Baryshnikov, Ruth Benedict, Josephine Baker, Carlos Chavez, Walt Whitman, Bob Dylan, Ralph Waldo Emerson, Judy Garland, Paul Gauguin, Allen Ginsberg, Benny Goodman, Bob Hope, Burl Ives, John F. Kennedy, Peggy Lee, Marilyn Monroe, Joe Namath, Cole Porter, Laurence Olivier, Harriet Beecher Stowe, Queen Victoria, John Wayne, Frank Lloyd Wright

CANCER: "Dear Abby," Lizzie Borden, David Brinkley, Yul Brynner, Pearl Buck, Marc Chagall, Jack Dempsey, Babe Didrikson, Mary Baker Eddy, Henry VIII, John Glenn, Ernest Hemingway, Lena Horne, Oscar Hammerstein, Helen Keller, Ann Landers, George Orwell, Nancy Reagan, Rembrandt, Richard Rodgers, Ginger Rogers, Rubens, Jean-Paul Sartre, O. J. Simpson

LEO: Neil Armstrong, James Baldwin, Lucille Ball, Emily Brontë, Wilt Chamberlain, Julia Child, William J. Clinton, Cecil B. De Mille, Ogden Nash, Amelia Earhart, Edna Ferber, Arthur Goldberg, Alfred Hitchcock, Mick Jagger, George Meany, Annie Oakley, George Bernard Shaw, Napoleon, Jacqueline Onassis, Henry Ford, Francis Scott Key, Andy Warhol, Mae West, Orville Wright

VIRGO: Ingrid Bergman, Warren Burger, Maurice Chevalier, Agatha Christie, Sean Connery, Lafayette, Peter Falk, Greta Garbo, Althea Gibson, Arthur Godfrey, Goethe, Buddy Hackett, Michael Jackson, Lyndon Johnson, D. H. Lawrence, Sophia Loren, Grandma Moses, Arnold Palmer, Queen Elizabeth I, Walter Reuther, Peter Sellers, Lily Tomlin, George Wallace

LIBRA: Brigitte Bardot, Art Buchwald, Truman Capote, Dwight D. Eisenhower, William Faulkner, F. Scott Fitzgerald, Gandhi, George Gershwin, Micky Mantle, Helen Hayes, Vladimir Horowitz, Doris Lessing, Martina Navratalova, Eugene O'Neill, Luciano Pavarotti, Emily Post, Eleanor Roosevelt, Bruce Springsteen, Margaret Thatcher, Gore Vidal, Barbara Walters, Oscar Wilde

SCORPIO: Vivien Leigh, Richard Burton, Art Carney, Johnny Carson, Billy Graham, Grace Kelly, Walter Cronkite, Marie Curie, Charles de Gaulle, Linda Evans, Indira Gandhi, Theodore Roosevelt, Rock Hudson, Katherine Hepburn, Robert F. Kennedy, Billie Jean King, Martin Luther, Georgia O'Keeffe, Pablo Picasso, Jonas Salk, Alan Shepard, Robert Louis Stevenson

SAGITTARIUS: Jane Austen, Louisa May Alcott, Woody Allen, Beethoven, Willy Brandt, Mary Martin, William F. Buckley, Maria Callas, Winston Churchill, Noel Coward, Emily Dickinson, Walt Disney, Benjamin Disraeli, James Doolittle, Kirk Douglas, Chet Huntley, Jane Fonda, Chris Evert Lloyd, Margaret Mead, Charles Schulz, John Milton, Frank Sinatra, Steven Spielberg

CAPRICORN: Muhammad Ali, Isaac Asimov, Pablo Casals, Dizzy Dean, Marlene Dietrich, James Farmer, Ava Gardner, Barry Goldwater, Cary Grant, J. Edgar Hoover, Howard Hughes, Joan of Arc, Gypsy Rose Lee, Martin Luther King, Jr., Rudyard Kipling, Mao Tse-tung, Richard Nixon, Gamal Nasser, Louis Pasteur, Albert Schweitzer, Stalin, Benjamin Franklin, Elvis Presley

AQUARIUS: Marian Anderson, Susan B. Anthony, Jack Benny, Charles Darwin, Charles Dickens, Thomas Edison, John Barrymore, Clark Gable, Jascha Heifetz, Abraham Lincoln, John McEnroe, Yehudi Menuhin, Mozart, Jack Nicklaus, Ronald Reagan, Jackie Robinson, Norman Rockwell, Franklin D. Roosevelt, Gertrude Stein, Charles Lindbergh, Margaret Truman

PISCES: Edward Albee, Harry Belafonte, Alexander Graham Bell, Chopin, Adelle Davis, Albert Einstein, Golda Meir, Jackie Gleason, Winslow Homer, Edward M. Kennedy, Victor Hugo, Mike Mansfield, Michelangelo, Edna St. Vincent Millay, Liza Minelli, John Steinbeck, Linus Pauling, Ravel, Renoir, Diana Ross, William Shirer, Elizabeth Taylor, George Washington

The Signs and Their Key Words

		POSITIVE	NEGATIVE
ARIES	self	courage, initiative, pioneer instinct	brash rudeness, selfish impetuosity
TAURUS	money	endurance, loyalty, wealth	obstinacy, gluttony
GEMINI	mind	versatility	capriciousness, unreliability
CANCER	family	sympathy, homing instinct	clannishness, childishness
LEO	children	love, authority, integrity	egotism, force
VIRGO	work	purity, industry, analysis	faultfinding, cynicism
LIBRA	marriage	harmony, justice	vacillation, superficiality
SCORPIO	sex	survival, regeneration	vengeance, discord
SAGITTARIUS	travel	optimism, higher learning	lawlessness
CAPRICORN	career	depth	narrowness, gloom
AQUARIUS	friends	human fellowship, genius	perverse unpredictability
PISCES	confine-ment	spiritual love, universality	diffusion, escapism

The Elements and Qualities of The Signs

Every sign has both an *element* and a *quality* associated with it. The element indicates the basic makeup of the sign, and the quality describes the kind of activity associated with each.

Element	Sign	Quality	Sign
FIRE	ARIES LEO SAGITTARIUS	CARDINAL	ARIES LIBRA CANCER CAPRICORN
EARTH	TAURUS VIRGO CAPRICORN	FIXED	TAURUS LEO SCORPIO AQUARIUS
AIR	GEMINI LIBRA AQUARIUS		
WATER	CANCER SCORPIO PISCES	MUTABLE	GEMINI VIRGO SAGITTARIUS PISCES

Signs can be grouped together according to their element and quality. Signs of the same element share many basic traits in common. They tend to form stable configurations and ultimately harmonious relationships. Signs of the same quality are often less harmonious, but they share many dynamic potentials for growth as well as profound fulfillment.

Further discussion of each of these sign groupings is provided on the following pages.

The Fire Signs

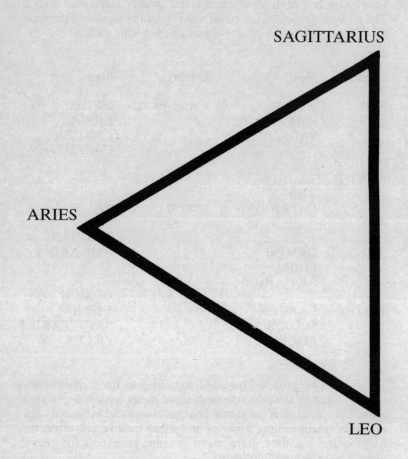

This is the fire group. On the whole these are emotional, volatile types, quick to anger, quick to forgive. They are adventurous, powerful people and act as a source of inspiration for everyone. They spark into action with immediate exuberant impulses. They are intelligent, self-involved, creative, and idealistic. They all share a certain vibrancy and glow that outwardly reflects an inner flame and passion for living.

The Earth Signs

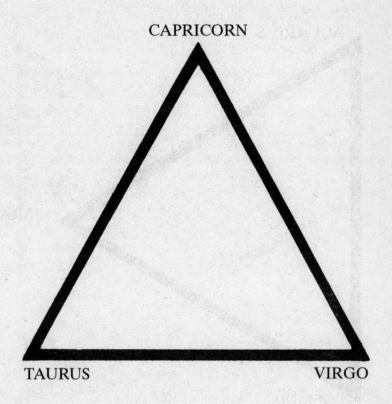

CAPRICORN

TAURUS

VIRGO

This is the earth group. They are in constant touch with the material world and tend to be conservative. Although they are all capable of spartan self-discipline, they are earthy, sensual people who are stimulated by the tangible, elegant, and luxurious. The thread of their lives is always practical, but they do fantasize and are often attracted to dark, mysterious, emotional people. They are like great cliffs overhanging the sea, forever married to the ocean but always resisting erosion from the dark, emotional forces that thunder at their feet.

The Air Signs

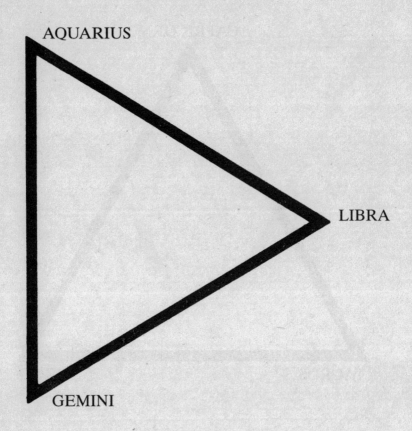

This is the air group. They are light, mental creatures desirous of contact, communication, and relationship. They are involved with people and the forming of ties on many levels. Original thinkers, they are the bearers of human news. Their language is their sense of word, color, style, and beauty. They provide an atmosphere suitable and pleasant for living. They add change and versatility to the scene, and it is through them that we can explore new territory of human intelligence and experience.

The Water Signs

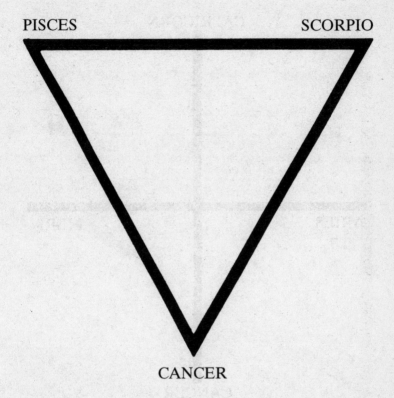

This is the water group. Through the water people, we are all joined together on emotional, nonverbal levels. They are silent, mysterious types whose magic hypnotizes even the most determined realist. They have uncanny perceptions about people and are as rich as the oceans when it comes to feeling, emotion, or imagination. They are sensitive, mystical creatures with memories that go back beyond time. Through water, life is sustained. These people have the potential for the depths of darkness or the heights of mysticism and art.

The Cardinal Signs

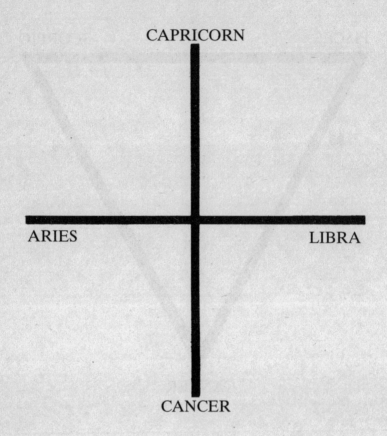

Put together, this is a clear-cut picture of dynamism, activity, tremendous stress, and remarkable achievement. These people know the meaning of great change since their lives are often characterized by significant crises and major successes. This combination is like a simultaneous storm of summer, fall, winter, and spring. The danger is chaotic diffusion of energy; the potential is irrepressible growth and victory.

The Fixed Signs

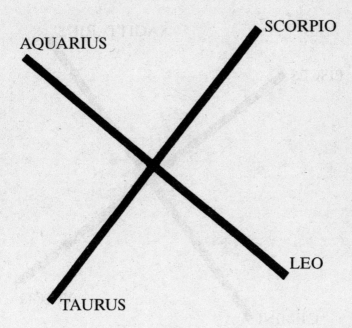

AQUARIUS

SCORPIO

LEO

TAURUS

Fixed signs are always establishing themselves in a given place or area of experience. Like explorers who arrive and plant a flag, these people claim a position from which they do not enjoy being deposed. They are staunch, stalwart, upright, trusty, honorable people, although their obstinacy is well-known. Their contribution is fixity, and they are the angels who support our visible world.

The Mutable Signs

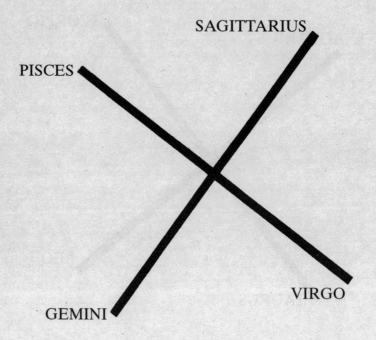

Mutable people are versatile, sensitive, intelligent, nervous, and deeply curious about life. They are the translators of all energy. They often carry out or complete tasks initiated by others. Combinations of these signs have highly developed minds; they are imaginative and jumpy and think and talk a lot. At worst their lives are a Tower of Babel. At best they are adaptable and ready creatures who can assimilate one kind of experience and enjoy it while anticipating coming changes.

THE PLANETS
OF THE SOLAR SYSTEM

This section describes the planets of the solar system. In astrology, both the Sun and the Moon are considered to be planets. Because of the Moon's influence in our day-to-day lives, the Moon is described in a separate section following this one.

The Planets and the Signs They Rule

The signs of the Zodiac are linked to the planets in the following way. Each sign is governed or ruled by one or more planets. No matter where the planets are located in the sky at any given moment, they still rule their respective signs, and when they travel through the signs they rule, they have special dignity and their effects are stronger.

Following is a list of the planets and the signs they rule. After looking at the list, read the definitions of the planets and see if you can determine how the planet ruling *your* Sun sign has affected your life.

SIGNS	RULING PLANETS
Aries	Mars, Pluto
Taurus	Venus
Gemini	Mercury
Cancer	Moon
Leo	Sun
Virgo	Mercury
Libra	Venus
Scorpio	Mars, Pluto
Sagittarius	Jupiter
Capricorn	Saturn
Aquarius	Saturn, Uranus
Pisces	Jupiter, Neptune

Characteristics of the Planets

The following pages give the meaning and characteristics of the planets of the solar system. They all travel around the Sun at different speeds and different distances. Taken with the Sun, they all distribute individual intelligence and ability throughout the entire chart.

The planets modify the influence of the Sun in a chart according to their own particular natures, strengths, and positions. Their positions must be calculated for each year and day, and their function and expression in a horoscope will change as they move from one area of the Zodiac to another.

We start with a description of the sun.

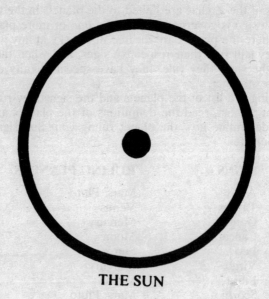

THE SUN

SUN

This is the center of existence. Around this flaming sphere all the planets revolve in endless orbits. Our star is constantly sending out its beams of light and energy without which no life on Earth would be possible. In astrology it symbolizes everything we are trying to become, the center around which all of our activity in life will always revolve. It is the symbol of our basic nature and describes the natural and constant thread that runs through everything that we do from birth to death on this planet.

To early astrologers, the Sun seemed to be another planet because it crossed the heavens every day, just like the rest of the bodies in the sky.

It is the only star near enough to be seen well—it is, in fact, a dwarf star. Approximately 860,000 miles in diameter, it is about ten times as wide as the giant planet Jupiter. The next nearest star is nearly 300,000 times as far away, and if the Sun were located as far away as most of the bright stars, it would be too faint to be seen without a telescope.

Everything in the horoscope ultimately revolves around this singular body. Although other forces may be prominent in the charts of some individuals, still the Sun is the total nucleus of being and symbolizes the complete potential of every human being alive. It is vitality and the life force. Your whole essence comes from the position of the Sun.

You are always trying to express the Sun according to its position by house and sign. Possibility for all development is found in the Sun, and it marks the fundamental character of your personal radiations all around you.

It is the symbol of strength, vigor, wisdom, dignity, ardor, and generosity, and the ability for a person to function as a mature individual. It is also a creative force in society. It is consciousness of the gift of life.

The underdeveloped solar nature is arrogant, pushy, undependable, and proud, and is constantly using force.

MERCURY

Mercury is the planet closest to the Sun. It races around our star, gathering information and translating it to the rest of the system. Mercury represents your capacity to understand the desires of your own will and to translate those desires into action.

In other words it is the planet of mind and the power of communication. Through Mercury we develop an ability to think, write, speak, and observe—to become aware of the world around us. It colors our attitudes and vision of the world, as well as our capacity to communicate our inner responses to the outside world. Some people who have serious disabilities in their power of verbal communication have often wrongly been described as people lacking intelligence.

Although this planet (and its position in the horoscope) indicates your power to communicate your thoughts and perceptions to the world, intelligence is something deeper. Intelligence is distributed throughout all the planets. It is the relationship of the planets to each other that truly describes what we call intelligence. Mercury rules speaking, language, mathematics, draft and design, students, messengers, young people, offices, teachers, and any pursuits where the mind of man has wings.

VENUS

Venus is beauty. It symbolizes the harmony and radiance of a rare and elusive quality: beauty itself. It is refinement and delicacy, softness and charm. In astrology it indicates grace, balance, and the aesthetic sense. Where Venus is we see beauty, a gentle drawing in of energy and the need for satisfaction and completion. It is a special touch that finishes off rough edges. It is sensitivity, and affection, and it is always the place for that other elusive phenomenon: love. Venus describes our sense of what is beautiful and loving. Poorly developed, it is vulgar, tasteless, and self-indulgent. But its ideal is the flame of spiritual love—Aphrodite, goddess of love, and the sweetness and power of personal beauty.

MARS

Mars is raw, crude energy. The planet next to Earth but outward from the Sun is a fiery red sphere that charges through the horoscope with force and fury. It represents the way you reach out for new adventure and new experience. It is energy and drive, initiative, courage, and daring. It is the power to start something and see it through. It can be thoughtless, cruel and wild, angry and hostile, causing cuts, burns, scalds, and wounds. It can stab its way through a chart, or it can be the symbol of healthy spirited adventure, well-channeled constructive power to begin and keep up the drive. If you have trouble starting things, if you lack the get-up-and-go to start the ball rolling, if you lack aggressiveness and self-confidence, chances are there's another planet influencing your Mars. Mars rules soldiers, butchers, surgeons, salesmen—any field that requires daring, bold skill, operational technique, or self-promotion.

JUPITER

This is the largest planet of the solar system. Scientists have recently learned that Jupiter reflects more light than it receives from the Sun. In a sense it is like a star itself. In astrology it rules good luck and good cheer, health, wealth, optimism, happiness, success, and joy. It is the symbol of opportunity and always opens the way for new possibilities in your life. It rules exuberance, enthusiasm, wisdom, knowledge, generosity, and all forms of expansion in general. It rules actors, statesmen, clerics, professional people, religion, publishing, and the distribution of many people over large areas.

Sometimes Jupiter makes you think you deserve everything, and you become sloppy, wasteful, careless and rude, prodigal and lawless, in the illusion that nothing can ever go wrong. Then there is the danger of overconfidence, exaggeration, undependability, and overindulgence.

Jupiter is the minimization of limitation and the emphasis on spirituality and potential. It is the thirst for knowledge and higher learning.

SATURN

Saturn circles our system in dark splendor with its mysterious rings, forcing us to be awakened to whatever we have neglected in the past. It will present real puzzles and problems to be solved, causing delays, obstacles, and hindrances. By doing so, Saturn stirs our own sensitivity to those areas where we are laziest.

Here we must patiently develop *method*, and only through painstaking effort can our ends be achieved. It brings order to a horoscope and imposes reason just where we are feeling least reasonable. By creating limitations and boundary, Saturn shows the consequences of being human and demands that we accept the changing cycles inevitable in human life. Saturn rules time, old age, and sobriety. It can bring depression, gloom, jealousy, and greed, or serious acceptance of responsibilities out of which success will develop. With Saturn there is nothing to do but face facts. It rules laborers, stones, granite, rocks, and crystals of all kinds.

THE OUTER PLANETS:
URANUS, NEPTUNE, PLUTO

Uranus, Neptune, Pluto are the outer planets. They liberate human beings from cultural conditioning, and in that sense are the lawbreakers. In early times it was thought that Saturn was the last planet of the system—the outer limit beyond which we could never go. The discovery of the next three planets ushered in new phases of human history, revolution, and technology.

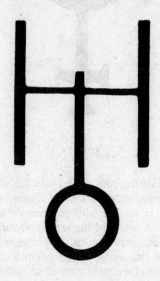

URANUS

Uranus rules unexpected change, upheaval, revolution. It is the symbol of total independence and asserts the freedom of an individual from all restriction and restraint. It is a breakthrough planet and indicates talent, originality, and genius in a horoscope. It usually causes last-minute reversals and changes of plan, unwanted separations, accidents, catastrophes, and eccentric behavior. It can add irrational rebelliousness and perverse bohemianism to a personality or a streak of unaffected brilliance in science and art. It rules technology, aviation, and all forms of electrical and electronic advancement. It governs great leaps forward and topsy-turvy situations, and *always* turns things around at the last minute. Its effects are difficult to predict, since it rules sudden last-minute decisions and events that come like lightning out of the blue.

NEPTUNE

Neptune dissolves existing reality the way the sea erodes the cliffs beside it. Its effects are subtle like the ringing of a buoy's bell in the fog. It suggests a reality higher than definition can usually describe. It awakens a sense of higher responsibility often causing guilt, worry, anxieties, or delusions. Neptune is associated with all forms of escape and can make things seem a certain way so convincingly that you are absolutely sure of something that eventually turns out to be quite different.

It is the planet of illusion and therefore governs the invisible realms that lie beyond our ordinary minds, beyond our simple factual ability to prove what is "real." Treachery, deceit, disillusionment, and disappointment are linked to Neptune. It describes a vague reality that promises eternity and the divine, yet in a manner so complex that we cannot really fathom it at all. At its worst Neptune is a cheap intoxicant; at its best it is the poetry, music, and inspiration of the higher planes of spiritual love. It has dominion over movies, photographs, and much of the arts.

PLUTO

Pluto lies at the outpost of our system and therefore rules finality in a horoscope—the final closing of chapters in your life, the passing of major milestones and points of development from which there is no return. It is a final wipeout, a closeout, an evacuation. It is a distant, subtle but powerful catalyst in all transformations that occur. It creates, destroys, then recreates. Sometimes Pluto starts its influence with a minor event or insignificant incident that might even go unnoticed. Slowly but surely, little by little, everything changes, until at last there has been a total transformation in the area of your life where Pluto has been operating. It rules mass thinking and the trends that society first rejects, then adopts, and finally outgrows.

Pluto rules the dead and the underworld—all the powerful forces of creation and destruction that go on all the time beneath, around, and above us. It can bring a lust for power with strong obsessions.

It is the planet that rules the metamorphosis of the caterpillar into a butterfly, for it symbolizes the capacity to change totally and forever a person's lifestyle, way of thought, and behavior.

THE MOON IN EACH SIGN

The Moon is the nearest planet to the Earth. It exerts more observable influence on us from day to day than any other planet. The effect is very personal, very intimate, and if we are not aware of how it works it can make us quite unstable in our ideas. And the annoying thing is that at these times we often see our own instability but can do nothing about it. A knowledge of what can be expected may help considerably. We can then be prepared to stand strong against the Moon's negative influences and use its positive ones to help us to get ahead. Who has not heard of going with the tide?

The Moon reflects, has no light of its own. It reflects the Sun—the life giver—in the form of vital movement. The Moon controls the tides, the blood rhythm, the movement of sap in trees and plants. Its nature is inconstancy and change so it signifies our moods, our superficial behavior—walking, talking, and especially thinking. Being a true reflector of other forces, the Moon is cold, watery like the surface of a still lake, brilliant and scintillating at times, but easily ruffled and disturbed by the winds of change.

The Moon takes about 27⅓ days to make a complete transit of the Zodiac. It spends just over 2¼ days in each sign. During that time it reflects the qualities, energies, and characteristics of the sign and, to a degree, the planet which rules the sign. When the Moon in its transit occupies a sign incompatible with our own birth sign, we can expect to feel a vague uneasiness, perhaps a touch of irritableness. We should not be discouraged nor let the feeling get us down, or, worse still, allow ourselves to take the discomfort out on others. Try to remember that the Moon has to change signs within 55 hours and, provided you are not physically ill, your mood will probably change with it. It is amazing how frequently depression lifts with the shift in the Moon's position. And, of course, when the Moon is transiting a sign compatible or sympathetic to yours, you will probably feel some sort of stimulation or just be plain happy to be alive.

In the horoscope, the Moon is such a powerful indicator that competent astrologers often use the sign it occupied at birth as the birth sign of the person. This is done particularly when the Sun is on the cusp, or edge, of two signs. Most experienced astrologers, however, coordinate both Sun and Moon signs by reading and confirming from one to the other and secure a far more accurate and personalized analysis.

For these reasons, the Moon tables which follow this section (see pages 86–92) are of great importance to the individual. They show the days and the exact times the Moon will enter each sign of the Zodiac for the year. Remember, you have to adjust the indicated times to local time. The corrections, already calculated for most of the main cities, are at the beginning of the tables. What follows now is a guide to the influences that will be reflected to the Earth by the Moon while it transits each of the twelve signs. The influence is at its peak about 26 hours after the Moon enters a sign. As you read the daily forecast, check the Moon sign for any given day and glance back at this guide.

MOON IN ARIES

This is a time for action, for reaching out beyond the usual self-imposed limitations and faint-hearted cautions. If you have plans in your head or on your desk, put them into practice. New ventures, applications, new jobs, new starts of any kind—all have a good chance of success. This is the period when original and dynamic impulses are being reflected onto Earth. Such energies are extremely vital and favor the pursuit of pleasure and adventure in practically every form. Sick people should feel an improvement. Those who are well will probably find themselves exuding confidence and optimism. People fond of physical exercise should find their bodies growing with tone and well-being. Boldness, strength, determination should characterize most of your activities with a readiness to face up to old challenges. Yesterday's problems may seem petty and exaggerated—so deal with them. Strike out alone. Self-reliance will attract others to you. This is a good time for making friends. Business and marriage partners are more likely to be impressed with the man and woman of action. Opposition will be overcome or thrown aside with much less effort than usual. CAUTION: Be dominant but not domineering.

MOON IN TAURUS

The spontaneous, action-packed person of yesterday gives way to the cautious, diligent, hardworking "thinker." In this period ideas will probably be concentrated on ways of improving finances. A great deal of time may be spent figuring out and going over schemes and plans. It is the right time to be careful with detail.

People will find themselves working longer than usual at their desks. Or devoting more time to serious thought about the future. A strong desire to put order into business and financial arrangements may cause extra work. Loved ones may complain of being neglected and may fail to appreciate that your efforts are for their ultimate benefit. Your desire for system may extend to criticism of arrangements in the home and lead to minor upsets. Health may be affected through overwork. Try to secure a reasonable amount of rest and relaxation, although the tendency will be to "keep going" despite good advice. Work done conscientiously in this period should result in a solid contribution to your future security. CAUTION: Try not to be as serious with people as the work you are engaged in.

MOON IN GEMINI

The humdrum of routine and too much work should suddenly end. You are likely to find yourself in an expansive, quicksilver world of change and self-expression. Urges to write, to paint, to experience the freedom of some sort of artistic outpouring, may be very strong. Take full advantage of them. You may find yourself finishing something you began and put aside long ago. Or embarking on something new which could easily be prompted by a chance meeting, a new acquaintance, or even an advertisement. There may be a yearning for a change of scenery, the feeling to visit another country (not too far away), or at least to get away for a few days. This may result in short, quick journeys. Or, if you are planning a single visit, there may be some unexpected changes or detours on the way. Familiar activities will seem to give little satisfaction unless they contain a fresh element of excitement or expectation. The inclination will be toward untried pursuits, particularly those that allow you to express your inner nature. The accent is on new faces, new places. CAUTION: Do not be too quick to commit yourself emotionally.

MOON IN CANCER

Feelings of uncertainty and vague insecurity are likely to cause problems while the Moon is in Cancer. Thoughts may turn frequently to the warmth of the home and the comfort of loved ones. Nostalgic impulses could cause you to bring out old photographs and letters and reflect on the days when your life seemed to be much more rewarding and less demanding. The love and understanding of parents and family may be important, and, if it is not forthcoming, you may have to fight against bouts of self-pity. The cordiality of friends and the thought of good times with them that are sure to be repeated will help to restore you to a happier frame of mind. The desire to be alone may follow minor setbacks or rebuffs at this time, but solitude is unlikely to help. Better to get on the telephone or visit someone. This period often causes peculiar dreams and upsurges of imaginative thinking which can be helpful to authors of occult and mystical works. Preoccupation with the personal world of simple human needs can overshadow any material strivings. CAUTION: Do not spend too much time thinking—seek the company of loved ones or close friends.

MOON IN LEO
New horizons of exciting and rather extravagant activity open up. This is the time for exhilarating entertainment, glamorous and lavish parties, and expensive shopping sprees. Any merrymaking that relies upon your generosity as a host has every chance of being a spectacular success. You should find yourself right in the center of the fun, either as the life of the party or simply as a person whom happy people like to be with. Romance thrives in this heady atmosphere and friendships are likely to explode unexpectedly into serious attachments. Children and younger people should be attracted to you and you may find yourself organizing a picnic or a visit to a fun-fair, the movies, or the beach. The sunny company and vitality of youthful companions should help you to find some unsuspected energy. In career, you could find an opening for promotion or advancement. This should be the time to make a direct approach. The period favors those engaged in original research. CAUTION: Bask in popularity, not in flattery.

MOON IN VIRGO
Off comes the party cap and out steps the busy, practical worker. He wants to get his personal affairs straight, to rearrange them, if necessary, for more efficiency, so he will have more time for more work. He clears up his correspondence, pays outstanding bills, makes numerous phone calls. He is likely to make inquiries, or sign up for some new insurance and put money into gilt-edged investment. Thoughts probably revolve around the need for future security—to tie up loose ends and clear the decks. There may be a tendency to be "finicky," to interfere in the routine of others, particularly friends and family members. The motive may be a genuine desire to help with suggestions for updating or streamlining their affairs, but these will probably not be welcomed. Sympathy may be felt for less fortunate sections of the community and a flurry of some sort of voluntary service is likely. This may be accompanied by strong feelings of responsibility on several fronts and health may suffer from extra efforts made. CAUTION: Everyone may not want your help or advice.

MOON IN LIBRA

These are days of harmony and agreement and you should find yourself at peace with most others. Relationships tend to be smooth and sweet-flowing. Friends may become closer and bonds deepen in mutual understanding. Hopes will be shared. Progress by cooperation could be the secret of success in every sphere. In business, established partnerships may flourish and new ones get off to a good start. Acquaintances could discover similar interests that lead to congenial discussions and rewarding exchanges of some sort. Love, as a unifying force, reaches its optimum. Marriage partners should find accord. Those who wed at this time face the prospect of a happy union. Cooperation and tolerance are felt to be stronger than dissension and impatience. The argumentative are not quite so loud in their bellowings, nor as inflexible in their attitudes. In the home, there should be a greater recognition of the other point of view and a readiness to put the wishes of the group before selfish insistence. This is a favorable time to join an art group. CAUTION: Do not be too independent—let others help you if they want to.

MOON IN SCORPIO

Driving impulses to make money and to economize are likely to cause upsets all around. No area of expenditure is likely to be spared the ax, including the household budget. This is a time when the desire to cut down on extravagance can become near fanatical. Care must be exercised to try to keep the aim in reasonable perspective. Others may not feel the same urgent need to save and may retaliate. There is a danger that possessions of sentimental value will be sold to realize cash for investment. Buying and selling of stock for quick profit is also likely. The attention turns to organizing, reorganizing, tidying up at home and at work. Neglected jobs could suddenly be done with great bursts of energy. The desire for solitude may intervene. Self-searching thoughts could disturb. The sense of invisible and mysterious energies in play could cause some excitability. The reassurance of loves ones may help. CAUTION: Be kind to the people you love.

MOON IN SAGITTARIUS

These are days when you are likely to be stirred and elevated by discussions and reflections of a religious and philosophical nature. Ideas of faraway places may cause unusual response and excitement. A decision may be made to visit someone overseas, perhaps a person whose influence was important to your earlier character development. There could be a strong resolution to get away from present intellectual patterns, to learn new subjects, and to meet more interesting people. The superficial may be rejected in all its forms. An impatience with old ideas and unimaginative contacts could lead to a change of companions and interests. There may be an upsurge of religious feeling and metaphysical inquiry. Even a new insight into the significance of astrology and other occult studies is likely under the curious stimulus of the Moon in Sagittarius. Physically, you may express this need for fundamental change by spending more time outdoors: sports, gardening, long walks appeal. CAUTION: Try to channel any restlessness into worthwhile study.

MOON IN CAPRICORN

Life in these hours may seem to pivot around the importance of gaining prestige and honor in the career, as well as maintaining a spotless reputation. Ambitious urges may be excessive and could be accompanied by quite acquisitive drives for money. Effort should be directed along strictly ethical lines where there is no possibility of reproach or scandal. All endeavors are likely to be characterized by great earnestness, and an air of authority and purpose which should impress those who are looking for leadership or reliability. The desire to conform to accepted standards may extend to sharp criticism of family members. Frivolity and unconventional actions are unlikely to amuse while the Moon is in Capricorn. Moderation and seriousness are the orders of the day. Achievement and recognition in this period could come through community work or organizing for the benefit of some amateur group. CAUTION: Dignity and esteem are not always self-awarded.

MOON IN AQUARIUS

Moon in Aquarius is in the second last sign of the Zodiac where ideas can become disturbingly fine and subtle. The result is often a mental "no-man's land" where imagination cannot be trusted with the same certitude as other times. The dangers for the individual are the extremes of optimism and pessimism. Unless the imagination is held in check, situations are likely to be misread, and rosy conclusions drawn where they do not exist. Consequences for the unwary can be costly in career and business. Best to think twice and not speak or act until you think again. Pessimism can be a cruel self-inflicted penalty for delusion at this time. Between the two extremes are strange areas of self-deception which, for example, can make the selfish person think he is actually being generous. Eerie dreams which resemble the reality and even seem to continue into the waking state are also possible. CAUTION: Look for the fact and not just for the image in your mind.

MOON IN PISCES

Everything seems to come to the surface now. Memory may be crystal clear, throwing up long-forgotten information which could be valuable in the career or business. Flashes of clairvoyance and intuition are possible along with sudden realizations of one's own nature, which may be used for self-improvement. A talent, never before suspected, may be discovered. Qualities not evident before in friends and marriage partners are likely to be noticed. As this is a period in which the truth seems to emerge, the discovery of false characteristics is likely to lead to disenchantment or a shift in attachments. However, when qualities are accepted, it should lead to happiness and deeper feeling. Surprise solutions could bob up for old problems. There may be a public announcement of the solving of a crime or mystery. People with secrets may find someone has "guessed" correctly. The secrets of the soul or the inner self also tend to reveal themselves. Religious and philosophical groups may make some interesting discoveries. CAUTION: Not a time for activities that depend on secrecy.

NOTE: When you read your daily forecasts, use the Moon Sign Dates that are provided in the following section of Moon Tables. Then you may want to glance back here for the Moon's influence in a given sign.

MOON TABLES

CORRECTION FOR NEW YORK TIME, FIVE HOURS WEST OF GREENWICH

Atlanta, Boston, Detroit, Miami, Washington, Montreal,
  Ottawa, Quebec, Bogota, Havana, Lima, Santiago..Same time

Chicago, New Orleans, Houston, Winnipeg, Churchill,
  Mexico City.. Deduct 1 hour

Albuquerque, Denver, Phoenix, El Paso, Edmonton,
  Helena .... Deduct 2 hours

Los Angeles, San Francisco, Reno, Portland,
  Seattle, Vancouver .... Deduct 3 hours

Honolulu, Anchorage, Fairbanks, Kodiak .... Deduct 5 hours

Nome, Samoa, Tonga, Midway.................... Deduct 6 hours

Halifax, Bermuda, San Juan, Caracas, La Paz,
  Barbados..Add 1 hour

St. John's, Brasilia, Rio de Janeiro, Sao Paulo,
  Buenos Aires, Montevideo..........................Add 2 hours

Azores, Cape Verde Islands...........................Add 3 hours

Canary Islands, Madeira, Reykjavik ....Add 4 hours

London, Paris, Amsterdam, Madrid, Lisbon,
  Gibraltar, Belfast, Rabat ....Add 5 hours

Frankfurt, Rome, Oslo, Stockholm, Prague,
  Belgrade..Add 6 hours

Bucharest, Beirut, Tel Aviv, Athens, Istanbul, Cairo,
  Alexandria, Cape Town, Johannesburg ....Add 7 hours

Moscow, Leningrad, Baghdad, Dhahran,
  Addis Ababa, Nairobi, Teheran, Zanzibar.........Add 8 hours

Bombay, Calcutta, Sri Lanka..................... Add 10 ½ hours

Hong Kong, Shanghai, Manila, Peking, Perth...... Add 13 hours

Tokyo, Okinawa, Darwin, Pusan.................... Add 14 hours

Sydney, Melbourne, Port Moresby, Guam.......... Add 15 hours

Auckland, Wellington, Suva, Wake................. Add 17 hours

1998 MOON SIGN DATES—
NEW YORK TIME

JANUARY		FEBRUARY		MARCH	
Day Moon Enters		**Day Moon Enters**		**Day Moon Enters**	
1. Aquar.		1. Aries		1. Aries	
2. Pisces	4:57 am	2. Taurus	4:26 pm	2. Taurus	0:01 am
3. Pisces		3. Taurus		3. Taurus	
4. Aries	7:44 am	4. Gemini	8:10 pm	4. Gemini	2:16 am
5. Aries		5. Gemini		5. Gemini	
6. Taurus	10:53 am	6. Gemini		6. Cancer	7:28 am
7. Taurus		7. Cancer	1:58 am	7. Cancer	
8. Gemini	2:43 pm	8. Cancer		8. Leo	3:47 pm
9. Gemini		9. Leo	9:58 am	9. Leo	
10. Cancer	7:44 pm	10. Leo		10. Leo	
11. Cancer		11. Virgo	8:10 pm	11. Virgo	2:36 am
12. Cancer		12. Virgo		12. Virgo	
13. Leo	2:46 am	13. Virgo		13. Libra	2:59 pm
14. Leo		14. Libra	8:18 am	14. Libra	
15. Virgo	0:32 pm	15. Libra		15. Libra	
16. Virgo		16. Scorp.	9:14 pm	16. Scorp.	3:52 am
17. Virgo		17. Scorp.		17. Scorp.	
18. Libra	0:45 am	18. Scorp.		18. Sagitt.	3:57 pm
19. Libra		19. Sagitt.	8:57 am	19. Sagitt.	
20. Scorp.	1:35 pm	20. Sagitt.		20. Sagitt.	
21. Scorp.		21. Capric.	5:31 pm	21. Capric.	1:44 am
22. Scorp.		22. Capric.		22. Capric.	
23. Sagitt.	0:26 am	23. Aquar.	10:11 pm	23. Aquar.	8:02 am
24. Sagitt.		24. Aquar.		24. Aquar.	
25. Capric.	7:40 am	25. Pisces	11:43 pm	25. Pisces	10:44 am
26. Capric.		26. Pisces		26. Pisces	
27. Aquar.	11:28 am	27. Aries	11:43 pm	27. Aries	10:50 am
28. Aquar.		28. Aries		28. Aries	
29. Pisces	1:09 pm			29. Taurus	10:07 am
30. Pisces				30. Taurus	
31. Aries	2:22 pm			31. Gemini	10:39 am

Summer time to be considered where applicable.

1998 MOON SIGN DATES—
NEW YORK TIME

APRIL		MAY		JUNE	
Day Moon Enters		**Day Moon Enters**		**Day Moon Enters**	
1. Gemini		1. Cancer		1. Virgo	
2. Cancer	2:11 pm	2. Leo	4:50 am	2. Virgo	
3. Cancer		3. Leo		3. Libra	10:18 am
4. Leo	9:37 pm	4. Virgo	2:48 pm	4. Libra	
5. Leo		5. Virgo		5. Scorp.	11:07 pm
6. Leo		6. Virgo		6. Scorp.	
7. Virgo	8:26 am	7. Libra	3:20 am	7. Scorp.	
8. Virgo		8. Libra		8. Sagitt.	10:35 am
9. Libra	9:05 pm	9. Scorp.	4:11 pm	9. Sagitt.	
10. Libra		10. Scorp.		10. Capric.	7:51 pm
11. Libra		11. Scorp.		11. Capric.	
12. Scorp.	9:57 am	12. Sagitt.	3:49 am	12. Capric.	
13. Scorp.		13. Sagitt.		13. Aquar.	3:04 am
14. Sagitt.	9:53 pm	14. Capric.	1:40 pm	14. Aquar.	
15. Sagitt.		15. Capric.		15. Pisces	8:32 am
16. Sagitt.		16. Aquar.	9:31 pm	16. Pisces	
17. Capric.	8:06 am	17. Aquar.		17. Aries	0:24 pm
18. Capric.		18. Aquar.		18. Aries	
19. Aquar.	3:42 pm	19. Pisces	3:04 am	19. Taurus	2:48 pm
20. Aquar.		20. Pisces		20. Taurus	
21. Pisces	8:07 pm	21. Aries	6:07 am	21. Gemini	4:27 pm
22. Pisces		22. Aries		22. Gemini	
23. Aries	9:31 pm	23. Taurus	7:07 am	23. Cancer	6:40 pm
24. Aries		24. Taurus		24. Cancer	
25. Taurus	9:10 pm	25. Gemini	7:26 am	25. Leo	11:05 pm
26. Taurus		26. Gemini		26. Leo	
27. Gemini	8:56 pm	27. Cancer	8:59 am	27. Leo	
28. Gemini		28. Cancer		28. Virgo	6:55 am
29. Cancer	10:58 pm	29. Leo	1:39 pm	29. Virgo	
30. Cancer		30. Leo		30. Libra	6:06 pm
31. Virgo	10:22 pm				

Summer time to be considered where applicable.

1998 MOON SIGN DATES—
NEW YORK TIME

JULY		AUGUST		SEPTEMBER	
Day Moon Enters		Day Moon Enters		Day Moon Enters	
1. Libra		1. Scorp.		1. Capric.	
2. Libra		2. Sagitt.	2:49 am	2. Capric.	
3. Scorp.	6:46 am	3. Sagitt.		3. Aquar.	4:22 am
4. Scorp.		4. Capric.	0:19 pm	4. Aquar.	
5. Sagitt.	6:25 pm	5. Capric.		5. Pisces	7:49 am
6. Sagitt.		6. Aquar.	6:32 pm	6. Pisces	
7. Sagitt.		7. Aquar.		7. Aries	8:53 am
8. Capric.	3:28 am	8. Pisces	10:05 pm	8. Aries	
9. Capric.		9. Pisces		9. Taurus	9:17 am
10. Aquar.	9:53 am	10. Pisces		10. Taurus	
11. Aquar.		11. Aries	0:11 am	11. Gemini	10:41 am
12. Pisces	2:23 pm	12. Aries		12. Gemini	
13. Pisces		13. Taurus	2:05 am	13. Cancer	2:21 pm
14. Aries	5:46 pm	14. Taurus		14. Cancer	
15. Aries		15. Gemini	4:47 am	15. Leo	8:49 pm
16. Taurus	8:34 pm	16. Gemini		16. Leo	
17. Taurus		17. Cancer	1:56 am	17. Leo	
18. Gemini	11:19 pm	18. Cancer		18. Virgo	5:53 am
19. Gemini		19. Leo	3:02 pm	19. Virgo	
20. Gemini		20. Leo		20. Libra	4:58 pm
21. Cancer	2:44 am	21. Virgo	11:22 pm	21. Libra	
22. Cancer		22. Virgo		22. Libra	
23. Leo	7:50 am	23. Virgo		23. Scorp.	5:23 am
24. Leo		24. Libra	10:03 am	24. Scorp.	
25. Virgo	3:35 pm	25. Libra		25. Sagitt.	6:06 pm
26. Virgo		26. Scorp.	10:26 pm	26. Sagitt.	
27. Virgo		27. Scorp.		27. Sagitt.	
28. Libra	2:15 am	28. Scorp.		28. Capric.	5:31 am
29. Libra		29. Sagitt.	10:56 am	29. Capric.	
30. Scorp.	2:45 pm	30. Sagitt.		30. Aquar.	1:54 pm
31. Scorp.		31. Capric.	9:24 pm		

Summer time to be considered where applicable.

1998 MOON SIGN DATES—
NEW YORK TIME

OCTOBER		NOVEMBER		DECEMBER	
Day Moon Enters		**Day Moon Enters**		**Day Moon Enters**	
1. Aquar.		1. Aries	6:28 am	1. Taurus	
2. Pisces	6:24 pm	2. Aries		2. Gemini	4:31 pm
3. Pisces		3. Taurus	6:13 am	3. Gemini	
4. Aries	7:33 pm	4. Taurus		4. Cancer	4:29 pm
5. Aries		5. Gemini	5:12 am	5. Cancer	
6. Taurus	6:58 pm	6. Gemini		6. Leo	6:56 pm
7. Taurus		7. Cancer	5:40 am	7. Leo	
8. Gemini	6:45 pm	8. Cancer		8. Leo	
9. Gemini		9. Leo	9:34 am	9. Virgo	1:22 am
10. Cancer	8:49 pm	10. Leo		10. Virgo	
11. Cancer		11. Virgo	5:38 pm	11. Libra	11:44 am
12. Cancer		12. Virgo		12. Libra	
13. Leo	2:26 am	13. Virgo		13. Libra	
14. Leo		14. Libra	4:59 am	14. Scorp.	0:17 am
15. Virgo	11:33 am	15. Libra		15. Scorp.	
16. Virgo		16. Scorp.	5:42 pm	16. Sagitt.	0:48 pm
17. Libra	11:03 pm	17. Scorp.		17. Sagitt.	
18. Libra		18. Scorp.		18. Capric.	11:56 pm
19. Libra		19. Sagitt.	6:14 am	19. Capric.	
20. Scorp.	11:37 am	20. Sagitt.		20. Capric.	
21. Scorp.		21. Capric.	5:46 am	21. Aquar.	9:18 am
22. Scorp.		22. Capric.		22. Aquar.	
23. Sagitt.	0:17 am	23. Capric.		23. Pisces	4:46 pm
24. Sagitt.		24. Aquar.	3:44 am	24. Pisces	
25. Capric.	0:06 pm	25. Aquar.		25. Aries	10:05 pm
26. Capric.		26. Pisces	11:15 am	26. Aries	
27. Aquar.	9:45 pm	27. Pisces		27. Aries	
28. Aquar.		28. Aries	3:35 pm	28. Taurus	1:06 am
29. Aquar.		29. Aries		29. Taurus	
30. Pisces	3:59 am	30. Taurus	4:54 pm	30. Gemini	2:23 am
31. Pisces				31. Gemini	

Summer time to be considered where applicable.

1998 PHASES OF THE MOON—
NEW YORK TIME

New Moon	First Quarter	Full Moon	Last Quarter
Dec. 29 ('97)	Jan. 5	Jan. 12	Jan. 20
Jan. 28	Feb. 3	Feb. 11	Feb. 19
Feb. 26	Mar. 5	Mar. 12	Mar. 21
Mar. 27	Apr. 3	Apr. 11	Apr. 19
Apr. 26	May 3	May 11	May 18
May 25	June 1	June 9	June 17
June 23	July 1	July 9	July 16
July 23	July 31	Aug. 7	Aug. 14
Aug. 21	Aug. 30	Sept. 6	Sept. 12
Sept. 20	Sept. 28	Oct. 5	Oct. 12
Oct. 20	Oct. 28	Nov. 4	Nov. 10
Nov. 18	Nov. 26	Dec. 3	Dec. 10
Dec. 18	Dec. 26	Jan. 1 ('99)	Jan. 9 ('99)

Each phase of the Moon lasts approximately seven to eight days, during which the Moon's shape gradually changes as it comes out of one phase and goes into the next.

There will be a partial solar eclipse during the New Moon phase on February 26 and August 21.

1998 FISHING GUIDE

	Good	Best
January	5-9-10-13-14-15-28	11-12-20
February	9-10-11-12-13-14	3-8
March	5-10-11-12-13-28	14-15-16-21
April	8-9-19	3-10-11-12-13-14-26
May	3-12-13-14-25	8-9-10-11-19
June	2-8-9-10-13-17	7-11-12-24
July	6-7-10-11-12-16-23	1-8-9-31
August	7-8-11-22-30	5-6-9-10-14
September	3-4-5-7-8-9-13-20-28	6
October	2-5-6-28	3-4-7-8-12-20
November	1-2-3-5-6-7-11-19-30	4-27
December	2-3-4-10-18-26	1-5-6

1998 PLANTING GUIDE

	Aboveground Crops	Root Crops
January	2-3-7-11-30	18-19-20-21-22-26
February	3-4-7-8-27	15-16-17-18-22-23
March	2-3-7-11-12-30	14-15-16-17-21-22-26
April	3-4-10-11-27-30	12-13-14-18-22-23
May	1-7-8-9-10-28	15-16-19-20-24
June	4-5-6-7-24-25	11-12-16-20
July	1-2-3-4-5-8-28-29-30-31	13-17-18-21-22
August	1-5-6-25-26-27-28	9-10-13-14-18
September	1-2-21-22-23-24-25-29	10-14-15
October	3-4-21-22-26-27-30-31	7-8-11-12-18-19
November	22-23-27	4-8-14-15-16-17-18
December	1-19-20-24-25-28-29	5-6-12-13-14-15

	Pruning	Weeds and Pests
January	21-22	13-14-15-16-17-23-24
February	17-18	12-13-20-21-24-25
March	16-17-26	19-20-24
April	13-14-22-23	15-16-20-21-24-25
May	19-20	12-13-17-18-22
June	16	10-13-14-18-22-23
July	13-21-22	11-15-16-19-20
August	9-10-18	8-11-12-15-16-20-21
September	14-15	8-12-16-17-18-19
October	11-12	6-9-10-13-14-15-16-17
November	8-17-18	6-10-11-12-13
December	5-6-14-15	7-8-9-10-17-18

MOON'S INFLUENCE OVER PLANTS

Centuries ago it was established that seeds planted when the Moon is in signs and phases called Fruitful will produce more growth than seeds planted when the Moon is in a Barren sign.

Fruitful Signs: Taurus, Cancer, Libra, Scorpio, Capricorn, Pisces
Barren Signs: Aries, Gemini, Leo, Virgo, Sagittarius, Aquarius
Dry Signs: Aries, Gemini, Sagittarius, Aquarius

Activity	Moon In
Mow lawn, trim plants	**Fruitful sign:** 1st & 2nd quarter
Plant flowers	**Fruitful sign:** 2nd quarter; best in Cancer and Libra
Prune	**Fruitful sign:** 3rd & 4th quarter
Destroy pests; spray	**Barren sign:** 4th quarter
Harvest potatoes, root crops	**Dry sign:** 3rd & 4th quarter; Taurus, Leo, and Aquarius

MOON'S INFLUENCE OVER YOUR HEALTH

ARIES	Head, brain, face, upper jaw
TAURUS	Throat, neck, lower jaw
GEMINI	Hands, arms, lungs, shoulders, nervous system
CANCER	Esophagus, stomach, breasts, womb, liver
LEO	Heart, spine
VIRGO	Intestines, liver
LIBRA	Kidneys, lower back
SCORPIO	Sex and eliminative organs
SAGITTARIUS	Hips, thighs, liver
CAPRICORN	Skin, bones, teeth, knees
AQUARIUS	Circulatory system, lower legs
PISCES	Feet, tone of being

Try to avoid work being done on that part of the body when the Moon is in the sign governing that part.

MOON'S INFLUENCE OVER DAILY AFFAIRS

The Moon makes a complete transit of the Zodiac every 27 days 7 hours and 43 minutes. In making this transit the Moon forms different aspects with the planets and consequently has favorable or unfavorable bearings on affairs and events for persons according to the sign of the Zodiac under which they were born.

When the Moon is in conjunction with the Sun it is called a New Moon; when the Moon and Sun are in opposition it is called a Full Moon. From New Moon to Full Moon, first and second quarter—which takes about two weeks—the Moon is increasing or waxing. From Full Moon to New Moon, third and fourth quarter, the Moon is decreasing or waning.

Activity	Moon In
Business: buying and selling new, requiring public support	Sagittarius, Aries, Gemini, Virgo 1st and 2nd quarter
meant to be kept quiet	3rd and 4th quarter
Investigation	3rd and 4th quarter
Signing documents	1st & 2nd quarter, Cancer, Scorpio, Pisces
Advertising	2nd quarter, Sagittarius
Journeys and trips	1st & 2nd quarter, Gemini, Virgo
Renting offices, etc.	Taurus, Leo, Scorpio, Aquarius
Painting of house/apartment	3rd & 4th quarter, Taurus, Scorpio, Aquarius
Decorating	Gemini, Libra, Aquarius
Buying clothes and accessories	Taurus, Virgo
Beauty salon or barber shop visit	1st & 2nd quarter, Taurus, Leo, Libra, Scorpio, Aquarius
Weddings	1st & 2nd quarter

CANCER

CANCER

Character Analysis

Cancer is generally rather sensitive. He or she is quite often a generous person by nature, and is willing to help almost anyone in need. He is emotional and often feels sorry for people less fortunate than he. He could never refuse to answer someone's call for help. It is because of his sympathetic nature that others take advantage of him now and again.

In spite of his willingness to help others, the Cancer man or woman may seem difficult to approach by anyone not well acquainted with their character. On the whole, he seems subdued and reserved. Others may feel there is a wall between them and Cancer, although this may not be the case at all. The person born under this sign, which is ruled by the Moon, is careful not to let others hurt him. He has learned through hard experience that protection of some sort is necessary in order to get along in life. The person who wins his confidence and is able to get beyond this barrier will find the Moon Child a warm and loving person.

With his family and close friends, he is a very faithful and dependable person. In his quiet way, he can be affectionate and loving. He is generally not one given to demonstrative behavior. He can be fond of someone without telling them so a dozen times a day. With people he is close to, Cancer is more open about his own need for affection, and he enjoys being pampered by his loved ones. He likes to feel wanted and protected.

When he has made up his mind about something, he sticks to it, and is generally a very constant person. He knows how to hold his ground. He never wavers. People who don't know him may think him weak and easily managed, because he is so quiet and modest, but this is far from true. He can take a lot of punishment for an idea or a cause he believes in. For Cancer, right is right. In order to protect himself, the person born under this sign will sometimes put up a pose as someone bossy and domineering. Sometimes he is successful in fooling others with his brash front. People who have known him for a while, however, are seldom taken in.

Many people born under this sign of the Crab are shy and seemingly lacking in confidence. They know their own minds, though, even if they do not seem to. He responds to kindness and encouragement. He will be himself with people he trusts. A good person can bring out the best in the Crab. Disagreeable or unfeeling people can send him scurrying back into his shell. He is a person who does not appreciate sharp criticism. Some Crabs are worriers. They are very concerned about what others may think of them. This may bother them so much that they develop a deep feeling of inferiority. Sometimes this reaches the point where he is so unsure of himself in some matters that he allows himself to be influenced by someone who has a stronger personality. Also, some Crabs may be afraid that people will talk behind his back if he doesn't comply with their wishes. However, this does not stop him from doing what he feels is right. The cultivated Cancer learns to think for himself and has no fear of disapproval.

The Cancer man or woman is most himself at home. The person born under this sign is a real lover of domesticity. He likes a place where he can relax and feel properly sheltered. Cancers like things to stay as they are; they are not fond of changes of any sort. They are not very adaptable people. When visiting others or going to unfamiliar places, they are not likely to feel very comfortable. They are not the most talkative people at a party. In the comfort of their own homes, however, they blossom and bloom.

The Cancer man or woman sticks by the rules, whatever the game. He is not a person who would ever think of going against an established grain. He is conventional and moderate in almost all things. In a way he likes the old-fashioned things. However, in spite of this, he is interested in new things and does what he can to keep up with the times. In a way, he has two sides to his character. He is seldom forgetful. He has a memory like an elephant and can pick out any detail from the past with no trouble at all. He often reflects on things that have happened. He prefers the past to the future, which sometimes fills him with a feeling of apprehension.

This fourth sign of the Zodiac is a motherly one. Even the Cancer man has something maternal about him. He is usually kind and considerate, ready to help and protect. Others are drawn to Cancer because of these gentle qualities. People in trouble often turn to him for advice and sympathy. People find him easy to confide in.

The Cancer person in general is very forgiving. He almost never holds a grudge. Still, it would not be wise to anger him. Treat him fairly and he will treat you the same. He does not appreciate people who lose patience with him. Cancer is usually proud of his mind and does not like to be considered unintelligent. Even if others feel that he is somewhat slow in some areas, he would rather not have this opinion expressed in his presence. He's not a person to be played with; he can tell when someone is treating him like a fool.

Quite often people born under this sign are musically inclined. Some of them have a deep interest in religious matters. They are apt to be interested in mystical matters, as well. Although they are fascinated by these things, they may be somewhat afraid of being overwhelmed if they go into them too deeply. In spite of this feeling of apprehension, Moon Children try to satisfy their curiosity in these matters.

Health

For the person born under the sign of Cancer, the stomach is the weak point. Chances are that Cancer is easily susceptible to infection. Sometimes his health is affected by nervousness. He can be quite a worrier. Even little things eat at him from time to time, which is apt to lower his resistance to infectious illnesses. He is often upset by small matters.

A Cancer as a child is sometimes sickly and weak. His physique during this period of growth can be described in most cases as fragile. Some develop into physically strong adults, others may have the remnants of childhood ailments with them for a good part of their adult lives. They are frightened of being sick. Illness is a word they would rather not mention. Pain is also a thing they fear.

They are given to quick-changing moods at times, which often has an effect on their overall health. Worry or depression can have a subliminal effect on their general health. Usually their illnesses are not as serious as they imagine them to be. They sometimes find it easy to feel sorry for themselves.

On the whole, the Cancer man or woman is a quiet person. He is not one to brag or push his weight around. However, let it not be thought that he lacks the force that others have. He can be quite purposeful and energetic when the situation calls for it. However, when it comes to tooting their own horn, they can be somewhat shy and reticent. They may lack the get-up-and-go that others have when it comes to pushing their personal interests ahead.

Some Cancers are quite aware of the fact that they are not what one would call sturdy in physique or temperament. Some may go through life rather painfully trying to cover up the weak side of their nature.

Sons and daughters of the Moon may not be very vigorous or active. As a rule, they are not too fond of physical exercise, and they have a weakness for rich and heavy foods. As a result, in later life they could end up overweight. Some Cancers have trouble with their kidneys and intestines. Others digest their food poorly. The wise Cancer man or woman, however, adheres to a strict and well-balanced diet with plenty of fresh fruit and vegetables. Moreover, they see to it that they properly exercise daily. The Cancer man or woman who learns to cut down on rich foods and worry often lives to a ripe old age.

Occupation

Cancer generally has no trouble at all establishing himself in the business world. He has all those qualities that make one a success professionally. He is careful with his equipment as well as his money. He is patient and he knows how to persevere. Any job where he has a chance to use his mind instead of his body is usually a job in which he has no trouble succeeding. He can work well with people—especially people situated in dire straits. Welfare work is the kind of occupation in which he usually excels. He can really be quite a driving person if his job calls for it. Cancer is surprisingly resourceful. In spite of his retiring disposition, he is capable of accomplishing some very difficult tasks.

Cancer can put on an aggressive front, and in some cases it can carry him far. Quite often he is able to develop leadership qualities and make good use of them. He knows how to direct his energy so that he never becomes immediately exhausted. He'll work away at a difficult chore gradually, seldom approaching anything head-on. By working at something obliquely he often finds advantages along the way that are not apparent to others. In spite of his cautious approach, Cancer is often taxed by work that is too demanding of his energy. He may put up a good front of being strong and courageous while actually he is at the end of his emotional rope. Risks sometimes frighten the Crab. It is often fear that exhausts him. The possible dangers in the world of business set him to worrying.

Cancer does not boast about what he is going to do. He or she just quietly goes ahead and does it. Quite often he accomplishes more than others in this quiet way.

The person born under this sign enjoys helping others. By nature, he is quite a sympathetic individual. He does not like to see others suffer or do without. He is willing to make sacrifices for someone he trusts and cares for. Cancer's maternal streak works wonders with children. People born under the fourth sign of the Zodiac often make excellent teachers. They understand young people well and do what they can to help them grow up properly.

Cancers also are fairly intuitive. In business or financial matters, they often make an important strike by playing a strong hunch. In some cases they are able to rely almost entirely on their feelings rather than on reason.

Water attracts the Cancer person. Often they have connections with the oceans through their professions. Cancer homemakers experimenting in the kitchen often are very successful creating new drinks and blending liquid recipes. Overseas trade and commerce also appeal.

The average Cancer has many choices as far as a career is concerned. There are many things that he can do well once he puts his mind to it. In the arts he is quite likely to do well. The Cancer man or woman has a way with beauty, harmony, and creativity. Basically, he is a very capable person in many things; it depends on which of his talents he wants to develop to a professional point. He has a rich imagination and sometimes can make use of it in the area of painting, music, or sculpture.

When working for someone else, Cancer can always be depended upon. He makes a loyal and conscientious employee.

It is important for Cancer to select a job that is well suited to his talents and temperament. Although he may feel that earning money is important, Cancer eventually comes to the point where he realizes that it is even more important to enjoy the work he is doing. He should have a position that allows him to explore the recesses of his personality and to develop. When placed in the wrong job, the Cancer man or woman might wish they were somewhere else.

Cancers know the value of money. They are not the sort of people who go throwing money around recklessly. Cancer is honest and expects others to be the same. He is quite modest in most things and deplores unnecessary display. Cancers have a genius for making money and for investing or saving it.

Security is important to the person born under this sign. He'll always see to it that he has something put away for that inevitable rainy day. He is also a hard worker and is willing to put in long hours for the money it brings him. Financial success is usually the result of his own perseverance and industry. Through his own need for security, it is often easy for Cancer to sympathize with those of like dispositions. He is a helpful person. If he sees someone trying to do his best to get ahead—and still not succeeding— he is quite apt to put aside his own interests temporarily to help another.

Sometimes Cancer worries about money even when he has it. Even the wealthy Cancer can never be too secure. It would be better for him to learn how to relax and not to let his worries undermine his health. Financial matters often cause him considerable concern—even when it is not necessary.

Home and Family

Cancers are usually great home lovers. They are very domestic by nature; home for them spells security. Cancer is a family person. He respects those who are related to him. He feels a great responsibility toward all the members of his family. There is usually a very strong tie between Cancer and his mother that lasts through his whole life. Something a Cancer will not tolerate is for someone to speak ill of a member of his family. This for him is a painful and deep insult. He has a great respect for his family and family traditions. Quite often Cancer is well-acquainted with his family tree. If he happens to have a relative who has been quite successful in life, he is proud of the fact. Once he is home for the weekend, he generally stays there.

Cancer is sentimental about old things and habits. He is apt to have many things stored away from years ago. Something that was dear to his parents will probably be dear to him as well.

Many Cancers travel near and far from time to time. But no matter what their destination, they are always glad to be back where they feel they belong.

The home of a Cancer is usually quite comfortable and tastefully furnished. Cancer men and women are romantic, which is usually reflected in the way their house is arranged.

The Cancer child is always attached to his home and family. He may not care to go out and play with other children very much but enjoys it when his friends come to his house.

The maternal nature of the Cancer person comes out when he gives a party. He is a very attentive host and worries over a guest like a mother hen—anxious to see that they are comfortable and lack nothing. He does his best to make others happy and at home, and he is admired and loved for that. People who visit are usually deeply impressed by their outgoing ways. The Cancer host prepares unusual and delicious snacks for visitors. Cancer is very concerned about them and sees to it that they are well-fed while visiting.

Homebodies that they are, Cancers generally do what they can to make their home a comfortable and interesting place for themselves as well as for others. They feel very flattered when a visitor pays them a compliment on their home.

Children play a very important part in the lives of people born under this sign. Cancers fuss over their youngsters and give them the things they feel that they need. They generally like to have large families. They see to it that their children are well provided for and that they have the chances in life that their parents never had. The best mother of the Zodiac is usually someone born under the sign of Cancer. They have a strong protective nature. They usually have a strong sense of duty, and when their children are in difficulty they do everything they can to set matters right. Children, needless to say, are fond of their Cancer parent, and respond lovingly to make the parent-child relationship a harmonious one.

Social Relationships

Cancer may seem rather retiring and quiet, and this gives people the impression that he is not too warm or sympathetic. However, most Moon Children are very sensitive and loving. Their ability to understand and sympathize with others is great. Cancer likes to have close friends—people who love and understand him as well as he tries to love and understand them. He wants to be well-liked—to be noticed by people who he feels should like him. If he does not get the attention and affection he feels he is entitled to, he is apt to become sullen and difficult to deal with.

The Cancer man or woman has strong powers of intuition and can generally sense when he has met a person who is likely to turn into a good friend. Cancer suffers greatly if ever he should lose a friend. To him friendships are sacred. Sometimes Cancer sets friends on too high a pedestal. He or she is apt to feel crestfallen when he discovers that they have feet of clay. He is often romantic in his approach to friendship and is likely to seek people out for sentimental reasons rather than for practical ones.

Cancer is a very sensitive person and sometimes this contributes to making a friendship unsatisfactory. He sometimes makes the wrong interpretation of a remark that is made by a friend or acquaintance. He imagines something injurious behind a very innocent remark. He sometimes feels that people who profess to be his friends laugh at him cruelly behind his back. He has to be constantly reassured of a friend's sincerity, especially in the beginning of a relationship. If he wants to have the wide circle of friends he desires, Cancer must learn to curb these persecution fantasies.

Love and Marriage

The Cancer man or woman has to have love in their life, otherwise their existence is a dull and humdrum affair. When they love someone, Cancer will do everything in their power to make a lover happy. They are not afraid to sacrifice in order to make an important relationship work. To his loved one he is likely to seem uncertain and moody. Cancer is usually very influenced by the impression he has of his lover. They may even be content to let their romance partner have his or her own way in the relationship. He may not make many demands but be willing to follow those of his loved one. At times he may feel that he is not really loved, and draw away somewhat from the relationship. Sometimes it takes a lot of coaxing before he can be won over to the fact that he is indeed loved for himself alone.

Cancer is often possessive about people as well as material objects. This often makes the relationship difficult to accept for his partner.

His standards are sometimes impossibly high and because of this he is difficult to please. The Cancer man or woman is interested in finding someone with whom he can spend the rest of his life. He or she is not interested in any fly-by-night romance.

Romance and the Cancer Woman

The Cancer woman is sincere in her approach to love. Her feelings run deep. Still, she's moody, tempestuous, and changeable. She is so sensitive in romance that her lover may find her difficult to understand at times. The Moon Child knows exactly the sort of man she is looking for. If she can find him, she'll never let him go.

The trouble is she frequently goes through a lot of men in her search for the perfect lover. She surrenders completely to her emotions. She can experience the whole melodrama of falling in love, longing to be with her man, then being desolate when parted from him. If she does find her ideal mate, she will take to marriage for the rest of her life without looking back or even at another man. If she can't marry the man of her dreams, or even live with him, she might carry a torch for the rest of her days. That is the tenacity of the Cancer woman's pure devotion to the man she loves.

Marriage is a union suited to the Crab's temperament, which needs a safe haven in which her feelings can be nurtured. She longs for permanence in a relationship, and usually is not fond of flings or meaningless romantic adventures. Because her emotions are so deep, she can easily feel wronged by a minor slight. Once she imagines she has been hurt, she can retreat rapidly and withdraw deep within herself to brood. It may be quite a while before she comes out of her shell. She desires a man who is protective and affectionate, someone who can understand and cope with her moods so that she does not feel threatened.

As a Moon Child, Cancer is very temperamental. She'll soar to the heights of ecstasy, then plunge into the depths of despondency all with dazzling speed. She'll sparkle like champagne, then fizzle out before the high wears off. Such marked changes of personality can be bewildering to a lover who may have done nothing to provoke them. Reason and logic will not coax her out of a bad mood. Only patient love will work. And if do you not have staying power or refined sensibilities, then you don't stand the ghost of a chance with the Cancer woman.

Cancer's intuition is usually right on. She can size up a situation instinctively, and more times than not she is right. What her gut feelings tell her can be the cause of many a quarrel and the occasion for nagging her mate about a myriad of things. Because she is possessive, there can be discord. And she more she loves, the more possessive and jealous she can become. The demands she is likely to make can be overbearing at times. But as long as she is reassured and appreciated, all will be well.

The Cancer woman makes a devoted wife and mother who will do everything to keep her family together. The only danger is that she may transfer all her love to the children, making her man feel useless and left out. As long as her man participates fully in family life, there will be harmony and affection.

Romance and the Cancer Man

The Cancer man may come on as the reserved type. It can be difficult for some women to understand him. Generally, he is a very loving person, but sometimes he will not let his sensitive side show. He is afraid of being rejected or hurt, so he tries to keep his true feelings hidden until he knows that the intended object of his affections is capable of taking him seriously.

For him, love is a serious business. And he is so serious about love that you might say he lives for love—to give it and to receive it. True to the symbol of the sign of Cancer, which is the Crab, he feels his way very carefully in any romantic alliance. He is not going to make any rash mistakes. But even if it's only a brief affair, the Cancer man will treat his lover as the only woman in the world. When he is convinced that you, too, are serious, then this sensuous idealist is all yours.

You must never play around with his feelings. Like the Crab, the Cancer man pretends to be tough and invulnerable on the outside, but on the inside he is so soft it hurts. He is perhaps the most sensitive person you have ever met. Your Moon Child is highly emotive and moody, reflecting the Moon's quick changeability and shifts of temperament. And, like his ruler the Moon, he is terribly responsive to the vibes coming from his lover. It's all or nothing with him, so jealousy and possessiveness can become a problem. He needs to be constantly reassured that you love him.

If you love him, tell him so often. And show him that you love him, not only with physical love but also with thoughtfully chosen fine gifts no matter how small. He is sentimental. He will treasure everything you give him. He will keep mementos of your happy moments together, especially souvenirs of the occasion when he became sure you would be the love his life.

When deeply in love, the Cancer man does everything in his power to hold the woman of his choice. He is very affectionate and may be extravagant from time to time with the woman he loves. He will lavish gifts upon you and will see that you never lack anything you desire to make your home life together warm and cozy.

Marriage is something the Cancer man sets as a goal early in his life. He wants to settle down with someone who will mother him to some extent. Often he looks for a woman who has the same qualities as his mother, especially if his early childhood revolved around his mother's central role in the family. The remembrance of things maternal makes him feel truly loved and secure.

The Cancer man is an attentive father. He is fond of large families. Sometimes his love for the children may be too possessive, and he can stifle their independence with smothering ways.

Woman—Man

CANCER WOMAN
ARIES MAN

Although it's possible that you could find happiness with a man born under the sign of the Ram, it's uncertain as to how long that happiness would last.

An Aries who has made his mark in the world and is somewhat steadfast in his outlooks and attitudes could be quite a catch for you. On the other hand, men under this sign are often swift-footed and quick-minded. Their industrious mannerisms may fail to impress you, especially if you feel that much of their get-up-and-go often leads nowhere.

When it comes to a fine romance, you want someone with a nice, broad shoulder to lean on. You are likely to find a relationship with someone who doesn't like to stay put for too long somewhat upsetting.

Aries may have a little trouble in understanding you, too, at least in the beginning of the relationship. He may find you too shy and moody. Aries speak their minds and can criticize at the drop of a hat.

You may find a Ram too demanding. He may give you the impression that he expects you to be at his beck and call. You have a barrelful of patience at your disposal and he may try every last bit of it. He is apt not to be as thorough as you are in everything that he does. In order to achieve success or a goal quickly, he will overlook small but important details—and regret it when it is far too late.

Being married to an Aries does not mean that you'll have a secure and safe life as far as finances are concerned. Not all Aries are rash with cash, but they lack that sound head you have for putting away something for that inevitable rainy day. He'll do his best, however, to see that you're adequately provided for, even though his efforts may leave something to be desired as far as you're concerned.

With an Aries mate, you'll find yourself constantly among people. Aries generally have many friends—and you may not heartily approve of them all. Rams are more interested in interesting people than they are in influential ones. Although there can be a family squabble from time to time, you are stable enough to take it all in your stride. Your love of permanence and a harmonious home life will help you to take the bitter with the sweet.

Aries men love children. They make wonderful fathers. Kids take to them like ducks to water. Their quick minds and behavior appeal to the young.

CANCER WOMAN
TAURUS MAN

Some Taurus men are strong and silent. They do all they can to protect and provide for the women they love. The Taurus man will never let you down. He's steady, sturdy, and reliable. He's pretty honest and practical, too. He says what he means and means what he says. He never indulges in deceit and will always put his cards on the table.

Taurus is very affectionate. Being loved, appreciated, and understood is very important for his well-being. Like you, he is also looking for peace, harmony, and security in his life. If you both work toward these goals together, they are easily attained.

If you should marry a Taurus, you can be sure that the wolf will never darken your door. They are notoriously good providers and do everything they can to make their families comfortable and happy.

He'll appreciate the way you have of making a home warm and inviting. Good meals and the evening papers are essential ingredients in making your Taurus husband happy at the end of the workday. Although he may be a big lug of a guy, he's fond of gentleness and soft things. If you puff up his pillow and tuck him in at night, he won't complain.

You probably won't complain about his friends. Taurus tends to seek out friends who are successful or prominent. You admire people, too, who work hard and achieve what they set out for. It helps to reassure your way of life and the way you look at things.

The Taurus man doesn't care too much for change. He's a stay-at-home of the first degree. Chances are that the house you move into after you're married will be the house you'll live in for the rest of your life.

You'll find that the man born under the sign of the Bull is easy to get along with. It's unlikely that you'll have many quarrels or arguments.

Although he'll be gentle and tender with you, your Taurus man is far from being a sensitive type. He's a man's man. Chances are he loves sports like fishing and football. He can be earthy as well as down to earth.

Taurus love their children very much but try hard not to spoil them. They believe in children staying in their places. They make excellent disciplinarians. Your children will be polite and respectful. They may find their Taurus father a little gruff, but as they grow older they'll learn to understand him.

CANCER WOMAN
GEMINI MAN

Gemini men, in spite of their charm and dashing manner, may unnerve you. They seem to lack the common sense you set so much store in. Their tendency to start something, then out of boredom never finish it, may exasperate you.

You may be inclined to interpret a Gemini's jumping from here to there as childish or neurotic. A man born under the sign of the Twins will seldom stay put. If you should take it upon yourself to try and make him sit still, he will resent it.

On the other hand, the Gemini man may think you're a slowpoke, someone far too interested in security and material things. He's attracted to things that sparkle and dazzle. You, with your practical way of looking at things, are likely to seem a little dull and uninteresting to this gadabout. If you're looking for a life of security and permanence—and what Cancer isn't—then you'd better look elsewhere for your Mr. Right.

Chances are you'll be taken in by his charming ways and facile wit—few women can resist Gemini magic. But after you've seen through his live-for-today, gossamer facade, you'll most likely be very happy to turn your attention to someone more stable, even if he is not as interesting. You want a man who is there when you need him. You need someone on whom you can fully rely. Keeping track of a Gemini's movements will make you dizzy. Still, you are a patient woman, most of the time, and you are able to put up with something contrary if you feel that in the end it will prove well worth the effort.

A successful and serious Gemini could make you a very happy woman, perhaps, if you gave him half a chance. Although you may think that he has holes in his head, the Gemini man generally has a good brain and can make good use of it when he wants. Some Geminis who have learned the importance of being consistent have risen to great heights professionally. Once you can convince yourself that not all Twins are witless grasshoppers, you'll find you've come a long way in trying to understand them.

Life with a Gemini man can be more fun than a barrel of clowns. You'll never have a chance to experience a dull moment. He lacks your sense when it comes to money, however. You should see to it that you handle the budgeting and bookkeeping.

In ways, Gemini is like a child himself. Perhaps that is why a Gemini father can get along so well with his own children, indeed with most of the younger generation.

CANCER WOMAN
CANCER MAN

You'll find the man born under the same sign as you easy to get along with. You're both sensitive and sensible people. You'll see eye-to-eye on most things. He'll share your interest in security and practicality.

Cancer men are always hard workers. They are very interested in making successes of themselves in business and socially. Like you, he's a conservative person who has a great deal of respect for tradition. He's a man you can depend on come rain or come shine. He'll never shirk his responsibilities as provider and will always see to it that you never want.

The Cancer man is not the type that rushes headlong into romance. Neither are you, for that matter. Courtship between the two of you will be a sensible and thorough affair. It may take months before you even get to that holding-hands stage of romance. One thing you can be sure of: he'll always treat you like a lady. He'll have great respect and consideration for your feelings. Only when he is sure that you approve of him as someone to love, will he reveal the warmer side of his nature. His coolness, like yours, is just a front. Beneath it lies a very affectionate heart.

Although he may seem restless or moody at times, on the whole the Cancer man is very considerate and kind. His standards are extremely high. He is looking for a partner who can measure up to his ideals—a partner like you.

Marriage means a lot to the Cancer male. He's very interested in settling down with someone who has the same attitudes and outlooks as he has. He's a man who loves being at home. He'll be a faithful husband. Cancers never pussyfoot around after they have made their marriage vows. They do not take their marriage responsibilities lightly. They see to it that everything in this relationship is just the way it should be. Between the two of you, your home will be well managed, bills will be paid on time, there will be adequate insurance on everything of value, and there will be money in the bank. When retirement time rolls around, you both should be very well off.

The Cancer man has a great respect for family. You'll most likely be seeing a lot of his mother during your marriage, just as he'll probably be seeing a lot of yours. He'll do his best to get along with your relatives; he'll treat them with the kindness and concern you think they deserve. He'll expect you to be just as considerate with his relatives.

Cancer is a very good father. He's very patient and understanding, especially when the children are young and dependent and need his protection.

CANCER WOMAN
LEO MAN

To know a man born under the sign of the Lion is not necessarily to love him—even though the temptation may be great. When he fixes most women with his leonine double-whammy, it causes their hearts to throb and their minds to soar.

But with you, the sensible Cancer, it takes more than a regal strut and roar to win you over. There is no denying that Leo has a way with women, even practical Cancers. If he sweeps you off your feet, it may be hard for you to scramble upright again. Still, you are no pushover for romantic charm when you feel there may be no security behind it.

He'll wine you and dine you in the fanciest places. He'll croon to you under the moon and shower you with diamonds if he can get ahold of them. Still, it would be wise to find out just how long that shower is going to last before consenting to be his wife.

Lions in love are hard to ignore, let alone brush off. Once mesmerized by this romantic powerhouse, you may find yourself doing things you never dreamed of. Leos can be vain pussycats when involved romantically. They like to be cuddled and petted, tickled under the chin, and told how wonderful they are. This may not be your cup of tea. Still, when you're romantically dealing with a Lion, you'll instinctively do the things that make him purr.

Although he may be big and magnanimous while trying to win you, he'll let out a blood-curdling roar if he thinks he's not getting the tender love and care he feels is his due. If you keep him well supplied with affection, you can be sure his eyes will never stray and his heart will never wander.

Leo men often tend to be authoritarian. They are born to lord it over others in one way or another, it seems. If he is the top banana of his firm, he'll most likely do everything he can to stay on top. If he's not number one, he's most likely working on it and will be sitting on the throne before long. You'll have more security than you can use if he is in a position to support you in the manner to which he feels you should be accustomed. He's apt to be too lavish, though, at least by your standards.

You'll always have plenty of friends when you have a Leo for a mate. He's a natural born friend-maker and entertainer. He loves to kick up his heels at a party.

As fathers, Leos may go from one extreme to another with their children. Leos either lavish too much attention on the youngsters or demand too much from them.

CANCER WOMAN
VIRGO MAN

The Virgo man is often a quiet, respectable type who sets great store in conservative behavior and levelheadedness. He'll admire you for your practicality and tenacity—perhaps even more than for your good looks. The Virgo man is seldom bowled over by glamour. When looking for someone to love, he always turns to a serious, reliable woman.

He'll be far from a Valentino while dating. In fact, you may wind up making all the passes. Once he gets his motor running, however, he can be warm and wonderful to the right lover.

The Virgo man is gradual about love. Chances are your romance with him will start out looking like an ordinary friendship. Once he's sure that you are no fly-by-night flirt and have no plans of taking him for a ride, he'll open up and rain sunshine all over your heart.

The Virgo man takes his time about romance. It may be many years before he seriously considers settling down. Virgos are often middle-aged when they make their first marriage vows. They hold out as long as they can for the woman who perfectly measures up to their ideals.

He may not have many names in his little black book; in fact, he may not even have a little black book. He's not interested in playing the field; leave that to the more flamboyant signs. The Virgo man is so particular that he may remain romantically inactive for a long period of time. The mate he chooses has to be perfect or it's no go.

With your surefire perseverance, you'll be able to make him listen to reason, as far as romance is concerned. Before long, you'll find him returning your love. He's no block of ice and will respond to what he considers to be the right feminine flame.

Once your love life with Virgo starts to bubble, don't give it a chance to die down. The Virgo man will never give a woman a second chance at winning his heart. If there should ever be a bad break between you, forget about picking up the pieces. With him, it's one strike and you're out.

Once married, he'll stay that way—even if it hurts. He's too conscientious to back out of a legal deal of any sort. He'll always be faithful and considerate. He's as neat as a pin and will expect you to be the same.

If you marry a Virgo man, keep your kids spic-and-span, at least by the time he gets home from work. He likes children to be clean and polite.

CANCER WOMAN
LIBRA MAN

Cancers are apt to find Libra men too wrapped up in their own private dreams to be romantically interesting. He's a difficult man to bring back down to earth, at times. Although he may be very careful about weighing both sides of an argument, he may never really come to a reasonable decision about anything. Decisions, large and small, are capable of giving Libra the willies. Don't ask him why. He probably doesn't know.

If you are looking for permanence and constancy in a love relationship, you may find him a puzzlement. One moment he comes on hard and strong with declarations of his love; the next moment you find he's left you like yesterday's mashed potatoes. It does no good to wonder what went wrong. Chances are nothing, really. It's just one of Libra's strange ways.

On the other hand, you'll probably admire his way with harmony and beauty. If you're all decked out in your fanciest gown, you'll receive a ready compliment and one that's really deserved. Libras don't pass out compliments to all and sundry. If something strikes him as distasteful, he'll remain silent. He's tactful.

He may not seem as ambitious as you would like your lover or husband to be. Where you have a great interest in getting ahead, Libra is often content just to drift along. It is not that he is lazy or shiftless. Material gain generally means little to him. He is more interested in aesthetic matters. If he is in love with you, however, he'll do everything in his power to make you happy.

You may have to give him a good nudge now and again to get him to recognize the light of reality. On the whole, he'll enjoy the company of his artistic dreams when you're not around. If you love your Libra, don't be too harsh or impatient with him. Try to understand him.

Libras are peace-loving people. They hate any kind of confrontation that might lead to an argument. Some of them will do almost anything to keep the peace—even tell a little lie.

If you find yourself involved with a man born under this sign, either temporarily or permanently, you'd better take over the task of managing his money. It's for his own good. Money will never interest a Libra as much as it should. He often has a tendency to be generous when he shouldn't be.

Don't let him see the materialistic side of your nature too often. It might frighten him off.

Libra makes a gentle and understanding father. He's careful not to spoil children or to demand too much from them. He believes that discipline should be a matter of gentle guidance.

CANCER WOMAN
SCORPIO MAN

Some people have a hard time understanding the man born under the sign of Scorpio. Few, however, are able to resist his fiery charm. When angered, he can act like an overturned wasps' nest; his sting can leave an almost permanent mark. If you find yourself interested in a Scorpion, you'd better learn how to keep on his good side.

The Scorpio man can be quite blunt when he chooses; at times, he'll seem like a brute to you. He's touchy—more so than you— and it can get on your nerves after a while. When you feel like you can't take it anymore, you'd better tiptoe away from the scene rather than chance an explosive confrontation. He's capable of giving you a sounding-out that will make you pack your bags and go back to Mother for good.

If he finds fault with you, he'll let you know. He might misinterpret your patience and think it a sign of indifference. Still and all, you are the kind of woman who can adapt to almost any sort of relationship or circumstance if you put your heart and mind to it.

Scorpio men are perceptive and intelligent. In some respects, they know how to use their brains more effectively than most. They believe in winning in whatever they do; second place holds no interest for them. In business, they usually achieve the position they want through drive and use of intellect.

Your interest in home life is not likely to be shared by him. No matter how comfortable you've managed to make the house, it will have little influence on making him aware of his family responsibilities. He does not like to be tied down, generally, and would rather be out on the battlefield of life, belting away for what he feels is a just and worthy cause. Don't try to keep the home fires burning too brightly while you wait for him to come home from work; you may run out of firewood.

The Scorpio man is passionate in all things—including love. Most women are easily attracted to him, and the Cancer woman is no exception, at least before she knows what she might be getting into. If you are swept off your feet by a Scorpio man, soon you find you are dealing with a carton of romantic fireworks. The Scorpio man is passionate with a capital P, make no mistake about that.

Scorpio men are straight to the point. They can be as sharp as a razor blade and just as cutting. Always manage to stay out of his line of fire; if you don't, it could cost you your love life.

Scorpio men like large families. They love children but they do not always live up to the role of the responsible, nurturing father.

CANCER WOMAN
SAGITTARIUS MAN

Sagittarius men are not easy to catch. They get cold feet whenever visions of the altar enter the romance. You'll most likely be attracted to Sagittarius because of his exuberant nature. He's lots of laughs and easy to get along with. But as soon as the relationship begins to take on a serious hue, you may feel let down.

Sagittarius are full of bounce, perhaps too much bounce to suit you. They are often hard to pin down; they dislike staying put. If he ever has a chance to be on the move, he'll go without so much as a how-do-you-do. Archers are quick people both in mind and spirit. If ever they do make mistakes, it's because of their zip. They leap before they look.

If you offer him good advice, he probably will not follow it. Sagittarius like to rely on their own wits and ways whenever possible.

His up-and-at-'em manner about most things is likely to drive you up the wall at times. And your cautious, deliberate manner is likely to make him seem impatient. He will tease when you're accompanying him on a hike or jogging through the park. He can't abide a slowpoke.

At times you'll find him too much like a kid—too breezy. Don't mistake his youthful zest for premature senility. Sagittarius are equipped with first-class brainpower and know how to use it well. They are often full of good ideas and drive. Generally, they are very broad-minded people and very much concerned with fair play and equality.

In the romance department, he's quite capable of loving you wholeheartedly while treating you like a good buddy. His hail-fellow-well-met manner in the arena of love is likely to scare off a dainty damsel. However, a woman who knows that his heart is in the right place won't mind it too much if, once in a while, he pats her on the back instead of giving her a gentle embrace.

He's not very much of a homebody. He's got ants in his pants and enjoys being on the move. Humdrum routine, especially at home, bores him silly. At the drop of a hat, he may ask you to dine out for a change. He's a past master in the instant-surprise department. He'll love keeping you guessing. His friendly, candid nature will win him many friends. He'll expect his friends to be yours, and vice versa.

Sagittarius is a good father when youngsters are old enough for rough-and-tumble sports. But with infants, Sagittarius may be all thumbs and feel helpless.

CANCER WOMAN
CAPRICORN MAN

The Capricorn man is often not the romantic lover that attracts most women. Still, with his reserve and calm, he is capable of giving his heart completely once he has found the right partner. The Cancer woman who is thorough and deliberate can appreciate these same qualities in the average Capricorn man. He is slow and sure about most things—love included.

He doesn't believe in flirting and would never lead a heart on a merry chase just for the game of it. If you win his trust, he'll give you his heart on a platter. Quite often, it is the woman who has to take the lead when romance is in the air. As long as he knows you're making the advances in earnest, he won't mind—in fact, he'll probably be grateful. Don't get to thinking he's all cold fish; he isn't. While some Capricorns are indeed quite capable of expressing passion, others often have difficulty displaying affection. He should have no trouble in this area, however, once he has found a patient and understanding mate.

The Capricorn man is very interested in getting ahead. He's ambitious and usually knows how to apply himself well to whatever task he undertakes. He's far from being a spendthrift. Like you, he knows how to handle money with extreme care. You, with your knack for putting pennies away for that rainy day, should have no difficulty in understanding his way with money. Capricorn thinks in terms of future security. He saves to make sure that he and his wife have something to fall back on when they reach retirement age. There's nothing wrong with that; in fact, it's a plus quality.

The Capricorn man will want to handle household matters efficiently. Most Cancers have no trouble in doing this. If he should check up on you from time to time, don't let it irritate you. Once you assure him that you can handle this area to his liking, he'll leave it all up to you.

Although he's a hard man to catch when it comes to marriage, once he's made that serious step, he's likely to become possessive. Capricorns need to know that they have the support of their women in whatever they do, every step of the way.

The Capricorn man likes to be liked. He may seem like a dull, reserved person. But underneath it all, he's often got an adventurous nature that has never had the chance to express itself. He may be a real daredevil in his heart of hearts. The right woman, the affectionate and adoring woman, can bring out that hidden zest in his nature.

Although he may not understand his children fully, Capricon will be a loving and dutiful father, raising his children with strong codes of honor and allegiance.

CANCER WOMAN
AQUARIUS MAN

You may find the Aquarius man the most broad-minded man you have ever met. On the other hand, you may find him the most impractical. Oftentimes, he's more of a dreamer than a doer. If you don't mind putting up with a man whose heart and mind are as wide as the universe and whose head is almost always up in the clouds, then start dating that Aquarius who has somehow captured your fancy. Maybe you, with your good sense, can bring him back down to earth when he gets too starry-eyed.

He's no dope, make no mistake about that. He can be busy making some very complicated and idealistic plans when he's got that out-to-lunch look in his eyes. But more than likely, he'll never execute them. After he's shared one or two of his progressive ideas with you, you'll think he's a nut. But don't go jumping to conclusions. There's a saying that Aquarius are a half-century ahead of everybody else in the thinking department.

If you decide to say yes to his will you marry me, you'll find out how right his zany whims are on or about your 50th anniversary. Maybe the waiting will be worth it. Could be that you have an Einstein on your hands—and heart.

Life with an Aquarius won't be one of total despair if you can learn to temper his airiness with your down-to-earth practicality. He won't gripe if you do. The Aquarius man always maintains an open mind. He'll entertain the ideas and opinions of everybody, though he may not agree with all of them.

Don't go tearing your hair out when you find that it's almost impossible to hold a normal conversation with your Aquarius friend at times. He's capable of answering a casual question with an imposing intellectual response. But always try to keep in mind that he means well.

His broad-mindedness doesn't stop when it comes to you and your personal freedom. You won't have to give up any of your hobbies or projects after you're married. In fact, he'll encourage you to continue your interests.

He'll be a kind and generous husband. He'll never quibble over petty things. Keep track of the money you both spend. He can't. Money burns a hole in his pocket.

You'll have plenty of chances to put your legendary patience to good use during your relationship with an Aquarius. At times, you may feel like tossing in the towel, but you'll never call it quits.

Aquarius is a good family man and father. He understands children as much as he loves them.

CANCER WOMAN
PISCES MAN

The Pisces man is perhaps the man you've been looking all over for, high and low—the man you thought didn't exist. As a lover, he'll be attentive and faithful.

The Pisces man is very sensitive and very romantic. Still, he is a reasonable person. He may wish on the moon, yet he's got enough good sense to know that it isn't made of green cheese.

He'll be very considerate of your every wish and whim. He will do his best to be a very compatible mate. The Pisces man is great for showering the object of his affection with all kinds of little gifts and tokens of his affection. He's just the right mixture of dreamer and realist that pleases most women.

When it comes to earning bread and butter, the strong Pisces man will do all right in the world. Quite often they are capable of rising to very high positions. Some do very well as writers or psychiatrists. He'll be as patient and understanding with you as you are with him.

One thing a Pisces man dislikes is pettiness. Anyone who delights in running another into the ground is almost immediately crossed off his list of possible mates. If you have even small grievances with any of your friends, don't tell him about them. He will be quite disappointed in you if you complain and criticize.

If you fall in love with a weak Pisces man, don't give up your job at the office before you get married. Better still: hang onto it a good while after the honeymoon; you may need it.

A funny thing about the man born under the sign of the Fishes is that he can be content almost anywhere. This is perhaps because he is inner-directed and places little value on some exterior things. In a shack or a palace, the Pisces man is capable of making the best of all possible adjustments. He won't kick up a fuss if the roof leaks or if the fence is in sad need of repair. He's got more important things on his mind. Still and all, the Pisces man is not lazy or aimless. It's important to understand that material gain is never a direct goal for him.

Pisces men have a way with the sick and troubled. He'll offer his shoulder to anyone in the mood for a good cry. He can listen to one hard-luck story after another without seeming to tire. Quite often he knows what is bothering someone before that person, himself, realizes what it is. It's almost intuitive with Pisces, it seems.

Children are often delighted with Pisces men. As fathers, they are never strict or faultfinding. They are encouraging and always permissive with their youngsters.

Man—Woman

CANCER MAN
ARIES WOMAN

The Aries woman may be too bossy and busy for you. Aries are ambitious creatures. They can become impatient with people who are more thorough and deliberate than they are, especially if they feel such people are taking too much time. The Aries woman is a fast worker. Sometimes she's so fast she forgets to look where she's going. When she stumbles or falls, it would be nice if you were there to grab her.

Aries are proud women. They don't like to be told "I told you so" when they err. Criticism can turn them into blocks of ice. Don't begin to think that the Aries woman frequently gets tripped up in her plans. Quite often they are capable of taking aim and hitting the bull's-eye. You'll be flabbergasted at times by their accuracy as well as by their ambition. On the other hand, because of your interest in being sure and safe, you're apt to spot a flaw in your Aries' plans before she does.

You are somewhat slower than Aries in attaining what you have your sights set on. Still, you don't make any mistakes along the way; you're almost always well-prepared.

The Aries woman is sensitive at times. She likes to be handled with gentleness and respect. Let her know that you love her for her brains as well as for her good looks. Never give her cause to become jealous. When your Aries date sees green, you'd better forget about sharing a rosy future together. Handle her with tender love and care and she's yours.

The Aries woman can be giving if she feels her partner is deserving. She is no iceberg; she responds to the proper flame. She needs a man she can look up to and feel proud of. If the shoe fits, put it on. If not, better put your sneakers back on and quietly tiptoe out of her sight. She can cause you heartache if you've made up your mind about her but she hasn't made up hers about you. Aries women are very demanding at times. Some of them are high-strung. They can be difficult if they feel their independence is being hampered.

The cultivated Aries woman makes a wonderful homemaker and hostess. She's clever in decorating and color use. Your house will be tastefully furnished. She'll see to it that it radiates harmony. Friends and acquaintances will love your Aries wife. She knows how to make everyone feel at home and welcome.

Although the Aries woman may not be keen on the responsibilities of motherhood, she is fond of children and the joy they bring.

CANCER MAN
TAURUS WOMAN

A Taurus woman could perhaps understand you better than most women. She is very considerate and loving. She is methodical and thorough in whatever she does. She knows how to take her time in doing things; she is anxious to avoid mistakes. Like you, she is a careful person. She never skips over things that may seem unimportant; she goes over everything with a fine-tooth comb.

Home is very important to the Taurus woman. She is an excellent homemaker. Although your home may not be a palace, it will become, under her care, a comfortable and happy abode. She'll love it when friends drop by for the evening. She is a good cook and enjoys feeding people well. No one will ever go away from your house with an empty stomach.

The Taurus woman is serious about love and affection. When she has taken a tumble for someone, she'll stay by him—for good, if possible. She will try to be practical in romance, to some extent. When she sets her cap for a man, she keeps after him until he's won her. Generally, the Taurus woman is a passionate lover, even though she may appear otherwise at first glance. She is on the lookout for someone who can return her affection fully. Taurus are sometimes given to fits of jealousy and possessiveness. They expect fair play in the area of marriage. When it doesn't happen, they can be bitingly sarcastic and mean.

The Taurus woman is easygoing. She's fond of keeping peace. She won't argue unless she has to. She'll do her best to keep a love relationship on even keel.

Marriage is generally a one-time thing for Taurus. Once they've made the serious step, they seldom try to back out of it. Marriage is for keeps. They are fond of love and warmth. With the right man, they turn out to be ideal wives.

The Taurus woman will respect you for your steady ways; she'll have confidence in your common sense.

Taurus women seldom put up with nonsense from their children. They are not so much strict as concerned. They like their children to be well-behaved and dutiful. Nothing pleases a Taurus mother more than a compliment from a neighbor or teacher about her child's behavior. Although children may inwardly resent the iron hand of a Taurus woman, in later life they are often thankful that they were brought up in such an orderly and conscientious way.

CANCER MAN
GEMINI WOMAN

The Gemini woman may be too much of a flirt ever to take your heart too seriously. Then again, it depends on what kind of mood she's in. Gemini women can change from hot to cold quicker than a cat can wink its eye. Chances are her fluctuations will tire you after a time, and you'll pick up your heart—if it's not already broken into small pieces—and go elsewhere. Women born under the sign of the Twins have the talent of being able to change their moods and attitudes as frequently as they change their party dresses.

Sometimes, Geminis like to whoop it up. Some of them are good-time gals who love burning the candle to the wick. You'll always see them at parties and gatherings, surrounded by men of all types, laughing gaily or kicking up their heels at every opportunity. Wallflowers, they're not. The next day you may bump into her at the neighborhood library and you'll hardly recognize her for her sensible attire. She'll probably have five or six books under her arm—on five or six different subjects. In fact, she may even work there.

You'll probably find her a dazzling and fascinating creature—for a time, at any rate. Most men do. But when it comes to being serious about love you may find that your sparkling Eve leaves quite a bit to be desired. It's not that she has anything against being serious, it's just that she might find it difficult trying to be serious with you.

At one moment, she'll be capable of praising you for your steadfast and patient ways. The next moment she'll tell you in a cutting way that you're an impossible stick-in-the-mud.

Don't even begin to fathom the depths of her mercurial soul—it's full of false bottoms. She'll resent close investigation anyway, and will make you rue the day you ever took it into your head to try to learn more about her than she feels is necessary. Better keep the relationship fancy free and full of fun until she gives you the go-ahead sign. Take as much of her as she is willing to give; don't ask for more. If she does take a serious interest in you, then she'll come across with the goods.

There will come a time when Gemini will realize that she can't spend her entire life at the ball. The security and warmth you offer are just what she needs for a happy, fulfilled life.

The Gemini mother will be easygoing with her children. She'll probably spoil them and dote on their every whim. Because she has a youthful outlook, she will be a fun playmate for her kids.

CANCER MAN
CANCER WOMAN
The Cancer woman needs to be protected from the cold cruel world. She'll love you for your gentle and kind manner. You are the kind of man who can make her feel safe and secure.

You won't have to pull any he-man or heroic stunts to win her heart; she's not interested in things like that. She's more likely to be impressed by your sure, steady ways—the way you have of putting your arm around her and making her feel that she's the only girl in the world. When she's feeling glum and tears begin to well up in her eyes, you'll know how to calm her fears, no matter how silly some of them may seem.

The Moon Child, like you, is inclined to have her ups and downs. Perhaps you can both learn to smooth out the roughed-up spots in each other's life. She'll most likely worship the ground you walk on or place you on a very high pedestal. Don't disappoint her if you can help it. She'll never disappoint you. The Cancer woman will take great pleasure in devoting the rest of her natural life to you. She'll darn your socks, mend your overalls, scrub floors, wash windows, shop, cook, and do anything short of murder in order to please you and to let you know she loves you. Sounds like that legendary old-fashioned girl, doesn't it? Contrary to popular belief, there are still many of them around and the majority of them are Cancers.

Treat your Cancer mate fairly and she'll treat you like a king. There is one thing you should be warned about, though. Never be unkind to your mother-in-law. It will be the only golden rule your Cancer wife will expect you to live up to. Mother is something special for her. You should have no trouble in understanding this, for your mother has a special place in your heart, too. It's always that way with the Cancer-born. They have great respect and love for family ties. It might be a good idea for you both to get to know each other's relatives before tying the marriage knot, because after the wedding bells have rung, you'll be seeing a lot of them.

Of all the signs in the Zodiac, Cancer is the most maternal. In caring for and bringing up children, she knows just how to combine tenderness and discipline. A child couldn't ask for a better mother. Cancer women are sympathetic, affectionate, and patient with children. Both of you will make excellent parents, especially when the children are young. When they grow older you'll most likely be reluctant to let them go out into the world.

CANCER MAN
LEO WOMAN

The Leo woman can make most men roar like lions. If any woman in the Zodiac has that indefinable something that can make men lose their heads and find their hearts, it's Leo.

She's got more than a fair share of charm and glamour and she knows how to make the most of her assets, especially when she's in the company of the opposite sex. Jealous men lose either their cool or their sanity when trying to woo a woman born under the sign of the Lion. She likes to kick up her heels and doesn't care who knows it. She often makes heads turn and tongues wag. You don't have to believe any of what you hear—it's most likely just jealous gossip or wishful thinking. Needless to say, other women in her vicinity turn green with envy and will try anything to put her out of commission.

Although this vamp makes the blood rush to your head and makes you momentarily forget all the things you thought were important and necessary in your life, you may feel differently when you come back down to earth and the stars are out of your eyes. You may feel that although this vivacious creature can make you feel wonderful, she just isn't the type you planned to bring home to Mother. Not that your mother might disapprove of your choice—but you might after the shoes and rice are a thing of the past. Although the Leo woman may do her best to be a good wife for you, chances are she'll fall short of your idea of what a good wife should be.

If you're planning on not going as far as the altar with that Leo woman who has you flipping your lid, you'd better be financially equipped for some very expensive dating. Be prepared to shower her with expensive gifts and to take her dining and dancing to the smartest spots in town. Promise her the moon if you're in a position to go that far. Luxury and glamour are two things that are bound to lower a Leo's resistance. She has expensive tastes, and you'd better cater to them if you expect to get to first base with the Lioness.

If you've got an important business deal to clinch and you have doubts as to whether you can swing it or not, bring your Leo along to the business luncheon. Chances are that with her on your arm, you'll be able to win any business battle with both hands tied. She won't have to say or do anything—just be there at your side. The grouchiest oil magnate can be transformed into a gushing, obedient schoolboy if there's a charming Lioness in the room.

Leo mothers are blind to the faults of their children. They make very loving and affectionate mothers and tend to give their youngsters everything under the sun.

CANCER MAN
VIRGO WOMAN

The Virgo woman is particular about choosing her men friends. She's not interested in going out with anybody. She has her own idea of what a boyfriend or prospective husband should be. Perhaps that image has something of you in it.

Generally, she's quiet and correct. She doesn't believe that nonsense has any place in a love affair. She's serious about love and she'll expect you to be. She's looking for a man who has both feet on the ground—someone who can take care of himself as well as her. She knows the value of money and how to get the most out of a dollar. She's far from being a spendthrift. Throwing money around turns her stomach, even when it isn't her money.

She'll most likely be very shy about romancing. Even the simple act of holding hands may make her turn crimson—at least, on the first couple of dates. You'll have to make all the advances, and you'll have to be careful not to make any wrong moves. She's capable of showing anyone who oversteps the boundaries of common decency the door. It may even take quite a long time before she'll accept that goodnight kiss at the front gate. Don't give up. You are perhaps the kind of man who can bring out the warm woman in her.

There is love and tenderness underneath Virgo's seemingly frigid facade. It will take a patient and understanding man to bring it out into the open. She may have the idea that sex is reserved for marriage. Like you, she has a few old-fashioned concepts. And, like you, it's all or nothing. So if you are the right man, gentle and affectionate, you will melt her reserve.

When a Virgo has accepted you as a lover or mate, she won't stint in giving her love in return. You'll be surprised at the transformation your earnest attention can bring about in this quiet kind of woman. When in love, Virgos only listen to their hearts, not to what the neighbors say.

Virgo women are honest about love once they've come to grips with it. They don't appreciate hypocrisy—particularly in this area of life. They will always be true to their hearts—even if it means tossing you over for a new love. But if you convince her that you are earnest about your interest in her, she'll reciprocate your love and affection and never leave you. Do her wrong once, however, and you can be sure she'll call the whole thing off.

Virgo mothers are tender and loving. They know what's good for their children and will always take great pains in bringing them up correctly.

CANCER MAN
LIBRA WOMAN

It's a woman's prerogative to change her mind. This wise saying characterizes the Libra woman. Her changes of mind, in spite of her undeniable charm, might drive even a man of your changeable moods up the wall. She's capable of smothering you with love and kisses one day and on the next avoid you like the plague. If you think you're a man of great patience, then perhaps you can tolerate her sometime-ness without suffering too much. However, if you own up to the fact that you're a mere mortal who can only take so much, then you'd better fasten your attention on a girl who's somewhat more constant.

But don't get the wrong idea—a love affair with a Libra is not all bad. In fact, it can have an awful lot of pluses to it. Libra women are soft, very feminine, and warm. She doesn't have to vamp all over the place in order to gain a man's attention. Her delicate presence is enough to warm any man's heart. One smile and you're a piece of putty in the palm of her hand.

She can be fluffy and affectionate. On the other hand, her indecision about which dress to wear, what to cook for dinner, or whether or not to redecorate could make you tear your hair out. What will perhaps be more exasperating is her flat denial of the accusation that she cannot make even the simplest decision. The trouble is that she wants to be fair or just in all matters. She'll spend hours weighing both sides of an argument or situation. Don't make her rush into a decision; that would only irritate her.

The Libra woman likes to be surrounded by beautiful things. Money is no object when beauty is concerned. There will always be antiques and objects of art in her apartment. She'll know how to arrange them tastefully, too, to show them off. Women under this sign are fond of beautiful clothes and furnishings. They will run up bills without batting an eye—if given the chance.

Once she's cottoned to you, the Libra woman will do everything in her power to make you happy. She'll wait on you hand and foot when you're sick, bring you breakfast in bed on Sundays, and even read you the funny papers if you're too sleepy to open your eyes. She'll be very thoughtful and devoted. If anyone dares suggest you're not the grandest man in the world, your Libra wife will give that person a good sounding-out.

Libras work wonders with children. Gentle persuasion and affection are all she uses in bringing them up. Her subtlety sets a good example for them to follow.

CANCER MAN
SCORPIO WOMAN
When the Scorpio woman chooses to be sweet, she's apt to give the impression that butter wouldn't melt in her mouth . . . but, of course, it would. When her temper flies, so will everything else that isn't bolted down. She can be as hot as a tamale or as cool as a cucumber when she wants. Whatever mood she's in, you can be sure it's for real. She doesn't believe in poses or hypocrisy.

The Scorpio woman is often seductive and sultry. Her femme

fatale charm can pierce through the hardest of hearts like a laser ray. She doesn't have to look like Mata Hari (many of them resemble the tomboy next door) but once you've looked into those tantalizing eyes, you're a goner.

The Scorpio woman can be a whirlwind of passion. Life with her will not be all smiles and smooth sailing. If you think you can handle a woman who can spit bullets, try your luck. Your stable and steady nature will most likely have a calming effect on her. You're the kind of man she can trust and rely on. But never cross her—even on the smallest thing. If you do, you'd better tell Fido to make room for you in the doghouse—you'll be his guest for the next couple of days.

Generally, the Scorpio woman will keep family battles within the walls of your home. When company visits, she's apt to give the impression that married life with you is one big joyride. It's just her way of expressing her loyalty to you—at least in front of others. She believes that family matters are and should stay private. She certainly will see to it that others have a high opinion of you both.

Although she's an individualist, after she has married she'll put her own interests aside for those of the man she loves. With a woman like this behind you, you can't help but go far. She'll never try to take over your role as boss of the family. She'll give you all the support you need in order to fulfill that role. She won't complain if the going gets rough. She knows how to take the bitter with the sweet. She is a courageous woman. She's as anxious as you are to find that place in the sun for you both. She's as determined a person as you are.

Although Scorpio loves her children, she may not be too affectionate toward them. She'll make a devoted mother, though. She'll be anxious to see them develop their talents. She'll teach the children to be courageous and steadfast.

CANCER MAN
SAGITTARIUS WOMAN

The Sagittarius woman is hard to keep track of: first she's here, then she's there. She's a woman with a severe case of itchy feet. She's got to keep on the move.

People generally like her because of her hail-fellow-well-met manner and her breezy charm. She is constantly good-natured and almost never cross. With the female Archer you're likely to strike up a palsy-walsy relationship. You might not be interested in letting it go any farther. She probably won't sulk if you leave it on a friendly basis. Treat her like a kid sister and she'll love it.

She'll probably be attracted to you because of your restful, self-assured manner. She'll need a friend like you to help her over the rough spots in her life. She'll most likely turn to you for advice frequently.

There is nothing malicious about a woman born under this sign. She is full of bounce and good cheer. Her sunshiny disposition can be relied upon even on the rainiest of days. No matter what she says or does, you'll always know that she means well. Sagittarius are sometimes short on tact. Some of them say anything that comes into their heads, no matter what the occasion. Sometimes the words that tumble out of their mouths seem downright cutting and cruel; they mean well but often everything they say comes out wrong. She's quite capable of losing her friends—and perhaps even yours—through a careless slip of the lip. Always remember that she is full of good intentions. Stick with her if you like her and try to help her mend her ways.

She's may not be the quiet, home-loving woman you'd be interested in marrying, but she'll certainly be lots of fun to pal around with. Quite often, Sagittarius women are outdoor types. They're crazy about things like fishing, camping, and mountain climbing. They love the wide open spaces. They are fond of all kinds of animals. Make no mistake about it: this busy little lady is no slouch. She's full of pep and vigor.

She's great company most of the time; she's more fun than a three-ring circus when she's in the right company. You'll like her for her candid and direct manner. On the whole, Sagittarius are very kind and sympathetic women.

If you do wind up marrying this girl-next-door type, you'd better see to it that you take care of all financial matters. Sagittarius often let money run through their fingers like sand.

A Sagittarius mother may smother her children with love on the one hand, then give them all of the freedom they think they need. It can be very confusing.

CANCER MAN
CAPRICORN WOMAN

The Capricorn woman may not be the most romantic woman of the Zodiac, but she's far from frigid when she meets the right man. She believes in true love. She doesn't appreciate getting involved in flings. To her, they're just a waste of time. She's looking for a man who means business—in life as well as in love. Although she can be very affectionate with her boyfriend or mate, she tends to let her head govern her heart. That is not to say that she is a cool, calculating cucumber. On the contrary, she just feels she can be more honest about love if she consults her brains first. She wants to size up the situation first before throwing her heart in the ring. She wants to make sure it won't get stepped on.

The Capricorn woman is faithful, dependable, and systematic in just about everything that she undertakes. She is quite concerned with security and sees to it that every penny she spends is spent wisely. She is very economical about using her time, too. She does not believe in whittling away her energy on a scheme that is bound not to pay off.

Ambitious themselves, they are quite often attracted to ambitious men—men who are interested in getting somewhere in life. If a man of this sort wins her heart, she'll stick by him and do all she can to help him get to the top.

The Capricorn woman is almost always diplomatic. She makes an excellent hostess. She can be very influential when your business acquaintances come to dinner.

The Capricorn woman is likely to be very concerned, if not downright proud, about her family tree. Relatives are important to her, particularly if they're socially prominent. Never say a cross word about her family members. That can really go against her grain and she'll punish you by not talking for days.

She's generally thorough in whatever she does: cooking, housekeeping, entertaining. Capricorn women are well-mannered and gracious, no matter what their backgrounds. They seem to have it in their natures to always behave properly.

If you should marry a woman born under this sign, you need never worry about her going on a wild shopping spree. They understand the value of money better than most women. If you turn over your paycheck to her at the end of the week, you can be sure that a good hunk of it will go into the bank and that all the bills will be paid on time.

With children, the Capricorn mother is both loving and correct. She'll see to it that they're polite and respectful and that they honor the codes they are taught when young.

CANCER MAN
AQUARIUS WOMAN
The woman born under the sign of the Water Bearer can be odd and eccentric at times. Some say that this is the source of her mysterious charm. You may think she's just a plain screwball, and you may be right.

Aquarius women often have their heads full of dreams and stars in their eyes. By nature, they are often unconventional; they have their own ideas about how the world should be run. Sometimes their ideas may seem pretty weird—chances are they're just a little bit too progressive. There is a saying that runs: The way the Aquarius thinks, so will the world in fifty years.

If you find yourself falling in love with a woman born under this sign, you'd better fasten your safety belt. It may take some time before you know what she's like and even then, you may have nothing to go on but a string of vague hunches.

She can be like a rainbow: full of dazzling colors. She's like no other girl you've ever known. There is something about her that is definitely charming, yet elusive. You'll never be able to put your finger on it. She seems to radiate adventure and optimism without even trying. She'll most likely be the most tolerant and open-minded woman you've ever encountered.

If you find that she's too much mystery and charm for you to handle—and being a Cancer, chances are you might—just talk it out with her and say that you think it would be better if you called it quits. She'll most likely give you a peck on the cheek and say "Okay, but let's still be friends." Aquarius women are like that. Perhaps you'll both find it easier to get along in a friendship than in a romance.

It is not difficult for her to remain buddy-buddy with an ex-lover. For many Aquarius, the line between friendship and romance is a fuzzy one.

She's not a jealous person and while you're romancing her, she won't expect you to be, either. You'll find her a free spirit most of the time. Just when you think you know her inside out, you'll discover that you don't really know her at all. She's a very sympathetic and warm person. She is often helpful to those in need of assistance and advice.

She'll seldom be suspicious even when she has every right to be. If the man she loves makes a little slip, she's likely to forgive it and forget it.

Aquarius makes a fine mother. Her positive and bighearted qualities are easily transmitted to her children. They will be taught tolerance at an early age.

CANCER MAN
PISCES WOMAN

The Pisces woman places great value on love and romance. She's gentle, kind, and romantic. Like you, she has very high ideals, and will only give her heart to a man who she feels can live up to her expectations.

Many a man dreams of an alluring Pisces woman. You're perhaps no exception. Even though she appears soft and cuddly, she has a sultry, seductive charm that can win the heart of almost any man.

She will not try to wear the pants in the relationship. She'll let you be the brains of the family. She's content to play a behind-the-scenes role in order to help you achieve your goals.

She can be very ladylike and proper. Your business associates and friends will be dazzled by her warmth and femininity. Although she's a charmer, there is a lot more to her than just a pretty exterior. There is a brain ticking away behind that gentle, womanly facade. You may never become aware of it—that is, until you're married to her. It's no cause for alarm, however; she'll most likely never use it against you, only to help you and possibly set you on a more successful path.

If she feels you're botching up your married life through careless behavior or if she feels you could be earning more money than you do, she'll tell you about it. But any wife would.

No one had better dare say one uncomplimentary word about you in her presence. It could set the stage for an emotional scene. Pisces women are maddeningly temperamental and can go to theatrical extremes when expressing their feelings. Their reaction to adversity or frustration can run the gamut from tears to tantrums and back again.

She can do wonders with a house. She is very fond of dramatic and beautiful things. There will always be plenty of fresh-cut flowers around the house. She will choose charming artwork and antiques, if they are affordable.

She'll have an extra special dinner prepared for you when you come home from an important business meeting. Don't dwell on the boring details of the meeting, though. But if you need that big idea, to seal a contract or make a conquest, your Pisces woman is sure to confide a secret that will guarantee your success.

Treat her with tenderness and generosity and your relationship will be an enjoyable one. A bunch of beautiful flowers will never fail to make her eyes light up. See to it that you never forget her birthday or your anniversary. These things are very important to her.

If you are patient and kind, you can keep a Pisces woman happy for a lifetime. She, however, is not without her faults. You may find her lacking in practicality and good old-fashioned stoicism; you may even feel that she uses her tears as a method of getting her own way.

Pisces is a strong, self-sacrificing mother. She will teach her children the value of service to the community while not letting them lose their individuality.

CANCER
LUCKY NUMBERS 1998

Lucky numbers and astrology can be linked through the movements of the Moon. Each phase of the thirteen Moon cycles vibrates with a sequence of numbers for your Sign of the Zodiac over the course of the year. Using your lucky numbers is a fun system that connects you with tradition.

New Moon	First Quarter	Full Moon	Last Quarter
Dec. 29 ('97)	Jan. 5	Jan. 12	Jan. 20
6 9 4 7	7 2 5 8	0 3 8 6	1 0 4 2
Jan. 28	Feb. 3	Feb. 11	Feb. 19
5 9 3 7	7 1 4 8	4 6 1 0	7 5 8 3
Feb. 26	March 5	March 12	March 21
3 6 1 4	4 0 2 7	9 4 7 9	9 7 1 5
March 27	April 3	April 11	April 19
8 3 6 4	0 4 9 2	2 6 9 7	7 1 2 5
April 26	May 3	May 11	May 18
9 3 6 0	1 6 8 3	6 6 4 7	7 2 4 8
May 25	June 1	June 9	June 17
2 0 9 5	5 7 2 5	9 3 6 0	1 4 8 8
June 23	July 1	July 9	July 16
0 6 2 4	4 8 2 9	7 3 7 0	1 5 8 1
July 23	July 31	August 7	August 14
5 1 3 7	7 1 8 2	1 6 9 4	4 7 0 5
August 21	August 30	Sept. 6	Sept. 12
1 5 7 2	5 3 6 0	5 4 8 2	2 0 9 5
Sept. 20	Sept. 28	Oct. 5	Oct. 12
5 7 3 6	4 7 2 5	8 9 3 0	0 1 6 8
Oct. 20	Oct. 28	Nov. 4	Nov. 10
8 3 9 7	1 5 8 3	3 6 0 9	4 9 2 6
Nov. 18	Nov. 26	Dec. 3	Dec. 10
6 9 1 4	8 2 6 9	6 0 7 3	3 5 9 3
Dec. 18	Dec. 26	Jan. 1 ('99)	Jan. 9 ('99)
3 1 9 4	7 2 5 0	0 3 8 1	1 5 8 6

CANCER
YEARLY FORECAST 1998

Forecast for 1998 Concerning Business
and Financial Affairs, Job Prospects,
Travel, Health, Romance and Marriage
for Those Born with the Sun
in the Zodiacal Sign of Cancer.
June 21–July 20

For those born under the influence of the Sun in the zodiacal sign of Cancer, which is ruled by the Moon, this promises to be an ambitious and optimistic year. The emphasis is on streamlining your current life so that you can move on to new and more inspiring enterprises. Life in general is likely to start opening up to you in ways you have only dreamed about. This year you are apt to face more than your usual share of challenges. Much of the time you could feel that you are under a microscope and have to prove yourself, especially in career matters. However, your efforts to show just what you are made of are likely to pay off handsomely. Where business and professional matters are concerned, your greatest success will depend on your willingness to be patient. You need to allow time for the seeds you sow to grow and develop. This is not a year for making many impulsive decisions, nor for trying to hurry along projects which clearly require gradual cultivation and sustained effort. The financial picture during 1998 is promising. Clarifying your individual responsibility with regard to joint finances can free you to use your money in more productive ways. One long-term monetary burden can be finally paid off. Where routine occupational affairs are concerned, this is a year when the need to make a clean break becomes more urgent. Thoroughness both in your day-to-day work and in your general routine planning is the basic key to success. Travel opportunities are likely to increase. Having other people's resources at your disposal may open up more possibilities with regard to foreign travel, in particular. Where health is concerned, inner healing is a key theme this year. A long-term, persistent problem could be cleared up when you get a second or even a third opinion about the condition. Your romantic life is likely to flourish. One relationship in particular should deepen and be more mutually supportive and rewarding. Both single and attached Cancers have an opportunity to move closer to fulfilling romantic dreams and desires. Passion takes on more meaning in a close, ongoing relationship. For married Cancer people in particular, a substantial increase in your joint income is likely to allow you to spend more leisure time together.

For professional Cancer people this should be a highly successful year. You reap what you sow, although it may take longer than you expect for the results of your efforts to manifest fully. This year it is important to take more responsibility for the long-term development of business interests. A venture left to ride along at its own pace may well come to nothing. Lack of monitoring tends to mean that development opportunities are missed or timing is off. Your success lies in being vigilant and willing to put in extra hours in order to oversee a number of different major projects simultaneously. The best type of investment this year tends to be money plowed back into the business. Long-term, stable investments can be lucrative on an ongoing basis. It is wise, however, to work on strengthening your immediate position. Invest capital and profits in modern equipment to make the business run more smoothly and efficiently. Much of what has been put into a venture in the past may begin to be repaid this year. Charitable gestures toward both clients and competitors will earn you added respect and rewards, perhaps when you least expect it. You can call upon various contacts for favors at any point when you really need some help, without fear of a refusal. January 1 to 25 is an excellent period for making these requests. Between April 14 and May 24, keep an eye on your finances; you may be inclined during this period to spend money recklessly because you are expecting a big payoff. Wait until you have the money before you spend it.

Financially, this year you are able to cash in on other people's resources and good fortune. For married Cancer people, more funds may be available due to a partner's inheritance or increase in earnings. It is likely, however, that you also need to invest quite some time and energy in helping your partner get ahead. What you gain financially is likely to have been earned by you in a roundabout way, rather than being a simple handout. It is a good idea to become involved in a new investment scheme if you end the year with money to spare. Traditional savings and investment plans may not give you the return you want; innovative plans may have a lot more to offer, accompanied by a higher degree of risk. Younger children will probably be the focus of some extra expenditure during the year, or you may want to contribute to a child-oriented charitable organization. Vacations, too, can be costly. It is wise to survey the year well ahead in terms of financial requirements so that you can plan a suitable place and time to go away for a well-earned break and still be left with money in the bank. The period between August 21 and October 7 demands that you carefully monitor your cash flow; you are prone then to spending without sufficient planning.

Where routine occupational affairs are concerned, this is an eventful year due to your need to move away from what does not suit you. For some time you may have been feeling that you want to make a major change in direction. This year the need to break away and free yourself from burdensome constrictions becomes more urgent. An interesting career opportunity could arise, offering the chance to make that change without fear of regret or recrimination from other people who are affected by your move. In your day-to-day work, whether or not you end up making a significant change, it is important to be very thorough in your approach. This is not a year for trying to cut corners on a regular basis. Good planning and organization are the real keys to success. If you are trying to make major changes, the more organized you are in your everyday work, the more time you will have to plan your future course. Major projects which have been ongoing for some time can be brought to an end this year, leaving you less stressed mentally and with your hands less tied on a practical level.

There are likely to be a number of opportunities to journey far and wide during the year ahead. Other people's resources are the key to your being able to travel on a more global level. A family member with money to spare for leisure activities may be eager for you to join in traveling for pleasure. Friends moving or living abroad may extend invitations to you also, perhaps offering free accommodations to you. There should be less overall need to travel in connection with occupational affairs, but work between August 21 and October 7 could necessitate at least one long-distance business trip. The best times for a vacation this year are between January 26 and February 4 and again from October 24 to November 22; the latter dates are especially good for family-oriented travel.

With regard to your health, inner healing is the key focus at both an emotional and physical level. Closer attention to what you eat and drink can help clear away an external problem such as a skin condition. As a Cancer you often bottle up your emotions, which can create all sorts of minor health problems. It is a good idea this year to resolve to speak out more and brood less. Stomach problems often afflict Cancers; the less emotional stress you put on yourself, the less difficulty you will have with digestion. If you have been living with an ongoing health problem for a long time, this is the year to obtain a new diagnosis and try to find the real cause of the problem. You have the willpower from January 12 to April 3 to give up a habit that you know is unhealthy.

Your life should be very rewarding this year where romance and marriage are concerned. For single Cancers, new romance is likely to prosper, filling you with greater enthusiasm for all areas of life. An ongoing relationship should deepen as you and your partner make time to be together more often, doing the things you both love to share. An increase in your partner's income may enable the two of you to indulge yourselves and nourish your relationship by enjoying mutual leisure pursuits. Foreign travel together ought to be particularly rewarding, especially if one or both of you are venturing into new territory. Married Cancer men and women need to give more mutual support at both a practical and an emotional level. Your time will not be your own in this respect, but this giving and receiving should be highly rewarding. Passion is the key emotion which brings more meaning to life and helps guide you toward greater general fulfillment. Unplanned moments spent with your love partner are likely to be some of the most rewarding times you experience this year. January 1 to 29 and from October 11 to November 28 are likely to be especially romantic periods for all Cancer people. Throughout the year, take advantage of every opportunity to express your emotions in deeds as well as words.

CANCER
DAILY FORECAST

January–December 1998

JANUARY

1. THURSDAY. Good. You should be able to make good progress convincing your mate or another family member to join you in a heath-related resolution for this year. Losing weight, joining a health club or giving up a habit you know is bad for you both may top your list. Socially, you could meet someone who puts an interesting proposition to you. If you are anxious to begin a new project, first make an effort to clear up the loose ends of your previous work. It is beneficial to start with a clean slate. As the new year begins, you may be intent on improving future economic security for yourself and your loved ones. This is a favorable time to discuss a budget and savings plan with your family. The more you concentrate on organization, the better.

2. FRIDAY. Disquieting. This is one of those days when you may have too many tasks to cope with all at once. It is best to stop what you are doing and prioritize carefully. Rushed efforts are unlikely to satisfy you because you will tend to miss out on important details. It is vital to keep an eye on the future without neglecting the present. Work which can be adequately done by someone else should be delegated at the first opportunity. Try to free yourself from some everyday routine so that you can focus on an overall perspective of what you hope to achieve in the long run. Keep your distance from colleagues or neighbors who may be argumentative. A minor disagreement could escalate into a year long feud.

3. SATURDAY. Confusing. Conditions are not much different from yesterday in terms of having too much to do. There is a tendency to get caught up in trivial discussions and arguments which ultimately are just distracting. Try to maintain your focus on what is really important. If you are attempting a do-it-yourself project around the home, do not take on too much all in one day. It is better to complete a few small jobs rather than try to rush through one long, laborious task. Enterprising as you are at the moment, you need to slow down and see one job through to a satisfactory conclusion before getting involved in something else.

4. SUNDAY. Fair. This is a better day than yesterday for moving ahead with your plans, particularly to fulfill a long-range objective. Family members are especially helpful. Team up with someone who understands what you are aiming to accomplish; he or she may have some useful ideas and advice to offer. If you are striving to make progress in the business world, this is a key time for establishing a solid reputation. It is important to make an effort to get to know influential people through social contacts. You never know when you may need to call on them in the future. If attending a get-together, act naturally and you are sure to make a good impression.

5. MONDAY. Variable. Rigorous self-discipline is one key to success where career matters are concerned. It can be easy to be swayed and distracted by other people. Keep in mind that while certain bright lights are shining around you, they may also burn out quite quickly. Your own ideas and ways of working are likely to be more solid, although perhaps slower and less dramatic. Trust yourself; you are making substantial progress, however gradual. Your personal life needs to be handled gently. Be as good to yourself as you are to other people. Be careful not to emotionally squash a loved one by refusing to listen to their newest idea even if it does not seem practical to you.

6. TUESDAY. Deceptive. Other people cannot be relied upon to provide you with accurate information. Frustrating as this may be, you need to be patient and do some research on your own. Trust your own instincts as far as possible. You are naturally very intuitive; do not allow others to throw you off a scent which is very strong. A friend may irritate you by forgetting to repay money to you or failing to keep another commitment. However, this is not a day to make a scene. Let others go their own way today as far as possible. Attempts to control the situation through talking behind their back or brooding are unlikely to have a very positive effect on the situation.

7. WEDNESDAY. Changeable. As a Cancer you are always emotionally sensitive, but especially around people you do not know well. You could feel somewhat out of your depth in a social situation today. It is a good idea to keep conversations superficial if you sense that you might get into hot water discussing a subject you only know a little about. Attempts to catch up on a backlog of work could be thwarted due to a series of distractions. Nevertheless, one of these is likely to involve someone important to you who needs some immediate advice and emotional support. Be willing to drop what you are doing so that you can have an in-depth discussion and really be of help to them.

8. THURSDAY. Rewarding. Friendly gestures on your part are likely to pay off. Go out of your way for individuals who need a little help and you are likely to be rewarded in more ways than you might expect. Your involvement in a club or other organization may bring you into contact with one particularly interesting new person. This is a key day for broadening your social horizons. If you are in a group social situation, make an effort to speak to a number of different people rather than just those sitting next to you. An old photograph you come across could remind you of someone you have not seen in a long time. Consider getting back in touch by writing or phoning directly or through a mutual friend.

9. FRIDAY. Productive. Your energy should pick up as today progresses. You may wake up feeling you do not want to face the world but would rather focus on private matters. You are bound to make inroads either way. Later you may feel ready to mingle with people you do not know well. Friends are likely to be quite an inspiration if you spend time with them. If you are beginning a new venture on your own, it is a good idea to enlist some support, even if it is only moral support for your efforts. Other people's generosity is a real bonus, especially if you need a favor or some inside information. Keep evening plans simple and inexpensive.

10. SATURDAY. Misleading. You are apt to be frustrated trying to get things done but getting nowhere fast. This is not a time for being in a hurry. The less pressure you put on yourself, and the fewer the amount of tasks you hope to accomplish, the better. If you are going out socially this evening, avoid being too forward in your attempts to get to know other people. Deep down you probably want to keep to yourself, and you should trust the instinct to do so. Much time can be wasted trying to make polite conversation. Single Cancers need to be especially wary of getting involved in a romantic triangle.

11. SUNDAY. Frustrating. Progress moving ahead on personal projects is likely to be slow going. An authority figure may be hard to convince to see things your way, but keep trying. It is likely that you will make the most headway playing strictly by the rules rather than trying to proceed your own way. It may be tempting to be bullheaded about one particular issue, but this approach probably will not get you far. Pay attention to the advice of older people, however patronizing their words may seem to you at the time. There is a strong likelihood that they actually know better, especially if they have considerable experience in an area that you are just venturing into with the hope of making your mark.

12. MONDAY. Stressful. Authority figures may turn out to be a help to you in terms of offering helpful advice, even if they get in your way to begin with. At the same time, you need to trust your own judgment more than anything else. One particular person is probably misguided even though experienced. The one who talks loudest is not the best one to heed. Money matters need careful handling. There may be confusion over money that you owe, either in terms of payment for services rendered or in relation to a prior loan. Carefully check details of a contract or other pertinent document. Avoid lending money to a friend or an acquaintance unless you can really spare it now and for the next month or two.

13. TUESDAY. Variable. You may not get very far with your own projects because your partner or colleagues object and stand in your way. Nevertheless, there may be good reason for them being so difficult. Try to find out just what the problem is. A family member may feel neglected due to your increasing interest in personal pursuits that exclude them. If you are involved in a legal battle at the moment, do not expect an easy ride. You will have to do more than you expect to prove your case. At times like this you can feel very alone. Confide in someone you trust; you can count on them for support. Be sure you are building on a strong foundation that will not shift and leave you in the lurch.

14. WEDNESDAY. Mixed. Money matters are under helpful influences on the whole. However, take your time in making a decision in relation to your personal finances. It is not the time to invest in a dubious business scheme. Tempting as the promised returns may be, you may be required to make much more of an investment than actual future results warrant. Avoid any type of gambling. If you have the option to go for gradual returns where investments are concerned or an end-of-year lump sum, select the latter. You will be less tempted to squander a large payment and grateful at a future date that you made this decision. If a former spouse or business partner tries to opt out of payments, you may have to take them to court.

15. THURSDAY. Good. This is a good day for single Cancers to get out in order to meet new people. Accept an invitation which will put you in a new environment. It is apt to be a key opportunity to be introduced to a potential love partner. This is generally a favorable day for travel and a change of scene. Even running errands around town ought to be quite stimulating. You will be happiest when you focus on a variety of tasks. Make telephone calls that you have been putting off and catch up with correspondence, including that letter of praise or congratulations you have been intending to write.

16. FRIDAY. Pleasant. Mental and creative endeavors are the most stimulating, especially where work is concerned. Do some long-range planning. If you have been temporarily out of work, this is a favorable day for contacting new companies. An earning opportunity which comes through the mail could be promising. It is also well worthwhile to follow up any leads given to you by friends or former co-workers. Advertisements on notice boards and in newspapers may be another a source of inspiration. Life with your partner should be especially loving. This is a starred day for an engagement or wedding. Single Cancers ready to settle down can make new links socially through sports activities.

17. SATURDAY. Satisfactory. Joint endeavors which involve one or more family members are likely to be a source of stimulation and satisfaction. Whatever you choose to do with your time, you are apt to enjoy your day more if others are part of all your activities. If you are single, get out socially. While pursuing a personal hobby or other interest you could meet someone quite interesting. Local community activities are also favored as a way of making closer links to other people. If you have recently moved to a new area, this is a key time for getting to know your neighbors better. Take the initiative to chat with someone you meet in passing. Volunteering in your local hospital or at a nursing home can also help you adjust to new surroundings.

18. SUNDAY. Fair. This is a favorable day for getting on with tasks at home. As a Cancer you have a natural creative streak which you can turn to home decorating and do-it-yourself tasks. An old piece of furniture can become the focal point of a room. This should appeal to the side of your nature which favors recycling what you just cannot part with or allow to be taken away from a neighbor's garbage. Despite the fact that the item may appear to have outlived its use, you can restore it to full glory. Partners can be rather argumentative. Give them time to sort out their feelings in private. It is better to avoid confrontation until tempers have cooled down.

19. MONDAY. Frustrating. It can be difficult to make satisfactory progress with a home-based project due to lack of knowledge or expertise. It might be a good idea to get a professional person in on the act. However, make sure that this individual understands exactly what you want done. As a Cancer you sometimes hold back your true feelings and opinions until it is too late for others to change what they have started to do for you. Aim to be more upfront. In that way you should not wind up fretting over what could have been rectified if you had only spoken up in the first place. Your loved one is open to romantic suggestions if you set the stage.

20. TUESDAY. Mixed. This is a good day for finishing up work and getting tedious tasks finally out of the way. If you are trying to clinch a business deal, do not hesitate to make a final agreement and sign the contract. You should find it easier than usual to act decisively; take advantage of this. Luck is on your side. The children in your life can cause extra expense, perhaps due to their social activities at school. Because these ventures may be important, do all that you can to support them, even if it means budgeting a little harder. If buying sports equipment, get the best quality you can afford.

21. WEDNESDAY. Variable. Sparks may fly where romance is concerned, especially if you are asked or are expected to foot a bill you did not anticipate having to pay. Although you and your mate or partner may disagree about money matters, it is likely that an open discussion will sort out the situation amicably. This evening can be very romantic for both single and married Cancers. If you are not with anyone special at the moment, accept a social invitation which could lead to meeting a newcomer. This is a favorable day for making new contacts and for teaming up with people you already know in order to brainstorm a creative idea. Look for a way to break out of established patterns.

22. THURSDAY. Uncertain. Creative talents can come to the fore when you team up with other people. A business deal in the making may have to be put on hold because certain parties are refusing to make a decision. Try to be patient. If you have been temporarily out of work, this is a good time to consider new avenues of employment, perhaps overseas. Single Cancers looking for romantic happiness could meet someone new through pursuing a hobby or other special interest. And this is a favorable time for married Cancers to enjoy leisure activities together with a loved one. Such activity can be healing if any kind of rift has occurred between you in the past week or two. Despite the weather, try to get some physical exercise.

23. FRIDAY. Slow. Membership in an organization to which you belong may seem too expensive for what you are getting in return. It might be worth looking around for an alternative which is better value. Also reconsider a subscription to a magazine you seldom read. You should make good progress if undertaking research-related work. However, do not expect to move quickly on any one project. It is important to explore new ideas in depth and to view documents the same way, particularly if you are about to sign a contract of any kind. A partner may try to get the upper hand in your relationship. Aim to meet halfway, but do not give in just to keep the peace.

24. SATURDAY. Quiet. This is a favorable day for settling down to various routine tasks at home. There should be little pressure from outside sources to distract you. A pet can be a great comfort, especially if you need some love with no strings attached. If you are thinking of renting out part of your home or a separate property, perhaps a vacation cottage, think about where to advertise and what ground rules you need to set up. Make the most of any spare time to prepare especially nourishing and wholesome meals for the week ahead. You will be glad you have ready-to-eat food in the freezer during the busy next few days.

25. SUNDAY. Good. Going somewhere new and exciting with a friend or partner should lift your spirits. It is a good time for trying new activities and journeying to a place that takes you out of yourself. A change of scene is the ideal tonic if you are feeling hemmed in by routine and the same old same old. Socially, accept an invitation to an event you might normally avoid because you will not know many of the other guests. It is likely that you will meet interesting people who you find stimulating. Married Cancers should find their partner supportive where new ventures are concerned, but be sure to discuss any significant costs that might be involved.

26. MONDAY. Challenging. Yesterday your partner most likely supported your endeavors, but today you may have difficulty getting anyone to back you and to cooperate. It is worth persevering, however, if you feel strongly about what you want to do. A colleague at work may challenge you openly. Although you may feel that you are in direct competition with each other and that you do not have the upper hand, think again. You may not have as much training or experience as the other person, but you have a way of dealing with people which definitely works in your favor. Being diplomatic rather than going on the defensive should help.

27. TUESDAY. Deceptive. Do not place too much emphasis on what others say or do. This is one of those days when various individuals can unintentionally give you the wrong information. If a partner is being vague about arrangements, make a point of demanding specifics. This is likely to be the only way to avoid confusion over future plans and double booking. Conditions favor getting down to work which requires intense concentration and attention to detail. Research tasks ought to go especially well. Search and you shall find is a key phrase to bear in mind. People expect you to take a leadership role, but that does not mean you can dictate to them.

28. WEDNESDAY. Promising. New business possibilities which come your way are likely to be exciting. You can profit by joining forces with other people who are interested in the same idea. If you need approval from an authority figure there ought to be no problem obtaining it. This is a favorable time for asking for references from current or previous landlords or employers, and also for requesting financial references. If you have been thinking of applying for credit or a loan, hesitate no longer. You are likely to get what you want now. The advice of an expert should be useful if you adapt it to your own special situation.

29. THURSDAY. Disconcerting. This is one of those days when you cannot help but get angry with certain individuals. Try to keep out of the way of people you usually find stressful to be around. Your feelings are more intense than usual. Although your instinct may be to keep them to yourself, that may not be easy. You may overreact to the slightest provocation. Past experiences could be haunting you more than you realize. If you end up reacting out of proportion to an event that occurs, try to think what it reminds you of and why. Some self-analysis can help you break a negative pattern of behavior.

30. FRIDAY. Calm. If you have the opportunity to get away early, do so. You are likely to have a wonderfully relaxing time if you go out of town with your mate or partner. If you normally spend time at home, a different environment can make a world of difference. Last-minute arrangements are apt to work out well. Single Cancers have more chance of meeting a new partner through distant social contacts. Journeying far away could lead to a new love match. Concentrate on broadening your horizons rather than limiting yourself in any way. A sporting event can be great fun, whether you are actively participating as a player or a spectator.

31. SATURDAY. Easygoing. As with yesterday, this is a great day for taking off to somewhere new. The ski slopes are likely to suit you at the moment, especially if you share the wonders of nature with a partner or close friend. Time spent away from the strains of everyday life could restore your vitality and inspire you. If you have been looking for the right time to bring up a difficult issue with a family member, this is it. Your loved one is likely to be more agreeable than usual, particularly about matters which you sense need sensitive negotiation. A promise is as good as a written contract. You can work out a new and better budget if you set priorities together with your mate or partner.

FEBRUARY

1. SUNDAY. Demanding. A wide variety of responsibilities are likely to weigh rather heavily on your shoulders. It is a good idea to utilize other people's help and resources as much as possible in order to lighten your burden. Family members may not be at their best, perhaps because they feel neglected since your time has recently been taken up so much with obligations to other people. Take a few minutes to soothe and reassure those who matter most to you. If you have tax or other financial matters to settle, this is an excellent time to do so. A problem that has been worrying you can be sorted out by looking into a new approach to solve it. Do not cling to a proposed solution that has been tried without success.

2. MONDAY. Confusing. Responsibilities are likely to take up most of your time, but the situation is improving by the hour. This is a good time for new financial investment. An offer which promises big returns in the future is well worth looking into. A friend of yours may prove quite unreliable. This could be due at least in part to a mix-up in arrangements. When discussing plans with other people, be careful that you are specific about meeting place and time.. It is worth going over such details twice so that everybody gets the word and has a chance to ask questions. Do not believe all that you read or are told. Not all information will be entirely accurate despite the informant's best intentions.

3. TUESDAY. Unsettling. This is another day when friends can be rather unreliable. The cause is more likely to be their wanting to do their own thing at the last minute rather than any mix-up in arrangements. Although it is likely to irritate you that others cannot be depended upon to stick with plans, it is important to remain as flexible as you possibly can. Have options in mind so that you are not left feeling stranded. There is little point attempting to control the lives of other people. As a Cancer you can be hard on them or on yourself when things go wrong, and you can lay on a guilt trip or two when you are let down. It is probably better to just let the matter slide now.

4. WEDNESDAY. Variable. You may be increasingly annoyed by the lack of commitment from someone you considered to be a stalwart friend or a very good acquaintance. However, brooding on this will not do you much good. Think the situation through again. It may be time to acknowledge that one particular relationship or connection is no longer working and there is probably not much point trying to hang onto it. If you feel that you are overinvested in some way in a particular a relationship, now is the time to pull out. Try not to focus too much on regrets regarding what once was. An older person can be a wonderful adviser.

5. THURSDAY. Changeable. Much as you may wish to keep a low profile, it could be difficult to do so. Work pressures can keep you very busy. A number of telephone calls may demand your immediate attention. You may feel like running away from it all when the going gets tough. However, it is worth your while to see a difficult project through to the end. The more problems you can tie up and say goodbye to once and for all, the better. An authority figure is likely to be surprisingly helpful. A compliment which comes your way in relation to your efforts is bound to boost your confidence and renew your determination.

6. FRIDAY. Quiet. Today is much better than yesterday when it comes to hiding yourself away so that you can focus on deadline tasks. It may be necessary to do some backtracking in order to solve a problem through a new approach. However, you should have sufficient time to be able to do so. If you have been neglecting certain areas of your work or life in general, this is a favorable day for getting back to them. Something that has been nagging at the back of your mind can be resolved now. If you feel that you did not act in the best way in one particular situation or relationship, do what seems necessary to make amends. Even if you were only partially to blame, do not hesitate to apologize first.

7. SATURDAY. Productive. This is an excellent day for pushing ahead with your personal interests. If you have been thinking about changing your image in some cosmetic way, you should now have the confidence to go ahead and do it. If you feel restless, get away from your usual weekend environment in search of excitement. A trip to fulfill a personal goal promises to be especially stimulating and rewarding. In-depth research of any kind is likely to produce encouraging results, even if it means a lot of detailed work. If you have felt in a rut lately, your current vitality and increased sense of purpose should help you break out of it. There is a strong element of luck putting you in the right place at the right time.

8. SUNDAY. Stressful. You are likely to be asked to help out with duties that involve doing a lot of running around on behalf of other people. Because you probably feel obliged to help, try not to plan to do too much else that is time-sensitive. You could create problems if you try to hurry through everything. It is much better to allow extra time so that you can pace yourself. Deep thinking about a matter that is troubling you can lead to unexpected insights. It may also be worthwhile talking things over with a good friend. Voicing problems sometimes makes the solution much more obvious. Test out a new idea in a small way before investing a lot of time and money in it.

9. MONDAY. Deceptive. This is not a very favorable day for making major financial decisions. Whether you are thinking of making a big purchase or of putting some money into a business, postpone the decision making to another day if you can. Overly idealistic thinking at the moment means that you may not see a hyped bargain or golden deal for what it really is. If you have made arrangements for an evening get-together, double-check the time and place. One person may forget to let you know of a change of plan. Avoid lending anything of value to other people. If you do, it could end up lost despite the other person's care, or might be never returned due to an oversight.

10. TUESDAY. Mixed. Arguments about money can put pressure on your relationship with your mate or partner. However, all is likely to work out well if you figure out between you who is to hold the purse strings in the long run. If you are thinking about making an important investment soon, it is a good idea to obtain professional advice directly or through reading. Individuals who think they know what they are talking about but are actually not qualified may be more of a hindrance than a help to you. Rely on tried-and-tested methods when trying to sort out a tricky work matter. This is one of those days when an attempt to test out a new technique might backfire on you. Cancel evening plans in favor of going to bed early.

11. WEDNESDAY. Disconcerting. Once again, avoid making any important financial investment at the moment. Figure out a way to repay an outstanding debt before committing any further large sum of money. Once this obligation is out of the way, you should feel that a heavy burden has been lifted from you. There may be difficulties in relation to recovering money which is owed to you. This is not the right time to be too aggressive. Instead, try to talk your way around the situation firmly but diplomatically. Be prepared to fall back on your own resources if someone who has been full of promises turns out to be full of nothing but hot air.

12. THURSDAY. Rewarding. Accomplishing everything which you set out to do may be a struggle because you need to give more in-depth attention than you expect. Nevertheless, your efforts will eventually prove useful. It really does pay to be thorough in all of your undertakings at the moment. Negotiations in relation to your finances should work out well, especially if you are acting as a result of professional advice. If you need a loan, putting forward a strong case for yourself ought to bring positive results. An older person whom you respect could be quite helpful when it comes to sorting out priorities which are difficult to put in order. Focus on doing one thing at a time rather than scattering your efforts.

13. FRIDAY. Pleasant. This is a favorable day for contacting distant people by letter or telephone. If you have an important message to convey, do not put it off. Finalize arrangements for a social event you have planned for the weekend and all should go smoothly. A loved one may make a special effort to let you know just how much you are appreciated, which ought to boost your self-confidence considerably. If you have no special plans for this evening, get together with a friend or neighbor whose company you enjoy. Catching up on gossip and discussing your individual plans ought to be quite stimulating. A trip somewhere special with your mate or another family member should bring you a lot of mutual pleasure and enjoyment.

14. SATURDAY. Useful. Try to be more organized at home this weekend. Get irksome chores out of the way early in the day so that you can fully relax later on. If you do some clearing you are likely to come across an item you mislaid some time ago. If you feel rather restless, stay on the go to expel some of that volatile energy. Vigorous exercise on your own or in a team sport could be good. If you and your partner have some do-it-yourself projects in mind, this is a good weekend to get started on at least one of them. Carefully plan the quantities of materials you will need, and buy the best quality you can afford.

15. SUNDAY. Frustrating. Older people, especially parents, can be difficult to be around. You may not see eye-to-eye on a few very basic matters. If you can manage to avoid discussing matters such as religion and politics, the air between you is likely to be clearer. As hard as you try to finish a home-based project, you may not be able to do so because you need someone else's expertise before you can move on. Try not to plunge ahead blindly or make a decision that you suspect you might regret later on. Do not be surprised if an old appliance stops working properly. You may have forgotten just how old it is but now realize you will soon have to replace it.

16. MONDAY. Misleading. This is a favorable day for completing a project around the home which could not be finished during the weekend. Obtain an estimate for any further work which needs to be done if you cannot handle it yourself. Get a second quote if in any doubt about the amount you are going to have to pay. It is also a good idea to ask for references from a company that you have not dealt with before. Beware if intending to buy a luxury item. What looks like a bargain could turn out to be poorly constructed or made from inferior materials. It is wiser to hold on to what you have until you can buy the best for yourself.

17. TUESDAY. Unsettling. Expenses that you have not budgeted for are likely to throw you for a loop. A child may want to go away on a school trip, and this might be quite costly. Try to juggle your finances to avoid having to deal with the guilt you are likely to feel if you sense that you are depriving a loved one of a valuable experience. As was true yesterday, be wary of buying a bargain that is not what it appears to be. A clever salesperson could try to fool you with a lot of talk and empty promises. Trust your instincts, which will probably tell you when to steer clear. Any promises should be put in writing.

18. WEDNESDAY. Good. If you have a chance to indulge in some fun entertainment, go for it even if you feel a bit shy. You are bound to enjoy yourself. Sporting activities, whether you are taking part or just sitting in the stands, promise to be a source of amusement. If you have been trying to create a romantic scenario for you and your love partner, this evening is a favorable time. The results of your creative endeavors, such as cooking or flower arranging, are likely to be highly appreciated. A compliment given to you should boost your self-esteem if you take it to heart. Although you may aim for perfection, other people do not expect unreasonably high results from you.

19. THURSDAY. Difficult. Strange rumors flying around in your neighborhood or at work can make you feel on edge. It is not a good idea, however, to try to pry in order to find out what is really going on. It is unlikely that you will get a satisfactory response. If anything, you could be closing a door which at the moment is at least slightly ajar. Trust your instincts and imagination, without allowing your thoughts to become exaggerated. Keep your eyes and ears open. You probably know more than you think you do. This is not a particularly good time to begin a new project. Aim to complete outstanding work first. Stay in the background in order to avoid new responsibility or increased scrutiny.

20. FRIDAY. Manageable. This is a good day for getting down to some hard work you want to get out of the way. You are your own best taskmaster at the moment and are also very good at organizing other people. It would probably be a mistake, however, to be overly ambitious. Avoid taking on more tasks or responsibilities just when you are trying to clear away a backlog of work. It is worthwhile keeping an eye on the future so that you do not lose sight of your longer term goals. Getting bogged down in petty details is likely to hold up your progress. You need to apply muscle power as well as brain power; guard against overdoing in either area.

21. SATURDAY. Happy. Today is excellent for getting together with your partner to talk about long-range mutual plans. This is especially important if you seldom have the time to discuss what you hope to do together as well as apart. It is the ideal moment to plan a summer vacation if you have not already done so. This is also a favorable time for going on a pleasure trip for the day with a loved one. You are bound to enjoy the time you spend together. Single Cancers may meet a prospective new romantic partner through educational or travel interests. It is worth striking up a conversation with someone to whom you are attracted without waiting to be formally introduced.

22. SUNDAY. Fair. You may get into an argument with a partner or close friend because one of you feels patronized by the other. Although your approach at the moment may be loving and giving, it may come across as overly protective to someone who is sensitive about their independence. Your best approach is to listen a lot and not do too much talking. If you have advice to offer, first consider if it is likely to be welcome. This should be a rewarding day if you immerse yourself in a new venture. Discussing an innovative plan could lead to putting it into action sooner than you expect. Be courageous when it comes to breaking away from a comfortable old pattern.

23. MONDAY. Enjoyable. Time spent with someone you admire is likely to be very fruitful. You should feel that you can take on the whole world if necessary. At a more realistic level, other people are apt to spur you on to achieve current goals. Your mate or partner is especially supportive now. Someone who owes you a favor is likely to be more than happy to repay it when you ask. Be wary of making any new financial investment at the moment. Even though a deal may look promising at first glance, there may be much more to it than meets the eye. If you can avoid doing anything in excess, life should proceed quite smoothly and enjoyably.

24. TUESDAY. Demanding. Sharing responsibilities with colleagues should help lighten your own load. However, you could have to offer something in exchange for what is given to you. This is a day of bargaining rather than freely given favors. There could be an unexpected change of plan, leaving you to cope with more tasks than usual. Fortunately, your closest associates are willing to help out. Unplanned and unexpected financial expenditure can deplete your savings. Look ahead and budget carefully for the next few months if you intend to make a major purchase such as a new car, household appliances, or carpeting.

25. WEDNESDAY. Profitable. All the hassles and worries of the past few days should drift away today. Your financial situation is looking better, even if you had to spend quite a lot recently. This is another good day for planning ahead. Figure out how you can balance your budget during demanding times in the future. This is a better day for shopping and buying, since you are likely to strike a fair deal. When it comes to trying to sell your services or product, you may find that purchasers are looking for a bargain and are not willing to pay full price. There is little point arguing with someone who is unwilling to negotiate. Guard against underselling yourself.

26. THURSDAY. Slow. You may be raring to begin a new project, but hold your horses if you can. It is worth thinking things through one more time, especially if you are launching a large-scale venture. This is a time for thinking on a broader perspective than usual. There could be an exciting opportunity coming your way which will allow you to expand your horizons in directions you have not explored before. Work responsibilities could hold up your plans. Read documents carefully. A current difficulty requires thorough research before you can progress with any degree of certainty. You may regret skimming over details or be called to account for your negligence.

27. FRIDAY. Variable. A desire to do something you have always dreamed of is likely to be consuming you at the moment. You can certainly achieve a lot, but do not take on too much all at once. It is better to put a lot of energy into one important project rather than scatter your attention by having several pots on the boil. Family members are likely to be charming and helpful. If you want to relax at the end of the day, do so in the arms of your loved one. If you are unattached, a low-key social event could bring you into contact with someone very attractive who is obviously also attracted to you. Pay your own way tonight but no one else's.

28. SATURDAY. Fortunate. The ambitious streak in your nature is unlikely to disappear just because it is the weekend. In fact, you are more in touch with your desires than usual. Do not hesitate participating in spontaneous, unplanned activities. These are likely to help you achieve your goals in some way. Through socializing you could meet people who have the resources or information that you need, Intensive work is likely to be especially fulfilling. Spend some time sorting through a closet or a room in your home which has been neglected for a while. A sporting event can be special fun this evening if you are playing or rooting for a player.

MARCH

1. SUNDAY. Sensitive. Being excluded from behind-the-scenes discussions can make you feel left out in the cold. One particular relationship not involving you is becoming stronger through a shared secret, which may make you a little jealous. If a relationship you were once deeply involved in is fading, consider whether you have given each other all that you have to give and now it is time to move on. There is still much going on which should give you a feeling of optimism. The more tactful and subtle you are in all of your relationships, the better. Play your cards close to your chest for the time being. Do not reveal future plans to someone who could become your competitor.

2. MONDAY. Fair. You may have a difficult time with a friend or acquaintance involving a loan made some time ago. It is vital to get the situation sorted out now. The sooner you attend to what are essentially trivial problems, the better. A loved one's unpredictable moves can make you nervous. Strive to expect the unexpected. Do not count on money that is owed to you arriving on time. Coming up with a contingency plan to allow for eventualities puts you in a much stronger position. Good communication is of prime importance. Choose your words carefully so that you leave no doubt about your meaning.

3. TUESDAY. Good. This is a better day than yesterday for both social and business relationships. You should be able to make useful new contacts. Single Cancers should not hesitate to accept an invitation from a neighbor or relative; it could lead to a romantic introduction. You are likely to be the center of attention in some special way. If you are interested in formulating a new business deal, contact with former colleagues could be the initial move that gets the ball rolling. Someone in your social circle is likely to take independent action that works in your favor. You will probably be quite touched by another person's thoughtfulness. Be gracious in accepting a gift or compliment.

4. WEDNESDAY. Variable. While this may begin as a noneventful day, conditions are likely to get more lively later on. Routine tasks demand attention this morning, and you can make good progress with them. Be careful, however, not to leave too much to chance. A flurry of telephone calls later in the day could set back your progress. A meeting is likely to drag on longer than expected. To some degree it suits you to take a back seat and let other people do the thinking and planning while you attend to more practical matters. It is important to try to achieve some kind of overall balance in order to protect your own interests without becoming the prime mover and shaker.

5. THURSDAY. Mixed. You can make gradual but steady progress with work and employment matters. The day starts off quietly and remains that way for most of the time. However, there is a distinct possibility that you will get in a mad scramble before the end of the day. Last-minute telephone calls to finalize arrangements can take a long time. Try to get important plans organized at the start of the day if you can. To avoid getting roped into taking on someone else's assignment, keep a low profile in your work environment. And if you are directly confronted with a request, make it clear that you already have more than enough to do.

6. FRIDAY. Deceptive. You may sense that conflict is arising in a close one-to-one relationship. You and your partner could disagree on financial or real estate issues. You are most likely to obtain encouragement and support for your plans from casual acquaintances. One problems that has been on your mind can be cleared up if you can devote enough time to thinking of various alternative solutions. You are not yet free to move in an entirely new direction, but the seeds of something new are starting to fall into place. Changing some of your basic attitudes now should have a positive effect on your closest relationships. Keep in mind, however, that you can only control yourself in the long term.

7. SATURDAY. Uncertain. Your close relationships should be easier than they have been the past few days. This is a starred time for talking problems through with your partner or another family member and for discussing mutual plans. It is likely that together you can find solutions and compromises without too much difficulty. Beware of a tendency to spend too much time focusing on the past. While what occurred earlier in your life may be important to you personally, it may irritate your partner to hear over and over again about a time when they were not on the scene. Keep your feet on the ground and your mind on the present. It is important to maintain a realistic perspective of your current situation.

8. SUNDAY. Manageable. Making plans for the future, especially in relation to finances, is likely to occupy you more than usual. Your main concerns probably revolve around creating more economic security for you and your loved ones. This is a time to do some forward planning. Be careful that you do not overestimate your potential income while underestimating your expenses. There may be factors which you overlook because of the time of year when particular expenses come due. For example, you could forget about an insurance payment due late in the year. Put a tentative budget together and review it later. Do not factor in a possible inheritance; it could be delayed.

9. MONDAY. Cautious. Be very careful when it comes to money matters. What at first looks like a bargain could turn out to be a con. If you are thinking of making an important investment, seek the advice of a reliable professional consultant. Someone who is recommended to you based on another person's experience may be a better bet than picking a name out of the phone book. Be wary of someone trying to undercut other practitioners. Work efforts should be very productive. Your efforts to thoroughly research an important plan or project are unlikely to go to waste. A trip canceled at the last moment may turn out to be a blessing in disguise.

10. TUESDAY. Calm. You should be able to move ahead with current projects without too many interruptions from outsiders. If you feel annoyed with the boss after a conversation, talk to someone else about what happened. It is likely that they will have a calming effect on you. Career developments may not be moving along as fast as you would like. It is in your best interests to encourage other people to move more quickly, but at the same time guard against coming across as too pushy. Money invested in training designed to advance your career prospects is likely to be a good investment. If you are in any doubt about this, look further into the course content and the instructor's qualifications.

11. WEDNESDAY. Disquieting. A conversation in connection with work matters may become quite heated. You and a colleague may not see eye-to-eye on the best working methods to use. Come up with more evidence for your case before launching into a full-scale battle about the situation. If you have a chance to attend a get-together organized by neighbors, work colleagues, or relatives, it is a good idea to go even if you do not feel like it. However, work and important practical tasks should take priority. You could even use the latter as a genuine excuse for not appearing at a gathering you suspect will bore you. Get to bed earlier than usual.

12. THURSDAY. Useful. Problems you have been experiencing at home could be resolved today. Difficulties are likely to come to a head, particularly in relation to your long-term plans. If you have been thinking about moving, it could happen after an in-depth discussion. Although you may feel that interim arrangements are just a temporary solution to current problems, the moves you make now are apt to have a much more permanent impact. There is a great deal to feel optimistic about, but you have to allow this feeling in yourself. Make every effort to tie up matters which have been hanging unresolved.

13. FRIDAY. Happy. Feelings of uneasiness in relation to your domestic situation are likely to be lessened. A final agreement can at last be made in connection with a property deal or an inheritance dispute. Cancer people already in the process of negotiations may be able to complete them rather sooner than expected. Events which have being taking place behind the scenes may be revealed to you, and the outcome ought to be a happy one for you. This is a key time to focus on creating a more secure future, especially in terms of real estate and joint financial investments. There is a chance to blaze a new trail if you follow your instincts and ignore prior rejection.

14. SATURDAY. Excellent. This is another favorable day for bringing negotiations to a positive conclusion. Around the home you should be able to get several chores out of the way. Do not pay too much attention to what an authority figure has to say, unless there are genuine legal implications involved. Older people can influence you more than is necessary. It is important to trust your own feelings. Disapproval of your actions from relatives can be unsettling, but they are not necessarily right and you should bear this in mind. If you explain the motivation for your actions, they are more likely to understand and offer whatever help you may need.

15. SUNDAY. Slow. This is one of those days when you feel relaxed one moment, tense the next. Worries about work responsibilities may be playing on your mind. If there is little that you can actively do to change things at the moment, try to find a way to switch off. Time spent with your family should be satisfying, but do not expect them to come to a quick decision about anything you propose. While your suggestion may seem watertight to you, it is likely that they need to think it through in their own time. Try to be sensitive to the way that other people operate, which may be quite the opposite of your own approach. Take criticism in the spirit in which it is offered.

16. MONDAY. Cautious. Your personal search for happiness could lead you into a tricky situation if you are not careful. Avoid becoming involved in dubious-looking enterprises; you will probably regret it later. Social acquaintances may try to talk you into going somewhere you have never been before. It probably does not suit you well to have no control over the planning and just have to go along with the crowd. Single Cancers need to think twice about accepting a social invitation from someone of the opposite sex who is new on the scene. To avoid future heartache, find out more about this person before getting involved in any way.

17. TUESDAY. Unsettling. Try to avoid mixing business and pleasure. This is one of those times when you can get yourself into hot water by being too naturally outgoing. A business associate may not appreciate it if you do not appear to take a meeting or conversation very seriously. Be careful what you say, and to whom. If you sense a situation is becoming too hot to handle, try to change the focus. Getting away from the circumstances entirely would be a good idea. It may surprise you how being in a different environment can sometimes help clear the air. If the opportunity arises to indulge in some light entertainment geared to make you laugh, do not miss it. Your sense of humor needs to be reinforced.

18. WEDNESDAY. Productive. This is a favorable day for a long-distance journey. Venturing far from your usual environment ought to be refreshing and enlivening. If you are stuck in your work environment, you should be able to make good progress with ongoing projects. However, avoid new starts now. Someone who has an easygoing attitude toward life is likely to be a healthy influence on you. You may start to envy this person's laid-back approach. In the business world, your efforts to improve sales and negotiating methods should pay off. Attention to detail is a must at the moment. Look for ways to take advantage of an emerging new trend.

19. THURSDAY. Fair. Get an early start this morning. Pay more attention to getting routine matters better organized. You will feel happier once you wrap up items that have been neglected lately. Whether it is the laundry and cleaning which need to be done at home, or general paperwork in the office, do your best to clear away the backlog. Having to make a long-distance trip may interfere with your plans. If you can get someone else to go in your place, so much the better. If you own a pet, it may need more attention than usual. If you have any doubt about its health, call your vet. Try to balance your time carefully.

20. FRIDAY. Good. This is a better day than yesterday for catching up on routine responsibilities that had to be shelved lately. You have sufficient time to plan and organize effectively. The distractions of yesterday ought to be well out of the way. The more forward plans you make, the more satisfied you are likely to feel. Try to come to grips with a new plan to protect your health. This is an excellent time for beginning a new diet or exercise program. This is also a favorable day to stop smoking or to try to kick some other bad habit. You have extra willpower now and can be successful even if you have failed in the past.

21. SATURDAY. Rewarding. Increased contact with your partner should be rewarding. Any difficulties that have occurred between you lately can be easily resolved. A change of scene continues to be good therapy if you are weary. If you can travel with someone whose company you enjoy, so much the better. If you are going by car, it is useful to share the driving. You can make more progress on a new or difficult project when you work with others. Do not try to shoulder too much at the moment. Teamwork is your key to ultimate success. Children can be a good diversion for you this evening.

22. SUNDAY. Confusing. The power balance in at least one of your relationships is likely to be a seesaw. You may feel that someone knows more than you do and that you are not in a very strong position. Worse still, it may seem that this person is being patronizing toward you. While you are willing to meet a partner halfway, it is questionable that they are doing the same. Take a step back and look at the fairness of the situation. It is important to speak your mind, even if doing so precipitates a showdown. Beware of salespeople who make claims for their product but do not actually appear to use it themselves. Do not purchase anything sight unseen.

23. MONDAY. Profitable. This promises to be a productive day where business interests are concerned. You may be signing papers for an important deal. If you are interested in developing a new project, consult a senior person who has more expertise than you. Authority figures tend to be working in your favor on the whole. If you need permission to proceed with a trip or a plan, it should be granted easily. Push ahead to bring a work-related project to an end; you are bound to be pleased with your results. This is an excellent time for making a new investment in property, stocks, or a collectible that you will enjoy living with. Jewelry, too, can be a worthwhile investment.

24. TUESDAY. Demanding. This is another day when business matters are favored. Put some energy into making financial plans and you are likely to come up with one or two especially good deals, particularly if you have the help of an unbiased financial adviser. You need to think more about future security not only for yourself but for your nearest and dearest as well. If you begin a long-term plan now you should start to feel much more secure about the future even if you only make a small investment. Do not seek advice if you have already decided what you want to do and are unwilling to consider other options.

25. WEDNESDAY. Pressured. Although you may feel a need for a change of scene, work priorities have to come first. This could potentially prevent you from fulfilling your more appealing plans, but not necessarily. If you can delegate routine responsibilities to someone else, you should be able to leave your usual environment for a while. Being in different surroundings can help clear your mind and put a problem into better perspective. It is vital that you set things up effectively enough so that you do not worry about them while you are away. Be sure to wear protective clothing if using any type of hazardous materials, including dye or cleaning fluid.

26. THURSDAY. Cheerful. Discuss your plans and dreams with other people. You are not only likely to be an inspiration to them, but voicing your thoughts can give you more motivation to fulfill your aims. Where you have had doubts before, now you should have increased faith, especially in your own abilities. Try to get more involved in cultural pursuits. Anything interesting which takes you away from everyday routine should be good for you, including crafts and musical pursuits. If you are interested in improving yourself and your career opportunities through academic study, consider signing up for a computer course or to learn to speak a foreign language.

27. FRIDAY. Challenging. You are reaching a turning point where career matters are concerned. This is a beneficial time for getting off to a brand-new start. Fresh opportunities are coming your way. This is especially helpful if you have been out of work. Increased inner confidence is vital when it comes to making the best possible impression in an interview. You should be able to make a very good impression on people who matter. Be willing to branch out into a new field. Business contacts from the past could be very helpful; it is worth getting back in touch with them.

28. SATURDAY. Successful. Today is similar to yesterday in many ways, particularly in connection with advancing an important goal. If you are hoping to gain a key role within an organization, there could be some very encouraging news, even an offer. Move ahead with career goals in any way that you can. A good opportunity to increase your status and your income may come along. You have little reason to doubt either your ability to succeed in the job or the role. Taking a more conventional approach to a social situation is likely to pay off. If you have any doubt about a dress code, opt for fairly formal clothing so that you do not offend your host.

29. SUNDAY. Useful. There is a rather confusing element to life today. Be careful of the commitments you make. It is possible that a friend will try to get you to go along with a plan of theirs without putting you fully in the picture. It is important to take your time, or even stall a little. Do not be in a hurry to make any major decision. Your social life may be stressful, largely because friends and acquaintances seem more needy than usual. While you may be ready and willing to help, try to find out first what kind of help is being sought. There is little point offering helpful advice if a loan is really needed, or offering money if someone actually needs encouragement.

30. MONDAY. Mixed. This should be a better day for friendships than yesterday. However, you still need to avoid making commitments in a hurry. Lack of funding for a key project could get you down, but do not despair. It is possible that trying a different approach will produce more encouraging results. Socially, you may start to wonder if you are mixing with the wrong people. New friends that you are making now may be more compatible with you. Do not be afraid to ease away from old acquaintances in quite a casual way if you feel that you are no longer a beneficial influence on each other. Someone at a distance is hoping you will call.

31. TUESDAY. Disconcerting. It is in your interests to play your cards close to your chest in any kind of meeting. If you are about to commit to a new deal, find out more about the other party before going ahead. Someone may not be revealing all the facts you need to know. Working behind the scenes should be unusually productive. Nevertheless, you may need to take center stage when an important visitor arrives. Be prepared to be flexible with your schedule and willing to help out as and when required. Keeping a low profile works some of the time but also can diminish your chances for success in a controversial encounter. Be willing to speak up even if your views are not currently popular.

APRIL

1. WEDNESDAY. Exciting. This is not a day for trying to keep a low profile. While you may not feel like putting your best forward and going out to conquer the world, circumstances may force you up to take center stage. People are looking to you for leadership. Where business matters are concerned, important contacts can be made and key deals advanced. Signing papers to finalize a deal is a distinct possibility. Do not count on having time to catch up with neglected personal responsibilities as much as you would like. There are other matters to attend to which suddenly become more compelling. Take everything one step at a time. Concentrate on what is before you, not what is to come.

2. THURSDAY. Demanding. You are definitely firing on all engines as your confidence increases by the minute. One success naturally leads to another. An important personal plan can be fulfilled if you put your mind to it. Long-distance travel is favored, especially if it is for personal reasons. It is good for you to get away from your everyday environment, if only for an hour or two. An authority figure, whether at work or elsewhere, could be stubborn and argumentative. This is not a propitious time to try to convince other people that you are right, even if you know you are. Your enthusiasm for a particular course of action, however, could be quite persuasive if you remain steady for the next few days.

3. FRIDAY. Successful. This is another very useful day for fulfilling personal plans. If you can move from your normal surroundings to somewhere more personally inspiring, do so. You
should find the inspiration to come up with some good ideas and
the solution to a longtime problem. Your ability to think on your
feet is a definite bonus, particularly in the business world. Be prepared to jump at a rare opportunity which comes your way. Do
not be too perturbed if the boss or another authority figure is
standing in your way at the moment. This is likely to be only a
temporary stumbling block. Give them time to mull over your
proposal until they think it was their idea all along.

4. SATURDAY. Disconcerting. You are likely to encounter opposition to your plans from people of influence or authority. Ag-
gravating as this will be, it is probably best to toe the line. Do not
attempt to create waves unless you feel you can handle the possible showdown that is bound to follow. Try not to be too hard
on yourself. Your tendency at the moment is to demand far too
much of yourself. It is pointless punishing yourself by going over
and over what you could have done differently. The better course
of action is to resolve to change the way you approach certain
people in the future.

5. SUNDAY. Variable. You have to exert a lot of effort in order
to get desired results today, but you should be pleased with the
outcome. Routine tasks can be completed in one fell swoop rather
than dragging them out. Aim for satisfactory results, not perfection. Immersing yourself in activity is likely to banish worries as
well as achieve a lot on a practical level. Be careful when it comes
to handling money. Avoid making snap decisions where investments are concerned. Sudden surprise developments may worry
you. Find out more details before getting too worked up. It is
possible that someone is trying to shock you into action against
your better instincts. Trust your good Cancer judgment.

6. MONDAY. Fortunate. This should be a better day than yesterday where financial matters are concerned. The opportunity to
move on to a better paying job may open up for you now. Although this is likely to involve taking on more responsibility, it
could be exactly what you are looking for. A salary increase in
your current job is also possible. You have the full support of
authority figures behind you. If you need a favor from the boss,
now is a good time to ask. Compliments and acknowledgments
that come your way are sure to boost your self-esteem. Circumstances at a distance are having a direct impact on you. Stay in
touch with an overseas contact.

7. TUESDAY. Disquieting. You may have an urge to do a number of different things. Variety is the spice of life for you at the moment. This is a favorable time for getting out to see people rather than waiting for them to contact you. However, be careful that you do not get too distracted from ongoing matters, particularly at work. Stay in touch until satisfied with the outcome. Keep an eye on situations you leave behind you when traveling. Time spent making telephone calls may be irritating but could be necessary. A problem with your car is a possibility, especially where long-distance travel is concerned. Allow yourself plenty of time whether driving or using public transportation.

8. WEDNESDAY. Manageable. Make an effort to get in touch with people who may be able to answer a question for you instead of you having to do a lot of research. However, try not to get involved in a long-winded conversation which would detract from matters foremost on your mind. It is all too easy to get wrapped up talking about trivia, which could waste a lot of time that you later regret losing. A neighbor's social gathering may be fun, but again do not spend too much time there if you have more important things to do. Someone you have not seen in a long time could get back in touch. This could turn into a fun reunion providing you schedule it for a day and time when you are not preoccupied with more important matters.

9. THURSDAY. Quiet. Today should be much easier going than yesterday. Getting out to see people is more possible because you have more free time on your hands. Conditions are excellent for advance planning, at least the immediate future. You may not be in the mood to focus on long-term aims, but you can easily address more immediate concerns. Catching up with people you have not seen for a while, either by telephone or in person, is likely to be worthwhile. Openly discussing any problem that is on your mind is the first step to finding a solution. Do not rule out any possibility for the future. What seems certain now is apt to become problematic in a few months.

10. FRIDAY. Fair. This promises to be a productive day for finishing work projects and tasks. You can make significant progress with a backlog of work. If you are thinking of doing some remodeling or redecorating at home, this is a favorable day for making a start. In the long run this work may turn out to be a much greater investment than you imagine. If you are involved in property negotiations, trust your instincts. There is a bargain to be had; when you spot it, you will probably recognize it right away. Look for ways to expand your circle of friends and acquaintances, perhaps through volunteer work at a hospital or coaching a sports team.

11. SATURDAY. Stressful. There could be some conflict and tension at home. This is one of those times when family members may insist that they are right and you are wrong. If their concern is in relation to your personal plans, it can make you begin to doubt yourself. If you are on the brink of completing a business or financial deal, try to be patient; there could be a snag or two to sort out before you can sign on the dotted line. Cancer people who are looking for real estate as an investment may be reaching a turning point in the negotiation process. Try to stop worrying about factors you cannot control and focus on finding an agreeable compromise.

12. SUNDAY. Mixed. This is another potentially tricky day where domestic matters are concerned. A difficult situation that has been brewing for some time is coming to a head. Do not become too flustered by this, since it is likely that a direct confrontation will clear the air. As the day advances, you are likely to become more frivolous and lighthearted. Spend some of your free time enjoying entertainment which does not cost too much. You cannot afford to withdraw money from your savings or add to your credit card balance just now, so the cheaper the social arrangements, the better. Just because you are not spending a fortune does not mean you cannot have a lot of fun.

13. MONDAY. Difficult. Your social relationships may be more up and down than usual. For single Cancers, a new romantic involvement could be obstructed by a jealous friend. If this friend is hanging around, stopping the two of you from getting together, try to arrange to meet in an environment where the friend is not so likely to turn up. Money can be a bone of contention in one particular relationship. A lingering disagreement is apt to come to a head now, bringing the opportunity to clear the air. If a friend or co-worker asks for a loan, recognize that despite their best intentions you may never be repaid.

14. TUESDAY. Calm. All the recent ups and downs you have been going through are now closer to being resolved. Cancer people should be in a much more lighthearted frame of mind. There is little to trouble you. As a Cancer you have a habit of brooding over problems rather than directly trying to solve them. With recent events pushing you to act, you have probably achieved a great deal in the last few days. Do not let up at this stage. Socially, you can relax and enjoy life more. If an invitation comes your way, accept it. You have good reason to celebrate but may not want to make a big deal out of your recent success. Treat yourself to something you have wanted for a long time.

15. WEDNESDAY. Deceptive. Yesterday was more relaxing than usual, but today you are apt to sense that this was more of a passing state than a long-term phase. This is a good day to focus on routine matters. There is a lot to get through in a little time. Try to handle small problems as they crop up; put major new issues on the back burner until another time. You cannot sort out everything in one day. Where difficult problems are concerned, you need time to think them through in order to come up with a plan of action. The first idea that pops into your head is unlikely to be the best one.

16. THURSDAY. Variable. You may again feel that you have more to do than you can really manage. Try to focus on immediate matters rather than longer term plans or problems for which you need to obtain specific information before acting positively or resolving them. You probably want to do other things instead of handling routine affairs, but it is best not to neglect these. Compromise by allowing yourself to take a reasonable break, without opting out of your responsibilities. An older person could be your best adviser. Keep all conversation with them as factual as possible. Make no promises that you may not want to keep or may not be able to honor in the future.

17. FRIDAY. Good. This should be an enjoyable day socially. You can get along harmoniously with family members and friends alike. It is favorable time for mixing generations if you are making the arrangements. For example, if planning a dinner party, invite neighborhood friends and their partners and some of your co-workers even if they have not met before. It is likely that there will be good rapport among everyone. At work it should be easy to get people to cooperate with you on a key project. Make the most of current harmonious influences which make negotiations very straightforward. Colleagues are likely to be more willing than usual to compromise. It is a good day for creative work, especially a project intended as a gift.

18. SATURDAY. Buoyant. So much is going your way you cannot help but be happy. You have a lot to be optimistic about where relationships are concerned. Increased cooperation in your closest partnership should make the relationship especially easy-going. This is a prime time for making plans with your loved one, especially joint long-term plans. If you can get away for a break with that person this weekend, so much the better; you are bound to have an enjoyable time together. Single Cancers may meet a potential new partner through academic interests or foreign travel. A recent decision that you struggled to make is proving to be the right one.

19. SUNDAY. Confusing. This promises to be a fun day for participating in group endeavors. Nevertheless, be careful that someone in your group is not attempting to lead you astray in some way. Their intentions may not be all that obvious, but they may encourage you to get involved in something that you do not really need or want. Other people are apt to agree readily to what you want at the moment, although it is likely that you are not really being given the commitment you seek. To be on the safe side, take what is said with a grain of salt. Where love is concerned, be prepared for disagreements, but nothing that cannot be resolved. Be sure to get approval before making any major changes at home.

20. MONDAY. Fair. There should be an equal amount of give-and-take in your relationships. Your partner is more willing than usual to accommodate you and adjust to your desires and plans. A lucky break may come your way where significant money is involved. A meeting concerning joint financial dealings should go better than you expect. An agreement is likely to be in your favor. This is a propitious time for starting up a new business or for making a business deal. Your hard work at researching markets and financial arrangements should pay off handsomely. One warning: do not count on someone doing what you should actually be doing for yourself.

21. TUESDAY. Manageable. Events which might normally unnerve or upset you are easier to cope with today. Turn to older more experienced people for help if you feel you are getting out of your depth. A change of scene promises to be very stimulating. If you are traveling you can extend your circle of acquaintances without having to try very hard. If you are thinking about making an important financial investment, first seek some professional advice. Any substantial sum of money which comes your way needs to be carefully handled. Look for ways to make positive things happen instead of merely reacting to developments after the fact.

22. WEDNESDAY. Challenging. You can make a lot of progress when it comes to broadening your horizons, whether socially or in relation to your career. You can expect the support you hoped would be available from various friends and acquaintances. Spend some time on a plan that has been important to you for some time. Finding new people who can help out is likely now. You should be able to move forward much faster than you expected. News should be encouraging; your recent optimism is likely to continue because of what you hear. Maintain a steady pace in all of your ongoing work. Divide your time carefully so that nothing gets neglected.

23. THURSDAY. Starred. You may be able to make a major move where your career interests are concerned. This is an excellent time to plan for the future. The opportunity to take a better paid job with increased responsibility could come your way. If you are ready and willing to change direction in your career, now is the time to grasp the opportunity. Your boss or another authority figure is likely to be very supportive. Discuss your aims and intentions openly so that you can make the most of the opportunities that influential people may direct your way. Be creative in solving a problem rather than expecting what worked in the past to again be successful.

24. FRIDAY. Rewarding. You are likely to make good progress by staying behind the scenes. If you have been feeling uncertain about your career direction, what you need to do should become clearer to you now. This is another day when interesting opportunities may come your way. One that seems rather unusual is worth serious consideration. Even if you do not accept the offer, it may point you in the direction you need to go. Your efforts to get ahead with work matters are likely to create a good impression among colleagues and bosses alike. Aim to be thorough in all that you do. Overlooking what seems like a minor detail could cause problems for you later.

25. SATURDAY. Frustrating. If you need favors from other people it is in your best interest to play by their rules. Protocol is important both at work and in a social context. Although there is a tendency for you to blur rules and regulations in your own mind, other people are likely to be very clear about them. Do not make the mistake of acting out of ignorance. If your career is not developing in the way you had hoped, try not to be too disappointed. It is likely that this is only a temporary setback. The key to success is to fulfill all of your responsibilities and see projects through to the very end. If asked for a charitable donation, consider giving your time rather than money.

26. SUNDAY. Disquieting. You are entering a new phase in a certain friendship. This could come as a relief if you have been having difficulty getting along. It is time to leave behind any non-productive situation and move on. If you owe money to a friend, you could be surprised at this person's sudden demand for repayment even though the original agreement was open-ended. Nevertheless, the person may have good reason for calling in the loan so soon. If you value the friendship, do your utmost to come up with the cash. Be wary of revealing a secret that has been confided to you.

27. MONDAY. Good. Your working life should be smoother if you deal only with behind-the-scenes matters. Other people are willing to team up with you if you need to share a certain burden. You can actually achieve much more this way and also save time instead of trying to work purely on your own. Avoid public speaking or making any public announcement. This is a favorable day for setting new goals for the not too distant future. If you are interested in making a significant financial investment, concentrate on formulating a plan. Keep focused on what you want to achieve in the future as well as keeping current responsibilities ticking over.

28. TUESDAY. Satisfactory. Unfortunately you may not have as much time to yourself as you would like, keeping you from planning and getting better organized. Pressing responsibilities need your full attention, and it is in your best interest to get them out of the way. If you end up neglecting major tasks now you will regret it later when you need to pick up the pieces. If you are thinking of making a new financial investment, seek some sound professional advice beforehand. Someone you have relied on in the past may no longer be able to help. Prove to them and to yourself that you can now stand on your own two feet.

29. WEDNESDAY. Unsettling. Working behind the scenes is favored again today. Nevertheless, you probably have to cope with a number of distractions from the outside. Everyone around you is in a hurry to get projects finished. They may need to interrupt you and ask for your help, even though it is obvious that it is inconvenient for you. The best you can do in the circumstances is keep as low a profile as possible. As a Cancer you often find it a relief to be able to turn to others for support, particularly when the going gets tough. Temporarily, you are the one who needs to do all the giving now. Plan on relaxing at home this evening rather than going out.

30. THURSDAY. Fair. Do not allow loneliness to get you down. Other people may not be there for you as much as you would like, but they are not against you either. You may feel put down by an authority figure and be able to find no one who would understand your feelings well enough to share them. Do not brood over the matter too much. Before long it should become obvious to you that other people will support you more when they have the time. This is a favorable day for moving ahead with personal plans so long as you do not allow yourself to be thrown off course by self-doubts. There is a good chance later in the day to finalize a deal with a handshake.

MAY

1. FRIDAY. Rewarding. This is an excellent day for making significant progress with personal plans. Your associates, both at work and in your personal life, are likely to be a great help to you. Someone you had temporarily crossed off your list of helpers may come back, raring to assist you with whatever you need. By discussing your plans openly with other people you are likely to be repaid with plenty of support and useful advice. The extra boost you receive in terms of moral support alone should help increase your personal confidence. If you are interviewing for a new job, be prepared to promote yourself wholeheartedly. Play up your strengths and past experience without any gross exaggeration.

2. SATURDAY. Tricky. This can be a tricky day where money matters are concerned. Be careful to balance your expenditures against your current income. You may not realize if you are overspending, particularly if you have not checked your accounts lately. Even if you generally keep a running tally when you write checks or use a credit card, there may be something you have forgotten to write down. This is a day when your desire to fulfill your innermost dreams and schemes can play havoc with your more practical sense. It is up to you to turn the tables by utilizing your natural, prudent streak that helps you to keep your feet planted firmly on the ground.

3. SUNDAY. Mixed. You should be in good form when it comes to a formal social situation. If your goal is to make a lasting impression on one particular person, you can do so through what you wear and how you act. With good manners you should have no problem achieving your aim. Be quite low-key about financial matters, and especially guard against excessive spending. A friend who needs to borrow may be asking at a time that is inconvenient for you, but you could feel too embarrassed to turn them down. It is likely to be better for both of you in the long run if you are honest about your own current situation. In that way resentment is less likely to result. If a certain family member recently was laid off, look for a way to help without causing embarrassment.

4. MONDAY. Manageable. This is a much better day than yesterday when it comes to money matters. Financial dealings should be fairly problem-free. Advice from an expert, either in person or perhaps from a newspaper column, is likely to be very helpful. At work, the boss may pay you a compliment, making you feel more appreciated for your efforts. If you have been temporarily out of work, a boost to your self-esteem can give you the motivation to forge ahead looking for a new job with much more confidence. Have the same faith in your own abilities that other people have. You have much to gain by taking the initiative in a social situation. Just be ready to adapt to new rules and changing customs.

5. TUESDAY. Happy. Information or news that comes your way is likely to be very heartening. If you feel an urge to get in touch with an old friend, do so; it could lead to a pleasant reunion. Differences with a relative can be sorted out if you take the initiative. This person may have been defensive and even hostile in the past. However, if you take time to explain your position, a new understanding can be worked out. It is possible that the reason you argued in the first place was because you touched on a sore spot in their life at the time. Your effort to make amends for anything you have done wrong will probably open up a new chapter that delights all of your family members.

6. WEDNESDAY. Useful. This is one of those days when Cancers are bound to be very lively and active. A lot of people could be in touch with you, and you are likely to feel the need to contact others more than usual. Without certain information you may not be able to move forward on a particular project. It may be difficult to ring down the curtain on a certain conversation occurring at a social event. All of this adds up to a lot of distractions. It is important at the moment for you to spend a small amount of time on each project or with each person. Set reasonable goals for yourself and avoid going off too far on a tangent. A lottery ticket or a raffle chance could surprise you.

7. THURSDAY. Fair. You probably need to become more involved in certain family affairs. Time spent with loved ones may not be entirely pleasant, especially if there are some quite serious issues to discuss. Try to find areas of compromise; guard against simply dismissing each other's points of view. A problem relating to finances and who owes what can be cleared up. It is likely that one of you was not sure when a sum was to be repaid, or has temporarily forgotten about the debt. Harmony should be restored when the matter is discussed and sorted out. Colleagues at work are ready and willing to cooperate. Joint effort is sure to be worthwhile.

8. FRIDAY. Variable. Family life ought to be a lot smoother than yesterday. You may be surprised by other people's eagerness to be supportive. If you need to borrow a piece of equipment, the answer is likely to be yes. Cancer people involved in property moves or negotiations should be able to make surprisingly good progress. However, choose your words with care when dealing with authority figures. Someone who is supposedly an expert on a particular matter may be full of talk but not able or willing to follow up. Trust your own instincts. A message from a higher-up could be misleading. Double-check facts and figures, and do not trust your own memory either.

9. SATURDAY. Misleading. You may feel that you are back to square one where a certain family dispute is concerned. Do not be swayed too much by the opinions of others, even if they speak with great authority. Trust your own inner feelings. Other people do not necessarily know better than you, although they may try to convince you otherwise. Be careful with money. This is one of those times when you can end up spending a lot on something which does not hold up for any length of time. If you are hoping to step into a higher position within an organization, perhaps heading up a committee, efforts made now are likely to earn you praise and recommendations. Volunteer your time to help a local charity.

10. SUNDAY. Disconcerting. This is another day for being watchful where your finances are concerned. Money matters can complicate your social life. The basic problem could be insufficient funds to do exactly what you want to do, forcing you to rethink your plans. However, by being inventive you could end up doing something even more fun. A romantic relationship, while enjoyable, could be more expensive than you expect in one way or another. You need to decide if you are willing to invest so much, both emotionally and financially. Discuss sharing costs if you are the one who up until now has been continually footing the bill. It is important to avoid going further into debt even if you anticipate a raise or a bonus later in the year.

11. MONDAY. Changeable. A friend may put you on the spot by asking to borrow money which you cannot spare. Cut through having to give a long-winded justification by explaining that you are temporarily short of cash. Overall, today should be easier than yesterday. A trip for business or pleasure is likely to be exciting and fulfilling. Romance is in the air. If you are single, accept any and all social invitations that come your way. One of them could lead to meeting somebody rather special. Do all that you can to make people sit up and take notice of you.

12. TUESDAY. Successful. Immersing yourself in work is likely to bring very positive results. This also applies if you are out of work and looking for a new job. Follow up every possible lead. Getting back into a normal routine and clearing up loose ends is a good idea. By going back to square one you can make a fresh start. Be realistic about the amount of future responsibilities you are in a position to take on; do not expect too much of yourself. It is vital to set realistic goals. You are apt to be feeling restless and can make good use of your extra energy. However, do not overcommit yourself for the future on the basis of expecting to have this extra energy all the time.

13. WEDNESDAY. Slow. Your efforts to be more organized than usual may go up in smoke due to outside distractions. If you are going on a long journey, there could be more delays than you expect. Try not to load up your schedule with too many appointments. If you are worried that you have already done so, attempt to postpone one of your engagements until a more convenient time. Because it is likely that whatever you undertake is going to be interrupted, the more free time you have, the better. By not putting too many demands on yourself in the first place the whole day ought to be a lot easier. This evening favors quiet time at home. A book can be your best companion.

14. THURSDAY. Manageable. Your working life is unlikely to be quiet but should be easygoing. There are deadlines to meet, but you should find that you can work faster than usual. This is a favorable time for planning, especially in terms of the long-term future. Put more effort into organization, especially if you have important documents to prepare and need to concentrate on them. The boss is likely to be willing to provide the resources that you need. If you would like more time to ponder a major decision, find a way to put the matter on hold for a while. Delaying tactics should work, at least for a few days.

15. FRIDAY. Sensitive. Try to avoid mixing personal and professional interests. If you need to sort out a domestic problem, co-workers may not be as understanding as you hope. A family powwow may resolve less than you expect; it may even bring up new issues that need to be addressed. It is best to stay out of the line of fire if you do not want to deal with conflict. The less involved you are in an ongoing battle, the better. Those at the top need to resolve problems between themselves before you can get any important information or approval from them. It could be difficult to get work colleagues moving on a new project. Try to be patient with them by focusing first and foremost on what you can accomplish on your own.

16. SATURDAY. Exciting. A one-to-one relationship is very special at the moment. Together you and your loved one can soar to heights you have never reached individually. An older person could be disapproving. It is up to you whether you react to their criticism or offer an explanation. It might be wise to ignore their words if you can. Your friends and your family, even if newly introduced, ought to get along well. This is a good time for mixing age groups at a party or other social get-together. A long-distance trip should be more enjoyable if you have good company during your travels. Use public transportation rather than driving.

17. SUNDAY. Variable. Life should be fairly smooth, especially if you are trying to finish a number of domestic tasks. You should be able to work faster than you expect. Where money matters are concerned, this is a good day for getting better organized. Consider putting together a new budget that is as realistic as you can make it. If you are involved in business dealings at the moment, this is a good time for going through the details of a contract. Reading the small print can be boring, especially if you are short of time. Use some of your free time today to do this before you are expected to sign the document. Do all that you can to avoid having to become involved in a lawsuit. The current air of uncertainty brings out your fighting Cancer spirit.

18. MONDAY. Sensitive. Powerful feelings, including a greater sense of determination, can help you along the road to career success. If there is a promotion in sight, make more of an effort to be considered for it. With friends, be careful not to upset someone important to you. It is all too easy to say the wrong thing because you have not thought matters through first. Be diplomatic and not too stubborn about getting everything your way. Examine your motives if a close associate accuses you of having acted out of character. After thinking about it you may tend to agree, and this could help explain what has been going on behind your back.

19. TUESDAY. Fair. You can make more progress if you put routine matters aside and concentrate on long-term planning. This may not be easy to do if people are putting pressure on you. Be firm in explaining to them that you cannot handle particular matters just now but will be able to do so at a certain later time. If you are planning a distant journey which involves visiting someone important, tie up last-minute arrangements thoroughly with the person involved. A discussion with the boss about your future is likely to be productive. Be honest but diplomatic in conveying what you want in terms of increased responsibility, title, and salary range.

20. WEDNESDAY. Rewarding. This promises to be a very positive day. You should feel encouraged by new opportunities that are starting to open up in several areas of your life. Conversations which revolve around your own long-term plans are likely to spark off useful new ideas. Your vision is working in your favor at the moment. There is less need to focus on routine matters, giving you freedom to plan for the future. There is little that is limiting you or standing in your way. The world is ready for you to make your move. By starting out in a small way you can make minor adjustments and revisions as you go along.

21. THURSDAY. Good. Clandestine discussions with authority figures or other influential people are likely to be helpful. Such people should be more willing than usual to help you out. While socializing you could be introduced to key figures who can help you expand your world. It is important to make a good impression on them; do not worry about this, as it should come easily. There is apt to be a positive development in relation to money matters. What has been vague or confusing is likely to clear up, especially when it comes to legal proceedings. Hard work can earn you excellent rewards. Avoid rushing what you instinctively recognize will take time to achieve.

22. FRIDAY. Unsettling. It is important to maintain a professional profile at work. Someone you do not yet know well could be making a mental note of your performance. A friendship may be under strain due to a disagreement regarding money matters. If you are asked to part with cash that you cannot really afford, put your foot down. In an honest and true relationship, friends do not coerce each other, they negotiate. If you feel that a certain person is asking too much of you, say so in a diplomatic way. A meeting in a public setting is likely to go well. Contact from a former associate may come as a surprise, but a welcome one once you realize how they have changed.

23. SATURDAY. Manageable. Friends and acquaintances cannot be relied upon wholeheartedly. Do not count too much on their promises; they may have a problem keeping their word. Financial matters can be deceptive. If you are planning an important purchase, think twice. A salesperson may not tell you the whole truth. There is a special quality developing in one of your closest relationships. Time spent together in private can lead to a highlight in your relationship so far. You could find that a small gamble pays off for you, but do not risk more than you can afford to lose or give up.

24. SUNDAY. Happy. Discussions with friends about current and future plans are likely to be productive. They may have useful ideas regarding how to move forward. A long-distance journey with a good friend or a new acquaintance is likely to be memorable. If you need commitments from other people, they are likely to give them now. Taking a philosophical approach to life can put you in touch with a deeper meaning to everyday events. Being away from your usual environment should be refreshing. Put worries and concerns out of your mind. Dwelling on them is unlikely to be productive. Your unconscious mind may come up with an answer that has eluded you.

25. MONDAY. Sensitive. You are apt to feel more sensitive and vulnerable than usual. Time spent alone should be most productive. As a Cancer you are entering a new phase, particularly regarding your health and general well-being. If you know you have been doing too much lately, the telltale signs mean that you should slow down. Take your time communicating important information. You can sort out a problem where money is concerned by putting your mind to it. For the best results in all activities, you need quiet, peaceful surroundings. Encourage family members to get involved in other activities if you find it difficult to concentrate with them around.

26. TUESDAY. Fair. Attend to current projects and try to iron out problems related to the past. This is not a day to try to get new plans up and running. As was true yesterday, you can make good progress when alone. Distractions from the outside can be a real nuisance. Stay in the background, doing your utmost to keep a low profile. An associate may need to communicate something of a sensitive nature. Be as helpful and supportive as you can. Serious issues which come up are best addressed as soon as possible. If you have an opportunity to settle one major matter once and for all, go for it.

27. WEDNESDAY. Disquieting. This is another day when you can get a lot done if you are able to be alone. The boss should give you all the support you need, including a free hand in delegating work if you need to do so. Extra attention paid to behind-the-scenes matters should be worth the effort. The more you deal with what has been neglected in private, the better. You do not have to be especially secretive, but try to handle delicate matters in an environment of peace and quiet, where you can concentrate best. Private and personal concerns may also need attention. Make sure you get some time purely to yourself to think things through and make definite plans for the future.

28. THURSDAY. Unsettling. Self-doubts and anxiety can creep into your thoughts more than usual. Try to block out as many of them as you can. As a Cancer you tend to worry a great deal about responsibilities which need to be fulfilled at a later date. The sooner you get around to handling them, the better. Be sure to give yourself sufficient breaks. Your inner determination should be a definite advantage in getting things done. Do not be surprised if you end up arguing with someone in a position of authority. This can clear the air, but do not allow it to throw you too far off course. Be alert to new trends that can keep you ahead of the competition.

29. FRIDAY. Cautious. Your tendency to go it alone with your plans is helpful in some ways but not in others. Authority figures may become angry if you try to break the rules or bend them too far. While you have some good ideas of your own, you also need to toe the line to some extent. Gaining the cooperation of other people may not be a simple matter; it will help if you make an effort to see things from their point of view. A degree of compromise is your key to success. You cannot expect to make much progress if you refuse to meet others halfway. Try also to be respectful of other people's time commitments. Avoid going into competition with someone who has always been on your side.

30. SATURDAY. Mixed. This should be a positive day where financial matters are concerned. There is a way to turn one of your dreams into reality if you set your mind to it. Shopping for supplies needed for a home repair or redecorating project will allow you to attend to matters that have been neglected. However, this is not a good time for making a major new investment. Try to stick to small projects. Money which you have saved up over a long period of time could be idling in the bank or may not be earning too good a rate of interest. Shop around for a safe but high-paying investment. A bond might be worthwhile. Do not rush to fill in an application form or commit to a new venture just yet. Give yourself time to think things through.

31. SUNDAY. Deceptive. Today is like yesterday in that money matters are up and down, but mostly positive. Friends who ask to borrow from you or do not pay their fair share of a bill can be a nuisance. Say something about this diplomatically, even if you feel awkward about doing so. This is especially true if it seems to be a habit on the other person's part. Expert advice regarding a major move you intend to make is a must. Make a list of who you might contact; friends or family members might know someone they could refer you to; it is likely to be useful to ask around. A new partnership, either personal or business, should be formalized with a written contract; a handshake does not provide you with enough security.

JUNE

1. MONDAY. Disquieting. If you have been hoping to settle a lawsuit, do not expect plans to go through smoothly. There could be extra details to sort out or tie up before a final agreement can be signed. It is important that all concerned parties feel satisfied with the agreement, or there could be problems later on. This is a tricky day where work matters are concerned. Many interruptions, including telephone callers who want to chat at length, can distract you from your main purpose. You need to be firm if you are to make any real progress. An element of luck can put you in the right place at the right time, but you have to be aware enough to take advantage of it.

2. TUESDAY. Difficult. This is another tricky day for business dealings. A potential partner could be stretching your patience, wanting to bend the rules more than you think is fair. If you are not happy with the way things are proceeding, think about opting out sooner rather than later. Your best work is apt to be done in an environment where you have plenty of peace and quiet. Conditions tend to improve halfway through the day. Later on, though, you may wonder if things are going downhill again when you cannot find the quiet space that you need. Do not push yourself too far or too fast. Put off until tomorrow what you cannot complete today.

3. WEDNESDAY. Productive. This is a much better day than yesterday for completing matters, especially in relation to a business deal. Having gone over and over the details, you should find it easier to come to a final decision or set of agreements. You are sure to benefit from disciplining yourself more than usual. Peace and quiet is still useful if you are trying to get a major project finished. However, you may also need other people's help off and on. Colleagues are likely to be particularly useful sources of information. This is a good time to take charge where a bad habit has gotten out of hand; you have the willpower now to overcome it.

4. THURSDAY. Variable. This is another key day for finalizing deals and finishing major work. Private negotiations could lead to one particular matter being settled once and for all. You still need quiet surroundings in order to do your best work; unfortunately, these can be hard to find. Keeping as low a profile as you can may help. Be careful about revealing a secret that has been confided to you. You could get yourself into a lot of hot water and damage your reputation. More attention paid to improving the future security of you and your family is likely to pay off. An unexpectedly good offer could come your way; snap it up before someone beats you to it.

5. FRIDAY. Sensitive. Try not to allow a dispute with family members to get you down. One of them may be sure you are wrong and they are right, but they may be badly mistaken. It could be better to let things blow over rather than try to solve the argument today. If you are considering investing in real estate, negotiations could be held up. Your bid may be too late or too low on a property, but this does not have to be the end of it. The current contract could fall through, giving you another chance. Even if you have your heart set on this particular property or parcel of land, another equally good opportunity could turn up soon. Try to remain positive. Your need for solitude continues today, and you also need sufficient space to spread out.

6. SATURDAY. Demanding. A social event ought to be stimulating. Single Cancer people, however could get a little frustrated with a friend who tries to thwart a romantic get-together. You need to be firm with this friend. Be careful if you are quickly getting involved with someone you hardly know. It is possible that this person has another life or a past that they have not told you about. Try to find out as much as you can, without appearing to be too inquisitive. Keep an eye on your wallet and other valuables in a public place. There is a danger of losing something due to carelessness or being too trusting.

7. SUNDAY. Exciting. This is a more positive day than yesterday in relation to romantic interests. The way that your loved one is acting at the moment should reassure you that all is well in the relationship. Do all that you can to develop more of your creative talents. A private discussion with a friend is likely to be useful. Any problem that you have on your mind should be aired, but only with someone you trust completely. As a Cancer you tend to be cagey around others at the best of times, but there are occasions when you need to talk; today is one of them. Do nothing that could arouse feelings of jealousy.

8. MONDAY. Mixed. Work ought to be fairly smooth on the whole. Cancer people who have been temporarily unemployed could get much closer to finding a new job. Trust your instincts; they are not going to steer you wrong. If you are not managing to get on top of a situation at work, it could be because you are distracted much of the time. Aim to keep a low profile so that other people do not have easy access to you. Delegating some of your workload could also be a help to you. Colleagues are more willing than usual to help out, although you will then owe them a return favor in the future.

9. TUESDAY. Stressful. This promises to be quite a productive day where work matters are concerned. You can achieve a lot once you put your mind to it. However, be careful not to over-exert without finding ways to restore some of that expended energy. A break from your normal surroundings could help. Rumors around the workplace may be a bit worrisome, but do not pay too much attention. It is likely that you will get the wrong impression if you eavesdrop on a phone conversation. Friends may be rather critical at the moment. Try not to notice unless you think their criticisms are valid. Restore your self-confidence by thinking of all that you have done well recently.

10. WEDNESDAY. Challenging. There may be some blurred areas in your working life which need to be sorted out. To avoid confusion in the future, make sure that communication with colleagues is clear and precise. If a message left for you is confusing, double-check with the person who took the message. Try to get to the bottom of a situation before taking any major action. A business arrangement may need revising because conditions have changed. Try to come up with new approaches likely to suit everyone involved. If you are seeking funding for a new project, this is a good day to apply for it. Do not underestimate your needs; ask for a little more than the basics.

11. THURSDAY. Lucky. Your partner is likely to also be your best friend. If there is a problem on your mind which you want to discuss, your beloved is sure to be understanding and quite a help to you. This is a lucky day for carrying out all kinds of endeavors hand in hand with other people. When you get together with one or more partners you are able to do more than you could ever do separately. Avoid spending too much time alone if you can help it; solitary activity does suit your current frame of mind. A friend can introduce you to someone new who soon becomes an active player on your stage of life. Welcome a newcomer like you would an old friend.

12. FRIDAY. Good. This is another very favorable day where partnership matters are concerned. For single Cancer people there is a chance to link up with a prospective new partner through academic interests or through traveling. Someone at or from a distance is beginning to have a strong influence on you. The way that partners act is likely to be enlightening. Talk about matters of the world which you do not usually have time to discuss. You could both benefit from going away together for the weekend to a locale where you have a complete change of surroundings and companions. Cancers who work on the weekends can make plans for a getaway later next week.

13. SATURDAY. Uncertain. Business interests are under helpful influences. Whatever you are working on at the moment, you are likely to make very good progress. If you are trying to tie up a business deal, you should meet with more success than you expect. Although you may be excluded from negotiations going on behind closed doors, try not to worry too much. When you need to know certain information it will probably be revealed to you. Be careful of making a friend feel excluded from a part of your life by acting too independently. This person may start to feel suspicious about your motives if you are being secretive or are not returning their phone calls or replying to their notes.

14. SUNDAY. Fair. You need to spend more time thinking about your financial future. This is especially true if a friend recently suffered a setback. Have a private conversation with someone who knows a lot about what you are considering investing in. If you need to borrow money temporarily, a friend may not be able to help out despite wanting to do so. Try not to take their refusal personally. Even if you have helped this person out in the past, this may be a bad time for them to try to return your favor. An older family member is a better bet if you need a loan to tide you over until next payday.

15. MONDAY. Satisfactory. A long-distance journey undertaken today is likely to go smoothly. You should have a more enjoyable and productive time if you travel with a companion. You have itchy feet at the moment and would benefit from a change of environment. If you do not already have a journey planned for any specific purpose, come up with a reason for getting away or a place to go. It is a good idea to visit a family member or longtime friend at a distance in order to maintain close ties. Time spent with friends and loved ones is bound to be enjoyable. If you are worried about leaving work responsibilities behind, delegate some tasks to someone else so that you are not overburdened when you return.

16. TUESDAY. Changeable. The same restlessness that got you up and moving yesterday is present again today. However, you may not be able to think as clearly or know quite what direction to take. Friends are likely to be good at guiding you. If you spend time on your own simply thinking about getting away for a change of scene, you may never get around to realizing your aims. Joining forces with other people is your key to success. This need for cooperation applies to work matters too. Teamwork is more helpful than trying to achieve a great deal on your own, particularly when making long-term plans. Consider the needs of others as well as your own.

17. WEDNESDAY. Disconcerting. If you have long-distance travel plans, ensure that you know the route you will be taking before leaving. This may mean doing some map studying and plotting. Better this than ending up lost. Also come up with an alternative route in case of traffic backups or road repairs. Something you have been hoping would happen may not reach the conclusion you desire, but do not be too disappointed. It is just a matter of time before you achieve your desired goal. If you are starting to feel that it is not worth investing any more of your energies in this matter, trust your instincts. Accept an offer of help even if you must share some of the glory.

18. THURSDAY. Productive. This is a more productive day than yesterday in many respects. Praise from a higher-up may surprise you, but it is probably due to your extra effort and dedication. There could even be a financial bonus involved. Going to a formal social occasion should be rewarding. Make an effort to look your best, especially if you are hoping to impress somebody important. You could become involved in talking to that particular person through a helpful introduction by another guest at the gathering. It is best if you can talk with a degree of privacy. Be careful of what you say in front of other people, particularly if the subject matter is sensitive.

19. FRIDAY. Tricky. This is a helpful day in respect to your current career matters and long-term goals. A private conversation with someone in a position of authority could do much to boost your prospects. Behind-the-scenes discussions can help you resolve problems which have been worrying you. If there are responsibilities which you want to pass on to other people, get them out of the way sooner rather than later. People in authority are taking note of your efforts, even if you are unaware of the fact. For this reason it is a good idea to do your best to maintain the highest standards of professionalism in your work and in your personal contact with colleagues.

20. SATURDAY. Unsettling. Friends are likely to be a lot of help to you in one way or another. If you have a problem that you want to discuss, talk it over with a friend. This is not a good time, however, to either lend or borrow money from a friend. Try to steer clear of any and all financial involvements and major fiscal commitments if you can. If it seems that an associate is being unduly selfish, it is probably best to discuss the matter openly. The less you hide problems from each other, the more chance of sorting them out. This way it is also less likely that resentments will build up between you and cause problems in the months ahead.

21. SUNDAY. Excellent. Relationships with friends which have been at all difficult lately are likely to be much improved today. This is an excellent time for making future plans. It is also a good day for going on a trip with a person or a group of people whose company you enjoy. Quiet time to yourself should also be enjoyable and may actually be necessary if you are trying to plan a move on business or financial matters prior to a meeting. Group activities in general ought to suit you. During the day get out to see and be seen. Use your Cancer talents as a peacemaker to resolve a family dispute.

22. MONDAY. Fortunate. Time spent away from the usual everyday distractions is likely to be helpful, particularly if you have a lot of work to get through. Meetings are best carried out in private behind closed doors rather than in a public environment such as a restaurant. It is not a particularly good idea to attempt to mix business with pleasure; avoid this if you can. If you are trying to solve a problem, look to the past for clues to the future. You may be surprised to realize that you have had the solution in the back of your mind all the time. It has just been a matter of listening to yourself at a deeper level and trusting your good Cancer judgment.

23. TUESDAY. Fair. Lately it has been helpful for you to be alone in order to sort out problems. Now, though, your imagination may run riot if you spend too much time in solitude. On your own risk getting things out of proportion and out of perspective. Avoid this by at least getting out and socializing for some part of the day. A walk in the open air may help clear your mind. A chat with someone you consider wise could also be helpful. This is not a particularly good day for getting down to paperwork that has been neglected since you may not feel up to focusing on details. Try tackling just a little of the stack so that you do not lose touch completely.

24. WEDNESDAY. Calm. This is an excellent day for pursuing your personal interests. You should have some time on your hands to fulfill goals which have little to do with other people. It is surprisingly easy to get your own way in most matters when you need to deal with others. Your self-confidence is high and you have greater determination to achieve your aims. Pursue personal interests as much as possible. You are not being inconsiderate in excluding other people from your activities when you know that what you accomplish will benefit them as well as yourself. Get to bed earlier than usual.

25. THURSDAY. Deceptive. This is another good day for pursuing personal and private interests. Talking over your goals and plans with other people can help to put them in clearer perspective. Long-distance travel is favored, especially if it gives you a break from matters that have become dull and all too routine. When it comes to social matters, a discussion with a friend may lead to finding resources which turn out to be very useful. Behind-the-scenes discussions in relation to money matters, particularly a loan or investment that you have applied for or hope to get, are likely to be productive. Be sure to continue to abide by the strong principles that have guided you so far.

26. FRIDAY. Variable. Money matters are likely to be up and down. Hard work and a great deal of effort can produce excellent rewards. This may be a compensation to you if you have a little bad luck as an investment suddenly takes a dive. It is difficult at the moment to predict how much money you may need to cover costs which are sure to come up in the future. If you have any doubt, it is a good idea to hold back on current spending until the situation becomes clearer. Keep a close watch on people who tend to play manipulative games. They may try to trick you into making an agreement you do not really want or need. First impressions are not totally reliable today.

27. SATURDAY. Good. If you need to sort out financial difficulties, it is best to do so in private. Use part of today to catch up with matters which have been neglected. If you have been meaning to work out a new budget, get to this now. A social function that is coming up soon needs a lot of careful planning, including arranging to hire a caterer or musicians if it is going to be a formal affair. The more time you devote to this now, the better. There is good opportunity to make special use of a talent that you have, one you have perhaps kept secret from other people. Investigate a possibility that you have been mulling over for a while.

28. SUNDAY. Sensitive. Do not pay too much attention to matters which come to your attention secondhand. If you only know half the story you may be quite misguided. Bear in mind that other people's interpretations may not be entirely accurate. A reliable friend is likely to be very reassuring regarding a matter which is troubling you. This is a favorable day for following your own initiative and pursuing your own interests, but try to do so away from the prying eyes of potential competitors. Teamwork and group involvement suit you better, especially if there is a lot to handle. Share burdens and discuss worries openly. Promises made to you now are not totally reliable.

29. MONDAY. Mixed. Get down to replying to correspondence and paying bills, particularly if they have been neglected lately. This is a key time for getting in touch with other people. Your current sociable frame of mind can be especially helpful to you in the business world. You can make some useful contacts by being more willing than usual to chat about quite trivial matters. Getting to know each other socially is a good start for a new partnership. A quiet atmosphere, contrary to what you might expect, may not be best for getting through a stack of work. You tend to have more energy to tackle a heavy load when you are around other people engaged in similar busy activity.

30. TUESDAY. Fair. You may be disturbed by people who are trying to compete with you. Something that you have said may have goaded a partner or associate into attempting to prove something to you. It is more likely, however, that this person is trying to prove something personally and it is not really your problem. Do not be the one to offer an apology if you feel that you are right, unless you sense that the situation could escalate out of proportion if you do not take some action. Paperwork could start mounting up at work. Try to keep up with it so that you do not end up with a huge backlog. Someone at a distance is hoping to hear from you.

JULY

1. WEDNESDAY. Misleading. A family member may need to discuss a private matter with you. Be extra attentive. What is said may be rather sensitive, and this person could need a lot of ongoing support. If you need to get something off your chest that you have so far kept secret from your family or the people you live with, this is as good a time as any. Nobody is likely to take offense at what you say. The only person who may be particularly hard on you at the moment is you yourself. However, you do not have as much cause for self-recrimination as you think; try to put the past behind you and look ahead with well-deserved optimism, especially now in the Cancer birthday month.

2. THURSDAY. Routine. This is a useful day for sorting out financial and property matters. You are apt to receive some assurance that a deal is right on track, even if final confirmation is not yet available. Do as much groundwork as you can to help matters continue to progress smoothly. After that it is up to others to handle the rest. Family life ought to be smooth. Being around other family members is likely to be quite soothing, especially if you are tired and need some extra rest. Try to avoid getting involved in any complicated scheme with friends. You may want to buy a surprise for someone who has recently suffered a loss.

3. FRIDAY. Deceptive. A social event you are thinking of attending may turn out to be rather expensive. Check the cost of tickets before making up your mind, and also the kind of attire you will be expected to wear. Knowing you have nothing in your closet that would be appropriate may make you change your mind. You may feel that you are entering a lighthearted phase, but do not be deceived. Some key issues need to be addressed before long, especially where money is concerned. Potential business associates may not be upfront about the extent of time you will need to commit to a new deal. Ask for more information before agreeing to anything, and get promises in writing.

4. SATURDAY. Fortunate. You are likely to continue to have the same problems to contend with that you had yesterday in relation to social matters and money. Continue to be on guard; avoid making commitments without thinking ahead. You should be able to make a dream come true with the help of someone you know you can rely on. Informal socializing is sure to be fun. Only where future arrangements are concerned do you need to be careful not to get too involved. Romance is in the air at the moment. This is a favorable day for single Cancers who are hoping to meet a prospective new partner. Try to be more outgoing than usual. Romantic sparks are apt to fly after dark.

5. SUNDAY. Good. A child, or a young adult in your family, is likely to be a real inspiration to you. This is an excellent time for going out with them for a day trip, particularly somewhere far away where you have not been before. Romance is in the air again today. For single Cancer people, a long-distance journey could bring you into contact with a potential new love partner. Married Cancers are likely to have an enjoyable time with their spouse if either traveling or in an environment different from your usual one. Find time to call or write a friend who is recovering from an accident or illness.

6. MONDAY. Disquieting. Your working life should be quite productive. There is an unpredictable element to have to cope with, but this does not mean that you will be kept from making significant progress. A break from routine is likely to be refreshing. If an offer comes to you out of the blue, do not turn it down as a reflex. While it may be wise to think the matter through, there are probably no real snags. It could offer you an opportunity to utilize your special talents to earn some extra money. You may also be able to get some on-the-job training to improve a skill that you already have. Watch what you say, and to whom. An outburst could come back to haunt you.

7. TUESDAY. Frustrating. Be wary of overcommitting yourself where work matters are concerned. You may be expecting too much of yourself, and probably of other people as well. Cancers temporarily out of work can afford to take job searching a little less strenuously today. A job you have already applied for may go to someone else, but do not allow this to deter you in the long run. Your application may lead to a different offer. This could be a busy day all in all. Be sure that you do not get overloaded with too many tasks. Be firm with people who insinuate that you could take on more work if you were better organized or not quite so finicky. It is vital not to lower your standards.

8. WEDNESDAY. Stressful. Life with your partner or family members may not be as easygoing and peaceful as you hope. There may be a power struggle going on between you, and the usual rapport is absent because of this. Before long today's feelings should blow over. In the meantime, try not to say anything out of turn; you may regret it later. Unattached Cancer people should make a point of not pursuing someone who is arrogant with you on first meeting. This is unlikely to be a person you will want to spend a lot of time with in the future. Someone from a different country or culture may soon be a major player in your life.

9. THURSDAY. Changeable. This is another tricky day where close partnerships are concerned. If the problem between you and a partner or loved one are long term, they must be addressed sooner or later. Matters are apt to come to a head now. Getting everything out in the open will probably help. A friend is likely to be a great support to you, particularly when it comes to fulfilling a personal goal or talking about a private problem. Do not worry if you find it hard to make definite decisions early in the day. Later on it should be easier to make up your mind, particularly if you have someone else's input in weighing the pros and cons of your situation.

10. FRIDAY. Variable. Conditions are improving where partnership matters are concerned. You should now know where your partner is coming from and what you want from the relationship. Getting away together to different surroundings for a while will probably be refreshing and a help in sorting out your problems. Your loved one is probably making more of an effort to pinpoint mutual priorities and find ways of achieving the goals you have set. Both of you need more personal space than usual. It is surprising how much can be clarified with a heart-to-heart discussion, but still there are no guarantees. Try to keep your options open.

11. SATURDAY. Tricky. This is a tricky day where financial negotiations are concerned. Unexpected expenses which crop up now may catch you by surprise. Be careful that you are not being forced into a commitment simply because you have not had sufficient time to think things through. It is likely that you can reach an amicable agreement with the other party in a joint financial setup, but only after you have covered all the bases. Quiet time spent alone gives you the chance to consider important matters in more depth. Taking a well-calculated chance can pay off, but guard against foolish risks.

12. SUNDAY. Fair. Check travel details thoroughly if you are going on a long-distance trip. This is one of those times when an omitted detail could mess up your arrangements. A journey with a friend should be most enjoyable. Being with someone may slow you down, but this should not matter to you very much. News from someone abroad is likely to be encouraging. A secret wish that you want to fulfill could start to come true as a result of this new information. Even major obstacles can be negotiated away if you are willing to compromise. Give a little and you will get a lot.

13. MONDAY. Quiet. You can look forward to a fairly peaceful day. This is a good time for making future plans since you have the time and freedom to look ahead, at least more so than you have done lately. This is a very positive time for long-distance travel, especially if you are going on a vacation trip. Where your social life is concerned, meeting new people can be very stimulating. You could be inspired to make some long-range plans with individuals you only recently met. If you cannot actually take a vacation now, arrange a trip for the not too distant future. At work concentrate on what you do best; avoid anything new.

14. TUESDAY. Exciting. You are likely to have the opportunity to fulfill a dream. This could be related to advancing in your chosen career field or a desire to travel somewhere special. Either way, do not hesitate to grasp the moment. A secret meeting with a loved one could reignite the spark in your relationship. For single Cancer people, a vacation romance may develop with someone from another part of the country or another part of the world. Cultural differences may seem slightly strange at first, but also quite charming. Keep all of your plans as flexible as possible so that you can take advantage of unusual openings.

15. WEDNESDAY. Demanding. Authority figures may oppose your actions. Be careful that you are not breaking rules, especially if legal implications could be involved. In addition, it is probably not worth the hassle that may ensue if you go toe-to-toe with a difficult person. A disagreement with someone you consider quite influential could anger you for quite a while. It is wise to think about what you intend to say before opening your mouth; otherwise anything you say could be misinterpreted. A financial difficulty can be resolved if you take greater initiative. Consider using a creative skill in a new way to make some money on the side.

16. THURSDAY. Tricky. You are again likely to find authority figures hard to deal with. You are probably not seeing things from the same perspective. Be careful not to be too self-centered. While you may have some positive plans and good creative ideas, you have to acknowledge that things have been done another way for a very long time. Getting people to even consider a change can be very challenging, especially at work. Choose another time or another context in which to push forward your own ideas. Time spent alone developing your plans is likely to be productive. Be sure important papers are filed away for future reference. Do not throw anything out that could be useful later.

17. FRIDAY. Uncertain. Friends are likely to be a great support to you both in emotional and practical terms. On the job, team efforts are likely to bring good results. If you have a backlog of work to get through, try to persuade others to lend a hand. If what you are asking is likely to benefit all of you, they will probably be glad to help. The more you are able to get other people to cooperate with you, the easier your life is likely to be. There may be unexpected developments in your financial life. Sudden expenses that crop up can be difficult to meet. Going off by yourself somewhere quiet may help you find a solution. Review all of your options with an open mind.

18. SATURDAY. Fair. Money matters need careful handling. This is one of those times when you can get carried away with expenditures relating to your social life. Group interests are favored so long as they do not involve a lot of spending on your part. You are likely to have more success fulfilling a personal goal if you get other people to support you beforehand, especially if you are attempting to lose weight. Cancer people can put on pounds just by looking at sweets. And if you have been going through any kind of a rough time you may have snacked your way through the problem. Make a start on a new diet now. Be sure to get some physical exercise every day; joining a health club can give you good incentive.

19. SUNDAY. Variable. This is a day for peaceful, quiet activity. You may want to tuck yourself away from the rest of the world and do your own thing. However, this may not be possible because you have things to do. Make a concerted effort to get practical tasks out of the way so that you can then rest fully. A lucky break where finances are concerned is sure to cheer you. There could be a check coming your way, quite unexpectedly. If you feel harried having too much to do, try taking frequent breaks to relieve some of the strain on you. By pondering a problem in detail you are likely to find a solution that works out well for everyone.

20. MONDAY. Optimistic. This is another day when you do not have as much time to yourself as you would like. Try to get an early start. People are apt to be in touch with you more than usual. If you lack confidence for a big event, you are likely to find that your nerves calm down and the situation improves once you get involved. A discussion about financial matters which is held behind closed doors is likely to be helpful. Try to help out a friend in need, but not if doing so means overstretching your own resources. Helping someone with their problem may indirectly help you come up with a way out of a difficult situation of your own.

21. TUESDAY. Useful. Catch up with neglected tasks. Because some important people in your office are away on vacation at the moment, you should have a peaceful atmosphere, unless it is up to you to answer everyone's telephone calls. Even if that is the case, you should not have too much trouble coping; the questions being asked may be right up your alley. Where more personal matters are concerned, it is a good idea to enlist the help of one or two friends. They can offer support which aids you in achieving a specific goal. Your mate or partner may come up with worthwhile suggestions that make your plans all the more successful.

22. WEDNESDAY. Successful. Be a little bit selfish and self-centered today. This is a key time for attending to your own needs and desires in ways which you usually neglect. You deserve some pampering and a chance to forward your own goals. If you have been thinking about changing your image, this is a good time to do so. Sorting through your closet and discarding outmoded clothing could be the best place to start. A new hair style or color can also enhance your appearance. If you are preparing for a special occasion where you want to look your best, bring out your good jewelry, or borrow some. Friends continue to support your aims and provide the help you need.

23. THURSDAY. Deceptive. You are beginning a new phase where financial matters are concerned. It is a good idea to review your budget and make sure that you are balancing your income against your expenses. Lack of funding may temporarily prevent a project from going forward or even from getting off the ground. Keep in mind that this is probably just a temporary hitch. Coming up with creative ideas for making more money could help. You may be able to make greater use of underutilized talents. Contacts in the business world may also help you indirectly. Focus on one specific project rather than scattering your efforts.

24. FRIDAY. Calm. Money matters should be much more settled than they have been for a while. If you are anxious to begin a new project which needs funding, use this time to apply for grants or loans. You may be surprised by the positive response that you get. Your own ability to create funds is a bonus at the moment. Search for ways to make money which utilize talents you have neglected or at least not made the best use of in recent times. This tends to be a better day for selling than for buying, although you may not make much of a profit. Be sure to keep careful profit and loss records for use when you have to prepare your tax return.

25. SATURDAY. Good. Encouraging news is coming your way in relation to financial developments. A discussion with a manufacturer or salesperson about a product you are thinking about buying is likely to be fruitful. If you intend to make a major investment, first seek professional advice. News from abroad is sure to give you a lift. There could be a love letter or romantic telephone call from that special person in your life who is out of town now. For single Cancer people that type of communication might be the first positive sign that someone you like is just as interested in you. Do not hesitate to express your feelings in actions as well as words.

26. SUNDAY. Difficult. This is another day when contact from someone a good distance away can be very welcome. If you have time on your hands, get in touch with someone you have not seen in a long time. If you have distant friends you write to only on holidays, exert that extra effort to get in touch now. For single Cancers, positive moves from a new partner are likely to convince you that you have found the right person. If you have been going together for a while, this is an excellent time to discuss plans for the future, possibly including a vacation together or formally meeting potential in-laws.

27. MONDAY. Unsettling. It is necessary to get your priorities in order right at the start today if you are to make reasonable progress. Communication from someone you do not usually hear from has the potential to throw you off your stride. Unless some specific action needs to be taken at once, it is best to stick to your original plans for the day. Do not worry if you do not hear from someone who promised to call; there is probably a very good reason for their failure to communicate. Single Cancers may have cause to be concerned if a new partner is not honoring a promise; there may be a lack of genuine interest. If you suspect this is so, do not kid yourself that the situation is going to improve over time.

28 TUESDAY. Rewarding. A quiet chat with your boss or another authority figure is likely to help solve a problem that has been on your mind. The answer to a difficult situation may be found through consulting individuals you consider to be older and wiser than you. Self-discipline is your key to success if you are attempting to get through a backlog of neglected or unfinished matters. There is no need to be hard on yourself. Simply decide what you want to achieve and go all-out to meet your goals. The more disciplined you are, the more you can get done in the shortest amount of time. Do not strive for perfection unless there is good reason to aim that high.

29. WEDNESDAY. Unsettling. This is not a good day for trying to get the upper hand in a personal relationship. You may wish you could take charge of matters between you and your partner to a greater degree than usual, but be very careful in how you go about this. If you come across as patronizing or bossy, you could lose out all around. Aim to be subtle and low-key. You may find yourself arguing with the boss because you do not see eye-to-eye on one particular matter. Keep in mind that while you may be persuasive in your role at times, you need to respect the other person's superior position. Someone you found difficult to work with in the past is now ready to cooperate with you.

30. THURSDAY. Tricky. This is a key day for making an important new financial investment. A discussion with a professional adviser or an expert in the field is likely to be very useful. You need to be wary in your friendships, which can be hard to handle. Someone you feel is taking you for granted may change their attitude if you talk to them honestly and from the heart. You may feel that there has been some deception going on, but be careful about accusing the other person. Try to find out the facts of the situation first of all. They may reassure you that no harm was intended. If this is not the case, stern words may be necessary or even a breakup.

31. FRIDAY. Disquieting. This is another day when you are apt to feel edgy about the way a relationship is developing. Your intuition in relation to possible double-dealing is probably right. Be quite diplomatic in handling the situation so that the other person has a chance to actually admit to any wrong that has been done. Direct confrontation is not the choice of Cancer people. In this instance it may be the best approach, helping you to cut through a tangle of red tape in your relationship. Insinuations tend to make other people feel guilty and try to cover up or make excuses. By being more direct in your approach you will probably get to the truth and be able to find common ground.

AUGUST

1. SATURDAY. Mixed. Contact with friends is likely to be especially stimulating. Get more involved in group activities related to a sport or hobby that interests you. However, avoid a costly venture even if you have some spare cash now; you may later regret the extra expenditure. This is not a good risk-taking day where money is concerned. Avoid any gambling activity, even a friendly wager. Pressure from friends can tempt you to gamble when stakes are too high for you. Also avoid attempting to prove anything to anyone else, particularly in a battle of physical endurance. Hearing from someone you have not seen in a long while is likely to be a pleasant surprise. Make plans to get together soon.

2. SUNDAY. Uncertain. If you need to handle some routine matters you should be more productive if you get off by yourself. Being alone with your thoughts can also help in addressing problems to which you have not been able to find a solution so far. If you are troubled by something to the extent that you are losing sleep over it, try to confront your worst fears. In so doing you are likely to realize that you have more options that you have considered up till now. Money matters ought to be less stressful than they have been lately. This is a key day for considering future personal investments. Where heavy work is concerned, take a friend up on an offer to help.

3. MONDAY. Rewarding. You can make good progress dealing with routine matters. As was the case yesterday, having more time to yourself is likely to be a bonus. Try to catch up with what you have recently been forced to neglect, especially paperwork. If there are bills to be paid or filing to do, get at least some of the backlog cleared away. One particular project that has been dragging on for a long time is finally coming to an end, which should lift a burden from your mind as well as your shoulders. Do not expect too much of other people; they may not be as resourceful as usual. You should do better relying on them less and on yourself more.

4. TUESDAY. Variable. Deal with business matters slowly and calmly. This is not a time to rush into anything. Other people may try to hurry you along, but it is in your best interests to stand your ground until you feel ready to proceed. New developments in a relationship are likely to make you feel very good about yourself. Your confidence is bound to increase because of a compliment from someone who means a lot to you. Single Cancers need to pay more attention to someone who is trying to show romantic interest. Although this person may not seem to be your type at first glance, a second look could reveal a more genuine attraction. Romance is starred with someone considerably older than you.

5. WEDNESDAY. Quiet. There is no reason to feel ruffled or hassled. Other people are likely to leave you alone but also not provide much assistance or support. This is an excellent time for getting on with personal matters. You can make good progress toward achieving a personal goal or aim that you know will raise your stature and probably your income as well. If you have been thinking about doing something to change your image, this is the day to move forward with your plans. Do not aim for anything too drastic, however. It is better to make an effort to groom yourself more effectively and improve your current look rather than go for an entire transformation so that you are not recognizable.

6. THURSDAY. Tricky. Make an effort to get in touch with a recognized authority or to consult an up-to-date reference book if you are looking for specific information. Think about who might be a useful contact. Call a former colleague or schoolmate to catch up on each other's news. Meeting with a financial adviser or with someone with whom you have joint financial dealings may turn out to be quite confusing. The other person could seem evasive and hard to pin down. Make an effort to be more businesslike during your meeting and you should have more success in achieving what you set out to attain. Do not take no for an answer.

7. FRIDAY. Stressful. Be careful if making any type of financial decision. This is one of those times when someone may try to talk you into an agreement that you would usually turn down on the spot. If you are thinking of making a major investment, such as purchasing a large item for your home or locking money into a long-term savings plan, be sure to find out more about the company. What looks innovative and worthwhile on the surface may turn out to be something quite different. The more thorough your research, the better. Try to repay money you owe sooner rather than later. Avoid buying on credit until your current bills are paid in full.

8. SATURDAY. Unsettling. This is another day for being on guard where financial matters, and investments in particular, are concerned. Someone could be trying to pull the wool over your eyes. If you hope to get through a number of different tasks, or even to complete one particular project, reconsider if you start the day feeling tired. You need to pace yourself carefully and take frequent breaks. Yesterday you may have been offered some valuable advice in relation to money. Today, however, revealing too much about your income or savings could put you at a disadvantage. Try to do more listening than talking. Keep an open mind but do not make a commitment.

9. SUNDAY. Disquieting. This is another day when it pays to keep your thoughts to yourself. While it may be tempting to reveal a secret, you are apt to feel embarrassed or awkward immediately afterward. Besides, this can put you in a vulnerable position, which as a Cancer you naturally find distressing. A short-distance trip can take longer than you expect, so allow plenty of time to reach your destination. There may be road detours which you did not know about or an accident blocking the road. Do not try to cope alone with deep-seated worries. To help relieve the anxiety, discuss your innermost thoughts with an older family member or a longtime trusted friend.

10. MONDAY. Enjoyable. Today you will enjoy extended conversations with people you see all too infrequently. You probably have a lot of news to catch up on, and you should feel more free to speak your mind than you did yesterday. Something that has been worrying you is likely to be resolved after a good night's sleep, perhaps as the result of a dream. For single Cancers, this is a starred time for meeting new people. You could be introduced through your social circle to someone to whom you are strongly attracted, and the attraction is likely to be mutual. Do not postpone buying a major item or investing in a company you know a lot about.

11. TUESDAY. Fortunate. This is a good day for behind-the-scenes activities. At work you can achieve excellent results by working alone. A private discussion could help you resolve a problem that has been at the back of your mind. An investment made for your family's security ought to be profitable in the long run, even if you make it in a hurry. Seek the advice of a broker or other financial adviser who is working in an independent capacity rather than part of a larger group. You will get positive results if you ask specific questions rather than seeking general information. Past performance is not a guarantee for the future.

12. WEDNESDAY. Fair. This is not a favorable day for trying to clear a backlog of work. You are reaching the end of a project, and this is likely to free up time to attend to matters which have been neglected. You can also make good progress with a home-based project. If you have been intending to get down to some do-it-yourself tasks, this is the day for planning and shopping for supplies. You could negotiate a very good deal. Get other family members involved in a project, but try to stay in charge or you could wind up arguing over work methods. Do not hire a professional to do work that you can handle yourself.

13. THURSDAY. Deceptive. You may start thinking that romance is in the air where a close associate is concerned, especially if you are single. Be careful, however. There are likely to be mixed messages. A new person you meet who pays you a lot of compliments may actually have an ulterior motive. Be especially wary if they ask about your financial affairs. If this person wants to know about property that you own, this is also a warning signal. Be extra careful where financial matters are concerned. This is one of those days when you can encounter someone who seems sincere but is actually a scam artist looking for a target.

14. FRIDAY. Disconcerting. A social event to which you have been invited could be a lot of fun but also very costly. Other people not paying their way could be the problem. In addition, you may not anticipate going out beforehand or afterward. If you do go to a restaurant or club, be sure that you do not get stuck with the bill for someone who claims to have no money. If you know you cannot afford to go out, come up with a reasonable excuse so that you do not feel embarrassed. Your relationship with your partner is likely to become more romantic in a social setting; you may not even know that other people are around.

15. SATURDAY. Satisfactory. You should be able to make surprisingly good progress with any practical tasks that you undertake. If you are thinking of buying practical items for your home, you could pick up some bargains. Interest-free credit deals are worth looking into; be sure to read and understand the fine print. Do not spend too much time in solitude; it may depress you and make you feel lonely. If you are single, or if your partner is away at the moment, consider visiting a good friend. Think of something fun that you can do together. Get to bed earlier than usual.

16. SUNDAY. Slow. This is another good day for focusing on routine, practical tasks. It is also a favorable time for catching up on correspondence of a business nature but separate from your working life. A health problem which has been worrying you ought to begin to show signs of improvement because you are under less pressure or are handling stress better. It could also be the result of experimenting with your diet. If you have allergies, try a food elimination diet. Just be careful that you are not missing out on any vital nutrients. Regular exercise can also make you feel better. It is best to seek medical advice before a problem escalates.

17. MONDAY. Good. A greater degree of romance is likely to make today seem extra special. Be sure to let that special person in your life know how you feel. For single Cancer people, there is a good chance of meeting someone new if you go out and socialize. In fact, there is a very good chance of meeting someone special. This is also a favorable day for finishing off work and tying up loose ends. If you are currently looking for work, update your resume. It is also worthwhile to go back to a company where you would like to be employed; there may now be an unadvertised opening.

18. TUESDAY. Calm. Partnership matters should be smooth and easygoing. This is not a day for acting like a loner in any respect. Where your job is concerned, you can benefit from sharing the work and getting more involved in team effort. You are seeing the world from a slightly different perspective today. In particular, you realize to a greater degree the benefit of being in a partnership. If you are single this is likely to encourage you to try to revitalize an old relationship or look for a new one even if you have been feeling cynical about marriage. Be honest if a friend comes to you for advice.

19. WEDNESDAY. Misleading. Discussions with your mate or partner are likely to be very productive, especially if you are making plans for the future. This is a good time to discuss a future vacation or possible relocation. Money issues are looming large. It is not a good idea to make long-term financial commitments if you are not sure what your situation will be later in the year. Try to base your plans on your current situation. An anticipated raise or bonus could be postponed. Social interests may take more of your time, energy, and money than you expect. Set limits for yourself and stick to them.

20. THURSDAY. Deceptive. This is another uncertain day where money matters are concerned. If money is owed to you, it may not be repaid on time. Even though the check is supposed to be in the mail, do not believe it until it is in your hands. Come up with a contingency plan so that you have other funds to fall back on temporarily. Avoid making a major investment for your home if you can. If you are in the midst of a home improvement project, its rising costs may start to worry you. If you have the option to scale back or to do some of the work yourself, do so; you can save a lot.

21. FRIDAY. Unsettling. This is a key day for improving your financial situation. You may feel that it is necessary to turn over a new leaf and start over with a new budget. This is a very good idea, particularly if you want to save for something specific. You probably cannot resolve all of your money problems overnight since your circumstances are subject to change at the moment. Keep an open mind. Before too long you could be altering the whole situation for the better. Begin with a few small steps in the right direction by striving to get out of debt before incurring new expense.

22. SATURDAY. Variable. This should be the most pleasurable day of the weekend. It is a great time to go away for a romantic break with your love partner. You are both bound to enjoy and appreciate the opportunity to relax and wind down. Single Cancer people could meet someone new while away for the weekend, especially if on a group outing away from everyday surroundings. It may surprise you how much people tend to let their hair down when they are in a neutral setting. Ideas are all around you, giving your natural creativity a chance to shine.

23. SUNDAY. Disquieting. Do not believe all that you hear or are told. A neighbor or relative is apt to exaggerate, probably for a good reason. This person may be worried about a mutual friend or a member of the family. Take what is said with a grain of salt, even if you express compassion. It might be a good idea to try to calm down this individual without dismissing their feelings or making light of them. What at first looks like a good opportunity for you to fulfill a personal dream could turn out to be something quite different. Do not become disillusioned; there is likely to be another chance in the near future. Try harder to find out what is bothering a loved one.

24. MONDAY. Excellent. Today is much better than yesterday for fulfilling personal goals and dreams. People who have made promises to you are more likely to keep them. Doors are opening up for you at the moment. It is not going to involve any great effort to walk through one of them, but it will require a little courage to take that first step. Entering new territory can be a little daunting. However, you have every reason to feel optimistic. A mature person having a traditional outlook is the best person to turn to for advice or reassurance. Stay on track until you achieve your goals.

25. TUESDAY. Good. This is a starred day for making financial investments. Discussions with a person from an established company should reassure you about the right plan to follow. It is also a key time for starting a new business venture or partnership. If an older person is involved in your plans, so much the better. You are likely to benefit from this person's greater experience and expertise in a particular field. Where romance is concerned, involvement with a person who is mature but not necessarily older is favored for Cancer singles. Married Cancers can benefit from sharing home responsibilities equally.

26. WEDNESDAY. Mixed. Work should move along smoothly. Although you may be trying to change careers, this is not the day to take any major steps. However, you can get your plans for the future sorted out in your head. Any important work that has been neglected ought to be attended to now. Try to avoid adding to your backlog. A romantic relationship is likely to move onto a more stable footing, which should be reassuring if you have been hurt in the past. This is also true for Cancers involved in a fairly young relationship. Try harder to accept other people as they are, not as you would like them to be.

27. THURSDAY. Difficult. Avoid either lending or borrowing from friends, whether it is money or possessions. Conflict could arise between you if a loan is not repaid on time or an item is not well looked after and returned in good condition. Do not offer advice unless specifically asked for it. It is also inadvisable to try to sell products to friends and acquaintances. If they know that you have goods available to sell, they will come to you if interested. A gentle reminder of a deadline should not be harmful, but do not push it further than that. On the social scene, be sure to pay your share of the bill if you go out for lunch or after work.

28. FRIDAY. Challenging. It is worthwhile taking your time in making financial decisions. Be careful that you do not end up spending a lot on something that you may not actually need or ever use. You could be strongly influenced by someone close to you, but it is important to follow your own initiative. Avoid spending much time with friends who are inclined to waste time and money. They could seriously get on your nerves, especially if it is your time and money that ends up being wasted. Find a way to be alone for part of the day in order to collect your thoughts and plan future moves.

29. SATURDAY. Buoyant. Friends are likely to be very supportive of your plans. It is a good time for taking the first step toward turning a dream into reality. Try not to worry too much about a difficult situation which, if you think about it long enough, frightens you. The matter is apt to work out in your favor in the end. If there is a financial settlement involved, you are likely to come out well. Social plans should go smoothly. Someone you are close to is likely to inspire you. This is a favorable time for group activities, particularly if you are pursuing a hobby. You can learn a lot from people who are more experienced than you.

30. SUNDAY. Promising. You can make good progress catching up on matters that have been neglected, particularly paperwork in relation to your personal finances. Make an effort to settle your outstanding accounts as soon as possible. If you have been spending freely, at least make sure that your expenditures are balanced against your income. An unexpected financial bonus could come your way, which may give you the freedom to do something you have only dreamed about. If you are worried about something you did or said in the past week which has upset another person, make amends without delay. Be the first to apologize even if you were not totally at fault.

31. MONDAY. Changeable. Review a past situation which resembles current circumstances so that you can be sure not to make the same mistakes all over again. You are likely to benefit from thinking through your actions very carefully. The more reflective you are, the more sound your decisions and actions are likely to be. Avoid gossiping about a situation which ought to remain private. If someone has told you a secret in good confidence, it is up to you to honor this trust that has been placed in you. Pay no attention to rumors which are flying around the workplace. It is highly likely that someone is exaggerating in order to gain attention. You can rely on a superior's promise even if it is not in writing.

SEPTEMBER

1. TUESDAY. Manageable. This is a helpful day for advancing personal plans. You should feel much more confident and positive about the future. A close relationship with a loved one is likely to make you feel especially happy. While you have your own individual plans to carry out, it helps to know that the person you love is behind you and is cheering you on. Any problem that has been causing some friction in your close relationships should be less difficult to handle now, mainly due to your newfound self-confidence. Also, you are in a stronger position for taking assertive action when you encounter resistance or any type of obstacle.

2. WEDNESDAY. Successful. This is an excellent day for promoting yourself in a situation where you hope to make an impact. In the business world, through advertising you can gain new customers and new contacts. In your more private life, you can increase your social circle by making more of an effort to get to know new people you meet. Conversation with partners should go smoothly. This is a positive day to discuss your more personal plans, or at least make them known. You now have a better feeling for what you want to achieve and can therefore communicate your aims and intentions more clearly to other interested persons. Teamwork is favored both on the job and at home.

3. THURSDAY. Unsettling. Beware of overspending. An unexpected or forgotten bill could resurface, worrying you if you do not have the funds to pay it. Contact from someone you owe money to and thought would not be able to track you down could come as a shock. Today is full of surprises, some perhaps not too pleasant but others decidedly favorable in the long run. Make a contingency plan in case you get into a similar situation in the future. A friend from your past could get in touch to discuss an interesting proposition which could become a money-maker for you.

4. FRIDAY. Difficult. This is another day to be watchful where money matters are concerned. A clever salesperson could talk you into making a purchase before you have time to think it over carefully. However, if you are on guard for this, the problem is less likely. Take your time before making any agreement, whether related to financial expenditure or your time and energy. It is not wise to overstretch your resources in any way at the moment. At an emotional level, it is important that you feel comfortable with what is being offered or suggested, particularly regarding any business venture you are interested in pursuing. Advice from an older family member is right on the mark.

5. SATURDAY. Variable. Time spent with loved ones should be enjoyable this weekend. If you are seeking greater commitment from a romantic partner, this is a good time to discuss your future together. This could lead to more security in your relationship. Cancer parents are likely to find children energizing to be around. Try to find time to take them to a park, movie, or sports event. Be sure that you know the route to take before setting off. It is not a good idea to depend upon signs, which could be misleading. You have to do a lot of running around but should make solid progress whittling down your to-do list.

6. SUNDAY. Mixed. This is another day when you are likely to be busy running around for one reason or another. There may still be a lot of errands to run, places to go, and people to see. While it is exciting having a lot of different things to do, try not to cram your schedule so full that you become emotionally or physically exhausted. If you do, you could feel quite temperamental by the end of the weekend. A long-distance journey could take more time than you expect. Do not assume that you can pay a flying visit to people you see all too infrequently. It is likely that your time will be taken up with general chitchat as much as anything else you hope to discuss.

7. MONDAY. Good. You should feel very confident about any public speaking that you have to do or important telephone calls that you have to make. This is a beneficial time to promote yourself in the eyes of others, particularly at work. You can get one step closer to fulfilling a personal dream through talking about it to someone in a position of authority. Putting your goals into words can make a powerful difference. Once you have said what is on your mind, your thoughts regarding your plan of action are likely to be set in motion, with no turning back. Home and family life ought to be smooth and easygoing. Your home is your best place of retreat and comfort at the moment.

8. TUESDAY. Quiet. This is another day when home and family life are easygoing. If you need time to yourself you should have it, both at work and in your private life. Try to finish up those things that usually get put to one side. A project which has been neglected for some time can be completed now if you put your mind to finishing it. Rely more on tried-and-tested methods rather than something new. Likewise, concentrate on finishing up old projects rather than beginning a new one. It is best to wipe the slate clean before moving on. If you drive, pay special attention to road signs, particularly the speed limit.

9. WEDNESDAY. Fair. This is apt to be a rather foggy day where social arrangements are concerned. If you are not clear about the plans that someone else has devised, double-check where, when, and what to wear. In this way you should be able to avoid any major mishap. A person you have teamed up with fairly recently may make a move to stabilize your relationship for the future. Because of this, you can feel more sure about making long-term plans. Distant travel promises to be stimulating, particularly if you are traveling in good company. You can get your way in most things by turning on your Cancer charm. Be free with compliments and stingy with criticism.

10. THURSDAY. Cautious. Going out for lunch or another group social event could turn out to be more expensive than you anticipate. The bill can shoot up quickly if drinks are included in the general tab. If you see a problem arising, opt to leave earlier than the rest. You are likely to enjoy yourself most in the company of people who have a lot to talk about. The last thing you need is to be in a situation where you cannot express the thoughts flitting through your mind. Try to avoid a noisy environment; having to shout above the crowd will get on your nerves. If noise from a neighbor or co-worker disturbs you, find a tactful way to approach them.

11. FRIDAY. Sensitive. A personal dream can come true if you follow your instincts. Become more involved in creative endeavors of all kinds. You may discover a new talent or skill, as well as having a generally enjoyable time. Spend part of the day in solitary surroundings, but do not isolate yourself too much. A discussion going on behind closed doors may worry you. Try not to get too serious about matters which remain open-ended at the moment; a lot could change in a short space of time. You will probably have little success attempting to keep a low profile, so do not bother to try. Be guided by your instincts if you have to make an immediate decision.

12. SATURDAY. Changeable. Make an effort to catch up on neglected tasks which you have avoided for too long. You should feel happy with the results. The fewer loose ends you leave hanging, the better. It may be necessary to elicit more facts or figures so that you can finish a current project or reach a decision. While this is likely to take some effort on your part, it is sure to be worthwhile. It is important not to take on more than you can comfortably handle at the moment. Overstretching yourself physically can be exhausting and, from a mental point of view, can tend to drain your creativity. Get to bed earlier than usual.

13. SUNDAY. Happy. This is a happy day where personal relationships are concerned. A certain partnership can be made more romantic by arranging a special treat for the two of you. For single Cancers, this is a good time for getting together with other people socially in order to make new friends and perhaps meet a prospective partner. Accept any invitation that comes your way, even if you receive it at the last minute. Your confidence is high, which is a boon to you in any type of social situation. If you are going out tonight, make an effort to dress so that you stand out in a crowd. Tonight's Moon rising in your sign of Cancer makes you especially mysterious and alluring.

14. MONDAY. Useful. If you have the chance to travel to a different city, jump at it. This is a very good day to visit people who live some distance away from you. Conversations with a loved one are likely to take on a philosophical angle. You may talk about the meaning of life and how you fit into the universal scheme of things. It is a favorable time for making long-term plans together. If you have academic aims, it is not too late to sign up for a course or to switch your major academic focus. Someone who has dropped out of a filled class may create room for you to enter now. Stay home tonight with a good book for company.

15. TUESDAY. Confusing. You may feel confused about exactly where to start with a current project. Do not make too many detailed plans, since things are likely to change on short notice. Exciting opportunity to do something very different could come your way. Working in collaboration with a partner promises unusually good results. This is another day when long-distance travel is favored, particularly if you are in the company of someone you admire. Avoid being vague if a friend or loved one wants to know your true feelings. Although it is sometimes hard for you to express your emotions, it is better to be upfront and totally honest about them.

16. WEDNESDAY. Sensitive. A financial bonus stemming from past investment or effort on your part could come your way today. With all that your finances are going through, it may help to get you past an unexpected lean patch. Avoid frittering away money, even if it is a windfall. Have confidence that you can handle a difficult financial situation by tightening your belt when necessary. If you are thinking of making major financial investments with spare money that you have, it is important to discuss your plans and intentions with a professional who can advise you well. Look to your past experiences in order to make a wise decision for the future.

17. THURSDAY. Calm. Your financial situation should be smoother than it has been lately. This is a propitious time for making plans for the future in relation to your finances. Consider investments you might be able to make to protect the future security of both you and your family. You can benefit from making an effort to reduce your everyday expenses, perhaps by carpooling or packing a lunch instead of eating out. Business meetings taking place now ought to yield positive results and firm decisions. Pooling resources with other people can potentially help you save money and time.

18. FRIDAY. Variable. Concentrate on making more plans for the future. If you have recently neglected your social life somewhat, try to pick up the pieces. Get back in touch with people you would like to see. If a current social arrangement is canceled, it may be a signal that one of your relationships is coming to an end. Do not worry about this; there are better things on the horizon. Broadening your interests is a good way of getting to meet new people and make new friends. You could become part of a whole new social circle. Maintaining your Cancer sense of humor is important in all social situations.

19. SATURDAY. Rewarding. This is another good day for efforts to broaden your social contacts. Give some general thought to which people from the past you would like to get in touch with again. More importantly, look to the future. Cultural pursuits, such as an interest in the theater or in art or crafts, should be more fully explored. Through these activities you may meet people who are more interesting to you than some of the friends you have spent a lot of time with in recent months. Some of those old relationships could feel a bit jaded, in which case it is definitely time for you to move on. Enjoy some outdoor exercise, especially a sport for the fun of it.

20. SUNDAY. Challenging. You are entering a new phase today where you are likely to feel the need to explore areas you have so far left untouched. You could discover a new way of looking at life if you become more involved in academic or religious interests. For some Cancer people there is likely to be a calling to serve. Despite your noble intentions and high ideals, it is important at the moment to be sure that you are not trying to run before you can walk. Take things one step at a time. Where work matters are concerned, you may be temporarily distracted from your longer term plans but can get back on track next month.

21. MONDAY. Stimulating. This is a positive day where your career interests are concerned. If you are going on an interview, dress conventionally so that you make the right impression, especially if the company you are applying to is well established and traditional. Make a point of carefully choosing your references if you think you may need them soon. Where routine occupational affairs are concerned, stick to familiar time-honored methods which will not tax you too much. Work superiors are likely to be extra supportive of your goals. Do not hesitate to apply for a promotion. If you need a favor or some advice, now is the time to ask.

22. TUESDAY. Productive. You should be able to make good progress with professional interests. There is much to be gained by entering into a business deal which appeals to you. As a Cancer you do not usually enter quickly into a new venture. However, snap decisions can work in your favor at the moment, especially since you need to think and act more quickly than usual. Long-distance travel is particularly favored in relation to your personal aims and desires. If you are interested in higher academic study, this is a key time to pursue your goal. Look into nontraditional courses, such as through television or via computer.

23. WEDNESDAY. Confusing. Disagreements with the boss at work are likely to involve a basic misunderstanding more than anything else. It would be smart to let the situation ride for a few days rather than attempt to sort it out now. It could be that your superior has too much to attend to at the moment to be able to devote sufficient quality time to answering the questions that you have. If you are experiencing difficulties with authorities outside of the workplace, the same principles apply. Call for an appointment rather than expecting to drop by and get an answer. A friendship with someone of the opposite sex may be stressful when it becomes obvious that the other person has romantic intentions. If these are not welcome, make a point of saying so firmly.

24. THURSDAY. Demanding. Friendships are much more straightforward and smooth flowing than they were yesterday. Your effort to make clear the nature of the relationship you desire should be paying off. Balance your priorities carefully. It is easy to get caught up in immediate but relatively trivial interests and miss out on something important. Try to keep your focus on the long-term future. If you are studying for an examination, keep your social involvements to a minimum for a while. Be wary of accepting an invitation if you might not be able to keep the date, or might not want to keep it.

25. FRIDAY. Lucky. If you are trying to turn a dream into reality it is likely to be helpful to enlist the support of friends. Practical help can be a real plus, but moral support and encouragement also tend to be quite valuable. You can make good progress catching up with a backlog of work. If you are trying to advance your career, make a point of going over old ground again. You may find new opportunities come your way through prior colleagues. This is a helpful day for approaching the boss in order to try to clear up a confusing situation. You should be able to clarify the matter in question to your satisfaction. Bring along extra cash if going out tonight.

26. SATURDAY. Exciting. You are likely to benefit from attempting to pin friends down to definite arrangements. Last-minute changes of plan should work out in your favor, but it helps to have some settled plans for the future. If you are worried about your current financial situation, talk it over with someone who has been in the same spot. An individual with unusual ideas about spending and saving may be able to offer new insights. If an important paper gets lost you may spend a long time looking for it. Your efforts should produce good results, plus an added bonus such as finding something else that you thought you had lost. Group activity is favored this evening rather than a twosome.

27. SUNDAY. Manageable. Be careful not to overexert, especially when it comes to mental work. While you may be eager to get a number of chores out of the way, it is a good idea to pace yourself. You may have problems focusing on your ideas for long-range action, possibly due to a lack of information. Do not waste time attempting to work out only half a plan, which could change quite quickly and drastically. It is more productive to go over the past with a fine-tooth comb than to try to map out a grand plan for the future. You can learn a lot from both past successes and mistakes. Allow time for change to be accepted gradually by all concerned.

28. MONDAY. Pleasant. Your social life ought to be especially stimulating. This is a beneficial time for getting more involved in creative interests; you could develop a hidden talent. Sports activities also give you a chance to show off abilities that you may not even know you have. The boss at work may not approve current plans immediately. Although you could be tempted to argue in order to strengthen your case, this is not the time to be pushy. Wait until the dust has settled a little. After a few days this person is apt to be more willing to see things from your point of view. Do not take no as a final answer.

29. TUESDAY. Challenging. Do all that you can to promote yourself in a situation where you want to make a good impression. If you are going on a job interview, your Cancer gift of gab is sure to be a boon that gives you a greater chance of success. Do not hesitate to talk about your past achievements and your ambitious future aims. The more candid you are, the more information a prospective employer has to go on. A higher-up is likely to be more supportive of your aims. You may be surprised by this turnaround, but there is no reason to question it; probably the boss has simply had more time to think it over and make a decision about your request.

30. WEDNESDAY. Fair. You are more in touch with your deeper dreams and ideals. It is worth making a greater effort to fulfill your aims, even if you suspect that others may not understand what you are trying to accomplish. Their opinions should not really matter in the long term, anyway. This is a day for looking to the future and trying to make step-by-step plans. A love partner could be inspired by the extent of your vision. Your social life may turn out to be rather costly, especially if you have to attend an important function. However, there is apt to be someone present whom you need to impress. Making the effort is sure to be rewarding in the long run.

OCTOBER

1. THURSDAY. Variable. It is important to stand by your principles in all business and financial matters. This is not time to cave in to other people's authority if you know that your instincts are right. A final agreement can be reached after an important discussion takes place. Practice all of the social graces both at an informal gathering and in the world of high society. If you are attending a key meeting, be sure that you are appropriately attired. Wearing a well-fitting suit is likely to make you feel more authoritative than if you turn up in casual clothing. Keep jewelry to one or two select but low-key pieces.

2. FRIDAY. Unsettling. Do not expect to be able to reach your desired goal or even a significant agreement regarding a joint financial situation. You have to bide your time while your partner or others make up their own mind. You may have to wait longer than you expect for a decision to be made. Try not to become too impatient or you could lose your current advantage. Neighborhood social events are likely to be particularly entertaining. Go along even if you go alone and find out what is happening. You may be introduced to someone you would like to get to know better. Avoid gossiping; what you say could be repeated in mixed company.

3. SATURDAY. Easygoing. This is an easygoing, sociable day. Expect a friendly visit from a neighbor or relative. If you have time on your hands, catch up on current news via a few telephone calls; you could learn something quite useful in the process. Some important information and insights can come through general chit-chat. You may make some new social contacts through your various activities. One of these could lead to a new partnership, especially if you are single. Make the most of all the social opportunities that are coming your way; do not turn down any invitation you receive.

4. SUNDAY. Calm. This is another good day fo[r] social contacts and for catching up on the news wit[h] Do all that you can to further an important perso[n] could find that talking to other people about what y[ou] do is the key to getting motivated. This could also your intentions in your own mind. With many ideas co[ming] ...g for attention in your mind, your key to success is to pick and choose among them so that they are not just fleeting thoughts. You may find it helpful to write down a few of the ideas for future reference. Make a list of long-term projects that need to be done which you sense may otherwise get neglected.

5. MONDAY. Pleasant. This is a useful day for bringing a project to a conclusion. You may have more time on your hands than you expect, plus more resources at your disposal. If you are interested in making a new investment, a good deal can be finalized. Cancer people already involved in negotiations should be able to move one step closer to success. Give a little and you will get a lot in return. Professional matters need to be handled with sensitivity. If you intend to have a discussion with the boss, having all the relevant facts and details straight in your mind can save time and strengthen your case.

6. TUESDAY. Deceptive. Be careful not to look at the world through rose-colored glasses when you know that there are hard facts to be faced. You can become your own worst enemy if you deceive yourself regarding a matter which is not working out the way you want it to. Single Cancers who are considering contacting a previous partner with a view of getting back together should think again. It is possible that you are not being realistic about the negative aspects of the relationship which were the main reasons for your breakup in the first place. Do not be pressured into making a decision before you are ready.

7. WEDNESDAY. Disconcerting. Unexpected financial obligations that crop up could potentially wreck your social plans. However, if you turn to someone who has money in the bank, they may be able and willing to help out. An upcoming social event could put you in the limelight. It is worth making the effort to attend even if the occasion is going to be rather costly. Last-minute changes of plan may not seem at first to work in your favor. However, if you can be innovative and think of alternatives, you can mold the change to suit yourself. Cancer ambition is at a peak. Be prepared for competition and a fight to the finish.

THURSDAY. Variable. This promises to be a wonderful day where social activities are concerned. As was true yesterday, you are likely to find yourself in the spotlight and, for a change, will probably enjoy it. As a Cancer you have a habit of hiding in your shell all too often. Now you can bask in the praise that is being showered on you. You may feel uncertain about a course of action you were firmly determined to follow a while ago. This could involve new business possibilities. While these may be confusing at first, take time to absorb them. Soon you will appreciate what a fortunate position you are in because of the varied options open to you.

9. FRIDAY. Good. This is a productive day where work matters are concerned. If you are thinking of obtaining some seasonal work, this is a favorable time to apply for a part-time position. Check local papers and store advertisements. To cure a minor health matter, alternative remedies could turn out to be more worthwhile than you expect. On most occasions it is a good idea to seek the advice of a professional medical practitioner, but at the moment it is likely to be more productive to first try an age-old remedy. If starting a diet, be sure you are getting all necessary nutrients. Avoid a fad diet in favor of a lifetime eating plan.

10. SATURDAY. Manageable. If you have been having problems with your landlord or with a tenant in your property, this is favorable day for trying to resolve the trouble. It is likely that the person in question will give in, even though you may doubt this initially. Being diplomatic will help bring the situation to a mutually satisfactory conclusion. A friendship has a better chance of becoming romantic if you get away together to neutral surroundings. Just a different view should bring you closer to each other. It is important to fulfill a commitment even if it is not convenient to do so.

11. SUNDAY. Misleading. Be careful not to rub authority figures the wrong way. A partner may encourage you to push for a decision when the matter ought to be left alone for now. Trust your own Cancer instincts, which are generally a very good guide. This is not one of your best days for attending to private matters and personal projects. You could lose your sense of direction and get lost along the way. It will not take much to throw you off course, especially if influential people are contradicting you. Slow down and aim to achieve significant results on another day. Try not to be too demanding of yourself or of others. In fact, give yourself a pat on the back for recent work well done.

12. MONDAY. Disquieting. You could get into an argument with a loved one over important matters. One of you devoting a lot of time to career advancement could strain your relationship. Whether this go-getter is you or your partner, it is likely to help if you talk about the situation openly. Do not sit and brood privately, an unfortunate Cancer habit. While it may be useful to dream and plan in private, brooding does you little if any good. You may not feel emotionally ready for a direct confrontation, but it might actually clear the air. A letter from a friend or relative at a distance may make you wonder who or what is influencing them.

13. TUESDAY. Mixed. If you are making plans for eventual retirement, an independent deal can be more advantageous than getting involved in a group scheme. You could end up with higher monthly income by making your own investments for the future. Be wary of people who try to impress you with gimmicks. An old-fashioned company that impresses you with its thoroughness is likely to be a good bet. If there are outstanding personal matters that you need to clear up, make a start on them today. The sooner you clear away a backlog, the sooner you can begin a new project. You do not need a partner in order to get ahead financially.

14. WEDNESDAY. Good. This is a good day for making a key financial investment. The advice of a professional accountant or other financial adviser could prove invaluable in the long run. Getting away from your usual surroundings for a while will probably do you a lot of good. A trip made with a group of people is likely to be particularly stimulating. If you are interested in furthering your career, devote some time to thinking how you want to do this. It could be useful to meet with a career counselor if you are unsure of the direction you want to go but strongly want to make a change. Work that involves direct public contact can be very satisfying.

15. THURSDAY. Changeable. If you are planning a long-distance journey be sure to make the usual checks before setting off. Bad weather conditions could necessitate carrying more than the usual equipment that you keep on hand for emergency situations. Study a map in detail to ensure that you know exactly what route you are taking before you leave. So long as you prepared well for the trip, you should have a very enjoyable time. Both friends and children are likely to be good company if you have a long way to go. Even if you are traveling for business reasons, try to squeeze in some sightseeing on your own.

16. FRIDAY. Quiet. If you are involved in any type of legal dealings at the moment, no news should be considered good news. There may be no distinctively positive developments in your favor, but neither should there be negative aspects brewing behind the scenes. Be a little wary about what you say and to whom. It might cause some embarrassment both to you and to the other person if you indirectly reveal information that ought to be kept secret for a while. Your career prospects look quite healthy, although there may be no major developments taking place just yet. Try to be patient at least until the end of this year. Do not make any demands or issue any ultimatums.

17. SATURDAY. Cautious. This is a good day for working toward completing an assignment. If you are considering the possibility of becoming more involved with a group, give it some serious thought. It is possible that teamwork could help you achieve your career aims. Higher-ups are aware of what you are doing and the leadership you are exerting. A dispute over money could arise with a friend. If this is a recurring situation in your life, you may need to question the nature of some of your friendships, which is probably not a bad thing. Think about whether a certain person is only using you without giving you anything in return.

18. SUNDAY. Rewarding. An older person is the best one to confide in if you have a secret to tell or a problem to sort out. Or they may come to you for advice. While it may surprise you to be put in the position of being a confidant, it is probable that you can help each other. Do not worry about being guarded in relation to what you say. It is likely that the person in whom you are confiding is less easily shocked than you expect. Bringing your deeper feelings out into the open can free you from worry and stress, particularly if you are brooding at the moment. It does not help to bottle things up and let them grow out of all proportion.

19. MONDAY. Routine. Conditions favor doing some forward planning in relation to your career. You should be able to make good progress with ongoing projects. An authority figure who has previously questioned your motives is likely to be more agreeable now to your ideas and plans. Your relationship with the boss, in particular, ought to be easygoing and harmonious. Cancer people who have been temporarily out of work should make a point of applying for jobs advertised in yesterday's newspaper. The more contacts you make, the more opportunities you have to be successful. Upgrading your computer skills could be a definite plus.

20. TUESDAY. Challenging. You are entering a fresh phase where career matters are concerned. More responsibility could soon land on your shoulders. If you feel you now have enough or too much, start now to reorganize your life. Do not accept new tasks on top of your current workload if you think they will make your life too difficult. As a Cancer you are happiest when your domestic situation plays a fairly large part in your life. Taking on more responsibility at work could mean that you have to sacrifice some quality time at home, and this probably will not suit you very well. Consider requesting to work at home one day a week or to travel with your family.

21. WEDNESDAY. Successful. Friends and acquaintances could be more than usually helpful when it comes to furthering your personal aims. It is a good idea to discuss with them what you intend to achieve. They may suggest alternative resources or approaches that you have entirely overlooked. Try to keep out of the way of an associate who tends constantly to drain both your financial reserves and your energy. Try to find some new friends among your social circle who will be better company for you. Group activities should be stimulating, but do not stay out too late tonight.

22. THURSDAY. Tricky. This is a key day for trying to put your ideals into action and turn dreams into realities. Do not attempt to do this all on your own, however. You are almost certain to meet with greater success if you organize a team effort. Your social life ought to be a source of great inspiration and enjoyment at the moment. It may be necessary to maintain a professional profile when socializing with business colleagues, but avoid being perceived as a stuffed shirt. If you are making a visit to in-laws, here too you need to be more aware of creating a good impression without losing your sense of humor and fun. Be sure to dress appropriately for any get-together.

23. FRIDAY. Disconcerting. Time spent alone is your key to solving a recurring problem. Make the effort to look inward in order to examine your deeper thoughts. It may seem that the solution to a big problem is to run away from it, preferably as far as possible. However, it is likely to be much more fruitful to stick with the issue and try to view it from a totally different perspective. A friend who keeps finding excuses not to keep a date with you is hardly doing you any favor. If there seems to be an increasing lack of balance in this relationship, it might be time to come right out and talk about it openly.

24. SATURDAY. Confusing. You are in for a rather busy day. Although you may want more time to yourself than usual, neighbors or relatives are apt to drop by or telephone to chat and gossip. It is not in your Cancer nature to turn people away when they want help or desire to be friendly. However, to obtain some peace for yourself you have to put your foot down and be firm. Try not to be overly influenced by a person who holds strong opinions and is not adverse to speaking out. They may not support you in your aims and ambitions, but do not let their views have the effect of knocking you entirely off course. If browsing at yard sales or in a secondhand store, inspect an item before you buy.

25. SUNDAY. Sensitive. Although today should be more restful than yesterday, you have more energy to put into personal projects. Push ahead with these. If you are going to an important social function you should be able to shine as one of the main attractions. People are likely to be almost magnetically drawn to you. You should not have much problem making new friends. For single Cancers, an informal get-together can be a passport to meeting someone new and exciting. Do not get so caught up in conversations with friends that you spoil your chances to mingle with people you have not met.

26. MONDAY. Good. If possible, take a break from the usual back-to-work scene. Jump at an opportunity to travel in connection with your work. If you have hopes of advancing in your current job, this is a favorable time for pressing ahead. You should have little problem getting authority figures to cooperate with you. Good communication is your key to long-term success. If you have been out of touch with a certain relative, make an effort to get in touch now; there is likely to be something to gain from doing so. You can move ahead surprisingly quickly with personal aims so long as you put your mind to them and remain focused until satisfied with your results.

27. TUESDAY. Tranquil. Cancers are likely to be in an especially dreamy frame of mind. Look to the future and make some plans, particularly where your social life is concerned. There may be some conflict at home. As a Cancer you are seldom happy having to cope with domestic difficulties. You do not thrive in a restless atmosphere, particularly at home where you feel most sensitive. Do all that you can to try to resolve the problem as soon as possible, even if you do not like the idea of an open confrontation. If you are making plans to do some home repairs or redecorating, make sure that you are being practical and realistic. Buy the best quality materials you can afford.

28. WEDNESDAY. Variable. Money can unexpectedly fall into your lap. However, it can just as easily slip away through the fingers of someone wanting to borrow from you. Or you could end up footing someone else's bill. If you see such a situation potentially developing, nip it in the bud by subtly mentioning that you are short of funds, even if you are not. There is no reason you should have to put up with bad behavior from people who are supposed to be friends. Review a past situation to try to find clues for solving this current problem. If you will be walking a lot today, wear your most comfortable shoes even if they are not stylish.

29. THURSDAY. Frustrating. The same kind of money-related problems that dogged you in a friendship situation yesterday may still be around. You may not feel like talking about this openly, but doing so could actually help. So long as you aim to be diplomatic, you should achieve positive results. However, if you let your anger build up for a long time you risk losing your temper when you finally say something. Try to sort out what you want to achieve before putting your irritation into words. This can help you sound more rational and logical rather than simply appearing to be in a bad mood about the situation. Do not be too trusting; your judgment is not as good as usual.

30. FRIDAY. Easygoing. Relationships with friends are much more easygoing than they have been lately. This is a favorable time for getting back in touch with people you have not seen in a while. You tend to enjoy reunions, and this is a fine time to arrange one. A meeting or telephone conversation with a distant relative promises to be lively and interesting. Spend some time catching up on their news. Relatives are likely to respond warmly to a social invitation. Be sure to include children in your social planning. All in all you should feel that your life is improving and that your relationships contain more positive potential than ever before.

31. SATURDAY. Mixed. This is another positive day where your social life is concerned. Once again, it is worth your while to get in touch with people you have not seen in a while, if only to catch up on their news. You may not feel too comfortable at home due to a degree of restlessness and uncertainty. You may not be able to immediately pinpoint what is worrying you. Deep down, it may be a fear that you might never fulfill one of your most cherished goals. Have faith. What is worth achieving can take a long time to develop and mature. Begin now to lay a solid foundation.

NOVEMBER

1. SUNDAY. Mixed. Both business and social arrangements are under helpful influences. In fact, going out socially is apt to lead to making new business contacts; the two seem to go hand in hand. This is a key day for finishing off a project started a long time ago which has been neglected for quite some time. You are likely to make good progress if you focus on it exclusively. Once old factors are out of the way, you can look forward to some new beginnings. This is also true when it comes to odd jobs you have been meaning to get around to but, for one reason or another, have yet to even begin. If you need to purchase some supplies, buy the best quality you can afford. You may be able to borrow equipment from a friend.

2. MONDAY. Quiet. This is another good day for catching up on matters which have been neglected for longer than you care to think about. You can make especially significant headway with home-based projects. Your domestic life ought to be quiet and peaceful even if you are involved in do-it-yourself tasks. The phone can be your enemy if you choose to chat rather than work. You tend to feel more peaceful at the moment. It is said that your home reflects your inner self and the state of your emotions. This is very fitting for Cancer people, ruled by the Moon, related to domesticity. The more organized your home life, the more peaceful and in control you tend to feel. Gather together items you no longer want and donate them to a local thrift shop, or plan to have your own garage sale.

3. TUESDAY. Uncertain. You may feel unclear about what you intend to achieve. Avoid making any major decisions while you are in this uncertain frame of mind. You could feel awkward or embarrassed at a social gathering when you realize that you are unexpectedly short of money, perhaps because you left your credit cards at home. Do not ask a friend or acquaintance to pay your way; doing so could put this person in a financial bind of their own even though they may not say so. Trying to laugh off the situation may only make it worse. Act as responsibly as you can under the circumstances. Coming up with an excuse to leave the gathering may be your best approach.

4. WEDNESDAY. Good. If you have some time on your hands, this is an excellent day for taking a special trip. Conversations with relatives, co-workers, and neighbors are likely to be useful. Keep one foot planted in the past and one ready to stride into the future. Talking about your ideas and plans can help make them happen more quickly. For single Cancer people, a new romantic involvement could begin with someone from a foreign background or recently returned from abroad. You may think that your different backgrounds could be a problem, but it is likely that the differences between you will make the relationship more interesting and intriguing. A wedding or engagement now is starred.

5. THURSDAY. Manageable. Where work matters are concerned, your progress may be held up due to frequent distractions from outsiders. A telephone that rings all day long can be very irritating. Nevertheless, there is little you can do if you are waiting for an important call. An unexpected financial windfall is likely, perhaps a bonus for recent work or a rebate for a purchase made some time ago. If you have not done so in a while, consider going out to buy yourself a treat. Try also to put some of this money in the bank for upcoming holiday expenses. A compliment from a colleague is likely to boost your confidence and put a smile on your face. You have something to celebrate tonight.

6. FRIDAY. Disconcerting. Do not worry if you cannot get as much done as you hope today; there is always tomorrow. If you are going on a job interview, you may find that the position is not quite what you thought it was. However, even if the job turns out to be unsuitable, the experience of the interview should be helpful in itself. Short-term commitments have to be handled before more exciting plans related to the future. Later in the month you can pursue your other aims with equally single-minded devotion. It is important to get your priorities right now so that you do not leave yourself open to criticism from the boss or from a family member or even from your own conscience.

7. SATURDAY. Difficult. Home life should be smooth and easygoing. However, you may not be feeling too sure of yourself and may worry about anything and everything. Keep in mind that you are supersensitive just now. This may be partly due to lack of sleep, especially if you have been suffering from insomnia lately. The cause could also be related to a deep-seated problem that you have not yet faced. If there is something troubling you and it is starting to come to light, talking it over with an older family member or a trusted friend could help. By bottling up your feelings and pretending everything is all right you are likely to intensify your difficulties.

8. SUNDAY. Excellent. Your relationship with a loved one should be very happy again today. There is an extra romantic and creative aura surrounding you at the moment. This is a good time for bringing together various friends at a get-together in your home. Be sure to invite a new neighbor. Focus on making plans for the future. This is an especially favorable day for planning a vacation with your partner or with friends. A reunion could be a memorable turning point. Accept an invitation that comes your way. A very special celebration is now being organized; get in on the planning stages unless it is in your honor.

9. MONDAY. Unsettling. That nice, easygoing atmosphere that you have shared recently with your partner may be slightly marred today. You could argue about basic matters, particularly in relation to dividing up domestic chores. However, this is not likely to turn into a full-scale argument. Avoid going off on your own and feeling sorry for yourself. Your loved one may not have the patience to try to drag you out of your shell if you go too far into it. Expressing a secret fear is likely to help clear the air. Being a bit more confrontational in the business world is likely to benefit you and win you renewed respect. If you have a certain degree of power, exercise it without regrets.

10. TUESDAY. Challenging. This is an exciting day where friendship and group activities are concerned. If you are undecided about some social arrangements, consider attending a lecture or seminar on a subject that interests you. Going along with a friend could make it all the more interesting, giving you a chance to discuss it afterward. That old problem of lending or borrowing among friends may be still haunting you. If you are waiting for an item to be returned, ask about it directly. Do all that you can to avoid getting involved in a financial wrangle. It is in your best interests to seek professional guidance regarding personal or business investments. A new offering looks promising.

11. WEDNESDAY. Favorable. This is a favorable day for making a business deal or financial investment which seems sound. Your Cancer intuition is not going to steer you wrong. Whatever you invest your energy and resources in now will pay dividends in the long term. While yesterday you tended to take what a friend or acquaintance did to heart, today you can better understand their motives and see them as separate from yourself. More consideration of your feelings by this person is likely to help mend a rift in your relationship. You can also put a new friendship on a more stable footing by going out together for lunch or later in the evening.

12. THURSDAY. Stressful. You may yearn to get away from your usual surroundings for a breath of fresh air. The only problem is that you tend to want to run away from the world at the same time. Feeling vulnerable does not mean that you have to sacrifice an opportunity to get out and socialize. Talking problems over with someone you consider wise may help you to resolve them, or at least to put them into better perspective. Try to overcome feelings of inferiority, which are probably only temporary. Attend a social event you were invited to some time ago, even if you have to go alone. You are likely to have a good time if you relax and mingle.

13. FRIDAY. Fair. This is a favorable day for making a long-distance journey, especially if it is connected with your business life or with a potential new opportunity. If you want to broaden your social circle, try expanding your personal interests. Going to an exhibit or seminar could bring you into contact with people on the same wavelength as you. You should be able to make good progress with mental and creative endeavors. If you are studying for a test, it is a good idea to get together with a friend to quiz each other. Although there is no need to worry about this date, avoid taking any reckless step that might make it seem like a bad-luck day.

14. SATURDAY. Satisfactory. If you are thinking of asking a favor of an older person, discuss the matter in private. You may also want to turn to this person if you need to discuss a personal problem. Self-doubts and anxieties which have been creeping up on you can be reduced by talking about them in an honest, open manner. You may also find that putting on a bit of a show for the benefit of others helps to get you out of this doubting frame of mind. Other people probably have more faith in you than you realize and are apt to communicate this to you today. Accept a well-deserved compliment without downplaying your contributions. If you have not yet been recognized and rewarded, give yourself a pat on the back.

15. SUNDAY. Good. This is another day when you are likely to benefit from discussing private, personal matters with someone you consider older and wiser than you. There is little point keeping problems locked away in your heart when you can clear them up through discussion. Friends are likely to be an inspiration to you, motivating you to go forward with a key project about which you are beginning to have doubts. If you are offered the chance to go out of town for the day, take it. The change of scenery is likely to be good for you, as is the company. Someone new is coming into your life through a friend of a friend.

16. MONDAY. Deceptive. Doubts that have been plaguing you off and on all month may come back again after having been temporarily reduced with the help of other people. Be careful not to set too high standards for yourself at the moment. If you do, you are likely to be creating a recipe for your own lack of advancement. Life on the domestic scene may not be as easygoing as you would like. Disagreements with those you live with are likely to relate to matters of principle. Try not to get too carried away attempting to prove that your approach or methods are far superior to other people's. You are probably wasting your breath. Instead, try to reach an acceptable compromise with them, or at least agree to disagree.

17. TUESDAY. Variable. Club or society dues which need to be paid can come as an unexpected debt. A raise in cost which you were not notified about could annoy you. Rethink the situation. Perhaps the group is not really worth the cost not only in money but time. Then again, do not be too hasty to cancel your membership before really thinking the matter through. A good friend may be influential in helping you to make a difficult decision. This person may also encourage you to move forward with a new project which you keep promising to begin. Accept their support while it is available; later you are left to proceed on your own.

18. WEDNESDAY. Fortunate. You are entering a new phase where friendships are concerned, making this a turning point for all Cancer people. Associates who have not cooperated with you should be left to get on with their own problems. Those that have been helpful deserve some recognition and appreciation from you. Make this as public as possible, perhaps with a ceremony or a newsletter article. You are at the point where you can enter into an entirely new social circle if you wish to do so. This is also a favorable time for taking up a new interest. Going to evening classes or getting more involved in community charitable endeavors should be fulfilling.

19. THURSDAY. Fair. A lot of matters which have been bothering you because they have been neglected can be attended to today. Sometimes the small things in life get you down, but it is just these that can be tackled and handled now. You should start to feel that life is becoming more organized as you assume greater control over tricky situations. With a backlog of work out of the way, you can then pursue new, more interesting projects. If you need more storage space at home, try clearing out a closet. In the process you may find some useful items that you had forgotten about. Do not expect praise or even appreciation for your efforts; self-satisfaction is your reward.

20. FRIDAY. Confusing. You will probably prefer to be left alone, but your wishes are unlikely to come true. You have to deal with interruptions not only from the constantly ringing telephone but by various people who show up in person. Although life probably seemed a lot smoother yesterday than today, you can still make significant progress clearing up outstanding matters. Contact with key people is likely to be helpful. Set some time aside purely for yourself this evening. Relaxing at home is likely to do you a lot of good. Be sure to keep a secret that has been entrusted to you, although you may be tempted to tell all.

21. SATURDAY. Variable. This is another good day for sorting out routine matters and tying up loose ends. You should be able to complete one important, major task if you plod along and stick with it. Although other people may be short on praise and encouragement, you should feel satisfied with your efforts by the end of the day. If you are trying to get a new project off the ground, give yourself extra time. There is little point being impatient if you do not feel up to moving full steam ahead at the moment. Putting yourself under a lot of unnecessary pressure could lead to false starts or unsatisfactory results that take time to undo as well as redo.

22. SUNDAY. Excellent. This is a day for tending to your own concerns rather than other people's. As a Cancer you naturally mother those you care about, but you also need time to yourself. Take advantage of today's opportunity to get ahead with a personal project. Friends continue to be supportive when it comes to furthering your goals. For single Cancers, a romantic match with someone who has so far been just a friend could turn out to be magical. There is a special quality today that offers an opportunity to fulfill a long-held dream. Do not turn down an offer of assistance, especially a loan. Whatever you can accomplish on your own can be easier if you accept help.

23. MONDAY. Disquieting. Do not give up on an important personal plan even if you end up feeling tired. There is plenty of moral support being offered by those around you, especially neighbors and relatives. Keep pushing ahead. Try not to spend too much time alone; your imagination can wander too much. It is best to be around people who you know have their feet planted firmly on the ground. A social event may be fun but could leave you exhausted if you do not know when to stop. Decide at the beginning about your personal deadline. Do not demand an answer to a long-term question. You know what you want, but other people have not yet made up their minds.

24. TUESDAY. Fair. Friends continue to be supportive when you need them. On the job it is a good idea to get more involved in teamwork, which could save a lot of time in the long run. Once again, try to avoid spending too much time alone. You can make better progress when you work alongside others. Your financial situation is apt to take a turn for the better, perhaps unexpectedly. Make an effort to catch up on matters which are starting to become neglected once again. Try to maintain a balance between your personal and professional goals. A suggestion made to you tonight may be intriguing. Look into it without committing yourself quite yet.

25. WEDNESDAY. Good. This is another profitable day when it comes to making an effort to finish up ongoing projects. Behind-the-scenes financial developments are likely to work out in your favor. Unreasonable demands could be dropped now and are unlikely to be repeated, even though a similar set of circumstances could arise. If you are involved in joint financial dealings and negotiations, be sure that you unearth all the facts you need to know. A private meeting could help you clarify matters. Be guided by logic rather than emotions. You are most persuasive when you predetermine what you want and then go after it.

26. THURSDAY. Mixed. A financial transaction which has been the subject of a lot of discussion could be speeded up with an offer of help from a relative. Trying to get any time to yourself may be difficult with all the Thanksgiving festivity. Neighbors and relatives may insist on keeping you informed about every passing development. Frustrating as this may be, try not to let it show. An interesting opportunity could arise following a family discussion. Trust your instincts in relation to this, but avoid making an impulsive decision. Romance is in the air later in the day. That special person in your life has an idea you do not want to turn down.

27. FRIDAY. Manageable. This is a helpful day when it comes to making new contacts, particularly in the business world. You may be surprised by the number of people who are interested in the work you do or in the same hobby that you find so intriguing. In your social life you need to pick and choose your associates with care. Someone who is quiet and mysterious may make an impression on you even though you do not feel comfortable around them. If your instincts are telling you to back off, do not overrule them. However, if the opposite is true, find a way to spend more time together. It is unlikely that your behavior will be viewed as aggressive or insulting.

28. SATURDAY. Fair. Make more of an effort to get home-based projects completed; you are likely to achieve very good results. This is also a good time for beginning a new project. Do not be swayed by the opinions of someone who is sure they know better than you what would be suitable for you. You know that best of all, even though you might not readily admit it. Somebody you respect a lot who is quite influential in your life may be critical of your current priorities. While this person may have some good arguments, overall they may be unfair. Think why they are being so difficult; they could be jealous or could fear loss of control over you.

29. SUNDAY. Exciting. This is another good day for working on projects around the home. You are likely to be surprised by the progress you make. Time spent alone is apt to be most productive, especially if you have a problem on your mind which you want to sort out in private. As a Cancer you can find it quite difficult to voice your innermost feelings to others and appreciate a chance to express them in a private setting. Make the most of an opportunity to do so now. If you intend to invest in real estate, you could come across a pleasant property for sale. If you have already made an offer to buy a place, completion of the deal is likely today. Try to lock in your interest rate as soon as possible.

30. MONDAY. Pressured. Concentrate on concluding business deals and projects. If you are not happy with the way an arrangement is shaping up, it may be best to terminate it rather than enter into another round of negotiations. Your social invitations are likely to include one costly but exciting event. Assess realistically whether you can afford to go before making a commitment. At long last you should get the time alone that you have wanted. Make the most of this period to set new personal goals and resolve old problems. The deeper you experience your feelings, the clearer the answer to a problem will be.

DECEMBER

1. TUESDAY. Satisfactory. A social event which you have been looking forward to or end up attending at someone else's urging could turn out to be a lot more expensive than you anticipate. You may be starting to wish you had a second job. On the other hand, you are probably already beginning to feel in a festive mood. If you want to buy tickets for a charity affair, make the effort to interest friends in attending with you. This is a good time to visit people, particularly someone recovering from an illness. Even when you are shopping, you could bump into a friend or acquaintance and spend some time catching up on their news. Be extra considerate of a child's feelings.

2. WEDNESDAY. Tricky. Work matters should go fairly smoothly. The rewards for your current efforts as well as those in the recent past are likely to be very good. The boss will tend to be full of praise and may even put you in for a promotion. Be careful about what you do behind closed doors. You have a tendency to overdo where your social life is concerned. This could lead to an embarrassing scene and the need to make a formal apology. Although Christmas is still a few weeks away, you may already have begun celebrating. Try to slow down your social pace so that you have the required energy to focus on more important long-term matters.

3. THURSDAY. Variable. Hard work is likely to bring excellent rewards once again today. You could be asked to put in some overtime; the extra money could be too tempting to turn down. However, at least consider the responsibilities you currently have. Adding to these could create so many additional problems that you wind up deciding the additional pay is not worth it. Colleagues can be a distraction when you are trying to concentrate on urgent priorities. Try to make your situation clear without insulting them or anyone else. Your tendency to sometimes become very irate can be alienating to others. Try to keep a grip on your emotions and avoid an outburst.

4. FRIDAY. Slow. You may be in workaholic mode, but bear in mind that your best results usually come from plodding along rather than trying to race to the finish line. Being thorough in all of your endeavors is more important than getting through them in a hurry. You and your partner may not be getting along too well, probably because one of you wants to take more control in the relationship. If you are impatient to see things develop in a new direction, ask yourself why. It may not seem to matter to your partner what you do or when. Better communication could be the key to improving your mutual understanding. Start now by listening more than you talk.

5. SATURDAY. Good. Social events you are hosting or attending this weekend are likely to go with a swing. Single Cancers should make more of an effort to socialize in order to meet new people. A gathering at a neighbor's should not be missed. Married Cancer people can also benefit from getting out and about more as a couple. You are bound to have an enjoyable time together. If you have not made a start on Christmas shopping, get to it today. If you wait until the last minute there may be a very poor selection for you to choose from. Time spent alone is likely to be useful. Make a point of getting some extra sleep; an afternoon nap can be especially refreshing.

6. SUNDAY. Sensitive. You and your loved one may tend to bicker and argue about trivial matters such as the color scheme for a room in your home or what to have for dinner. This can all seem important at the time, but what is likely to be going on is that one of you is trying to get the upper hand in the relationship. You can also expect to argue over money or a recent purchase. Try to get away somewhere quiet by yourself rather than get worked up about all of this. Be wary of telling a friend or older family member about your current upset. You do not want or need their advice now.

7. MONDAY. Fair. Be careful about taking money out of your savings account or writing a check for a large sum before you have checked your financial situation. There is a possibility that a recent deposit has not yet cleared through your account. Once you have sorted this out, shopping can be worthwhile, particularly if you shop alone. A store which allows customers to defer payments until next year might be your best bet. If you want to avoid crowds, go early in the morning or during dinner time. Mail order can also be a useful way of shopping if you are short on time needed to trek around yourself. Spend some quality time tonight with a child or pet.

8. TUESDAY. Fortunate. Behind-the-scenes developments in relation to an investment are likely to work out in your favor. If you need to discuss money matters in order to get advice, an independent, private adviser may produce the best results. Pooling resources with a family member can allow you to splurge on party preparations or buy a special gift. Do not allow the practical and financial side of things to become a burden on any one person, and especially not on you. Domestic disputes can be smoothed over if everyone is prepared to be a little more patient with one another. Excitement is brewing at home but you will probably manage to remain calm and the voice of reason.

9. WEDNESDAY. Unsettling. A trip away from your usual surroundings could turn out to be disorienting. It may be hard to get back in the swing afterward. Give yourself time to settle back into your everyday routine. You have recently had a number of interesting encounters which you need to absorb. Time spent at home ought to be relaxing. If you want to host a party, make it a sedate one so that you do not have to worry about neighbors being bothered or possible damage to your home. There could be an undercurrent of jealousy that you have not even noticed involving someone of the opposite sex who is new on the scene.

10. THURSDAY. Disquieting. This is another day when traveling far from home or undertaking any new experience can throw you off course. Do not venture away from your usual base of operations unprepared. People at a distance are unlikely to be understanding or cooperative. You need to rest more than usual in order to recuperate fully. It is not so much that you are upset as that you feel bone-weary. If you travel by air, jet lag is apt to be the problem. Squeezing more rest into your schedule is likely to be a help. Try to avoid active socializing, even if a party seems appealing. You would be wiser to get some extra sleep.

11. FRIDAY. Stressful. The same theme of being tired and worn out is likely to continue today. If you are unable to take a day off, all you can do is try your best to keep going. Natural herbal remedies and strict attention to your diet could be helpful. If you are trying to adjust to a different time zone, it may be better to fit into the new schedule rather than try to work around it. Make an effort to catch up on your sleep, even if this means napping through your lunch hour. If you are unsure how to handle a financial situation, seek professional advice from someone who has been reliable in the past. Avoid buying anything from a telephone salesperson or a TV shopping show.

12. SATURDAY. Successful. Professional help in relation to money matters is likely to assist you in solving the problem of how best to manage an unexpected inheritance, prize, or bonus. Behind-the-scenes negotiations are favored at the moment, particularly if you are handling a large sum of money on behalf of a group. If you experience difficulties carrying a project through to completion, it is probably because you need to obtain additional relevant information. Try to be patient. There is little point rushing ahead into a wrong move or decision which you could live to regret. You should not find it too difficult to find a way around obstacles rather than having to attack them head-on. The subtle approach is favored.

13. SUNDAY. Mixed. If you need a favor from someone in a position of authority, it is best to ask in private. This is a useful day for sorting out personal problems, particularly if you have access to an older and wiser person who is willing to advise you. Conflicts at home are possible. A certain family member is in a hurry for your decision. You may feel like taking it easy even though there are important matters awaiting your attention. It is probably best to get vital issues out of the way first thing this morning. A partner who is not feeling well may need more support from you than usual. Their demands could test your patience, but your help will no doubt be appreciated. If you have already bought some holiday gifts, be sure they are well hidden.

14. MONDAY. Changeable. If you need help with practical tasks such as shopping or with problems of a more personal emotional nature, turn to friends for support. Someone who has stood by you for a long time is still likely to be there when you need them. It may surprise you if this person refuses to take you into their confidence. Do not push the issue; the other person could find it somewhat offensive if you do. Simply be appreciative of what is being done for you and available if the time comes when you can return the favor. Cancers who are celebrating the start of Hanukkah will enjoy being surrounded by close kin.

15. TUESDAY. Exciting. A social gathering to which a lot of people that you know are going should be well worth attending. You could also make some new contacts there. For single Cancers, a get-together could provide a chance to meet someone with whom a relationship could develop next year. In-laws or another older relative could suddenly decide to help you out with a financial situation without first discussing it with you. Although you may feel a bit proud or guilty about accepting money, it is being given freely and with the best of intentions. Allow yourself to accept it in the spirit that it is being given to you. Find a way to help those in your community who are less fortunate than you, perhaps by donating food or toys.

16. WEDNESDAY. Manageable. Make an effort to get outstanding work matters finished completely, especially if you want to leave early. A conversation with someone who is special to you is likely to be very intimate. In fact, if you are single and recently met someone who feels right for you, you could find yourself revealing all sorts of secrets. Talking about money matters should be low on your list of priorities. Do not reveal how much you make or how much you have in the bank right now. A close friend may find a way to show you how much you are appreciated. Try to be as gracious taking a compliment as you are in giving them.

17. THURSDAY. Fair. There is a need to keep a recently revealed secret to yourself, whether it is your own or someone else's. While you may be acting as a temporary sounding post for another person's injured feelings, you probably will not mind. In fact, this is apt to bring out your natural Cancer nurturing instincts. A degree of self-sacrifice is necessary in relation to money, particularly if you want to help out someone you love, such as a partner or an old friend. It could take you by surprise, but an authority figure may decide that you are the right person to confide in. Do not offer any specific advice unless requested to do so.

18. FRIDAY. Tranquil. The end of this workweek marks the beginning of a new phase. First of all, clear away loose ends hanging around in all the major areas of your life. Your compassion toward someone you visit in a hospital is likely to extend to other people in difficult situations, even those you have never met. You could find yourself looking for ways to make personal sacrifices in order to help those who are less fortunate than you. Your home life should be very peaceful. You are more settled in yourself and can move forward with a greater sense of purpose and dedication. Help is available if you need it.

19. SATURDAY. Calm. If life becomes any more straightforward you could soon feel it is getting boring. This is an excellent day for pushing ahead with personal matters in a calm, collected manner. Although you are not in the mood to compromise quite as much as usual, this should not have a negative effect on your relationships. If anything, people are likely to respect you more because of your inner strength and determination. If you have been going through a difficult period, perhaps looking after a sick relative, this is definitely a day for you to rest. You need to keep your spirits high in order to be of real help.

20. SUNDAY. Variable. This is another good day for pursuing personal goals. You may find, however, that older, influential people oppose you and try to block your way. They probably think that they are working in your best interests. It is up to you to dig in your heels and refuse to be budged. A discussion with a neighbor or relative is likely to help you move forward with what you want to achieve. Generous gestures are likely from people you see on an everyday basis. Make the most of the support that is offered. Try to ignore any self-doubts. Draw on your inner reserve of vitality and strength. Other people are tending to notice you more and more as you prove your abilities.

21. MONDAY. Confusing. Domestic issues or other problems which need immediate attention may collide with the personal plans you have in mind. This does not mean that you have to ignore your social life. Instead, try getting a few necessary tasks out of the way and then put the rest on hold until the weekend. This is not a good time for trying to sort out financial matters. Avoid making any new investment that is not very clear to you in terms of the benefits offered. It is best to wait at least a few days before making major decisions. The clearer your thoughts, the better the decision you are likely to make.

22. TUESDAY. Stressful. Try to get financial matters clarified. Unless you make this effort, you could worry about current spending all day. Your partner is likely to be a great help, offering not only support but practical help as well. You may be very busy, but take the time to let this person know how much you appreciate their encouragement. You need time to yourself also. Alone you can think through a problem which has many facets and find the best solution. Other people can help to some extent, but the ultimate answers and decisions have to come from you. Someone at a distance is hoping to hear from you; do not disappoint them.

23. WEDNESDAY. Good. You should be able to finalize a deal even if it is at the eleventh hour. This is helpful since you do not want to have to think about it during the holiday break. You should also have luck bringing personal financial negotiations to a close. If you have been considering an important investment, it is likely that you now feel certain about what to do. Time spent alone is again likely to be useful for resolving problems. Discussions behind closed doors can be very productive. Listen carefully to the advice of an expert, although you are likely to follow some of it and ignore the rest.

24. THURSDAY. Fair. You can get more involved in Christmas Eve celebrations this year because work matters are out of the way and your shopping is complete. Concentrate on having an enjoyable time. An office party is likely to go with a swing. You could end up being the center of attention for reasons you do not suspect beforehand. It is advisable, however, to carefully maintain your good reputation. Avoid blurting out a secret to someone who could potentially stir things up and do some damage. Also be on your best behavior when higher-ups are present.

25. FRIDAY. Merry Christmas! This is likely to be a sociable Christmas day. A gathering which includes neighbors and relatives is bound to be lively and enjoyable, especially if you do not get to spend much time with some of these people all year round. The only likely problem is your inability or unwillingness to tear yourself away from a conversation with one particular person. Someone might become a little jealous or even make a scene. Getting out to visit other people is also a good idea. This can help to relieve any late afternoon boredom which sets in after the presents have been opened and dinner served. Be extra attentive if you are driving or reading a map.

26. SATURDAY. Mixed. Your mind is likely to be on financial matters even though Christmas celebrations are still officially happening. You need to get a long-term problem settled once and for all. Try to formulate a plan, but at the same time do not lose out on enjoying the festive atmosphere around you. Home and family life should be easygoing. However, you may miss not having as much time to yourself as usual. Family members may not be very understanding if you choose to rush off alone. At least leave at a reasonable time, rather than the crack of dawn, and ask if anyone wants to accompany you for the day.

27. SUNDAY. Productive. You are restless to get things done. Matters which were not entirely sewn up before the holiday may start to nag at the back of your mind. Try to avoid stirring up trouble with an authority figure. If you attempt to contact an official you may not get the most welcome response. It is best to put personal worries on the shelf if you can. Your family needs you more than is obvious, or perhaps you have not been listening to what they have been saying. Go out of your way to spend time with a young family member. You do not have to spend a lot in order to have a good time.

28. MONDAY. Demanding. If you are spending time with family members you could find them rather sensitive. And if you are trying to complete work matters you can find it tough going. Whatever you do, you are going to have to pull your own weight and not rely on obtaining support. Your social life is likely to be enjoyable but could be a lot more expensive than you anticipate. For single Cancers, a love relationship could start to seem like too much effort. Rethink what you are looking for and whether your current partner is able to fulfill your needs.

29. TUESDAY. Pleasant. Your social life promises to be a lot more easygoing and enjoyable than it was yesterday. You may not have actually resolved anything, but at least for now you can relax and enjoy yourself. Just thinking along new lines may have a beneficial effect which lasts into the future. You cannot count on changing other people, but you can change your own expectations. Taking more initiative in a love relationship can improve the situation tremendously. At work you are on a creative curve at the moment. Make the most of this energy to get a new project under way and to make concrete plans for the future.

30. WEDNESDAY. Sensitive. Your work efforts are likely to be productive and lucrative. However, you need to guard against a tendency to get a bit carried away. You need to rest and reflect as much as work to achieve positive results. Do not make the mistake of rushing into a deal which could potentially backfire because you have not done enough research. Look into a product or company to find out more information before making any kind of significant commitment. Try to find time for yourself. With so much activity going on, you are undoubtedly tired but may not recognize the symptoms. Extra rest tonight will give you more energy for partying tomorrow.

31. THURSDAY. Satisfactory. This is another day when your efforts are likely to be very productive, perhaps surprisingly so. Authority figures are right behind you when it comes to supporting your most important goals. In fact, thanks to them you may achieve sudden success. You again should take life easy. You need to recharge your batteries. A number of social invitations may be enticing, but choose carefully among them. Party hopping is apt to wear you out long before others are ready to call it a night. If you make any resolutions for the new year, keep them to yourself unless you want the added pressure of satisfying other people.

CANCER
NOVEMBER–DECEMBER 1997

November 1997

1. SATURDAY. Easygoing. This is a romantic day for both married and single Cancers. All close relationships have a special quality, whether you are lovers or not. If you are involved with a love partner, expect today to be truly magical. With little effort you could get to meet someone magnetic and charismatic with whom you could hit it off right away; a new romantic affair is beginning. For some Cancers the same heightened emotions can occur with work or with a hobby. You are apt to become engrossed in creative endeavors, especially if you spend time with someone you find inspiring on a variety of levels.

2. SUNDAY. Variable. This is an excellent day for burying your head in a good novel or murder mystery. The dark side of life appeals to you through fiction. It should be fun to lose yourself in the fantasy world that a good book creates. You have ample energy at the moment and may feel like handling practical tasks. If you have been intending to clean closets or the attic at home, get down to it today. You may uncover a few items which you thought were lost forever. Unexpected guests could interrupt your schedule, but practical tasks can wait; the guests are likely to be considerably more exciting.

3. MONDAY. Calm. You are naturally very imaginative, but do not worry if you find yourself lacking inspiration today. This is a time for concentrating on the real world and on practical, routine matters. You can make a lot of progress if you put your mind to completing a series of tasks. You should be able to concentrate on jobs that involve intricate details. If you are temporarily out of work, this is a good time for elaborating on your resume, or for condensing it if it is too lengthy. Be industrious about sending out job applications and following up on previous employment interviews.

4. TUESDAY. Pleasant. Conditions are excellent for all types of interviews. Your outgoing manner is sure to create a good impression. Attention to detail where your appearance is concerned could swing a situation in your favor, especially if you are competing with many other applicants. You may feel a little lazy when it comes to work matters. It is better for you to be directly involved with people rather than pushing papers. At a minimum, try to achieve a balance between the two. If you have been avoiding filing chores, try to get paperwork properly organized now. You are more methodical than usual.

5. WEDNESDAY. Mixed. This promises to be a good day, on the whole, for relationship matters. Your loved one is especially romantic. Single Cancers could meet somebody very attractive. One difficulty, however, is that you are likely to experience a power struggle in a partnership. You may feel pressured in some way by the other person, who wants to minimize your choices. At the moment you are good at compromising, but do not do so to the extent that you give up your own desires entirely. Socially you may be encouraged to spend more money than you intend. Pay your own way only unless you want to treat someone.

6. THURSDAY. Fair. This is a good day for relationships. If you are unattached, a neighbor could introduce you to somebody you instantly like. It is also a favorable time for a heart-to-heart talk with a loved one. Be aware that you tend to see partners through rose-colored glasses. There could be some deception on the other person's part that escapes your notice, at least at first. A business proposition could be very exciting. However, do not make a major commitment until you have a chance to think things through carefully. You could be out of your depth at work simply because there is so much going on.

7. FRIDAY. Useful. Concentrate on sorting out joint financial matters. The time is right for asserting your authority. Although you need to meet others halfway, you should be able to settle matters very much on your own terms. The support and encouragement of an experienced person could be very helpful. If you need advice on investments, turn to a traditional institution; such help will be more sound than a friend's off-the-cuff advice. Aim for a safe rather than risky investment. If you have been avoiding dealing with tax or insurance issues, now is the time to act. Officials and other authority figures are likely to be sympathetic and straightforward.

8. SATURDAY. Changeable. Cancers should have a high level of physical and mental energy. This is a good time for catching up with old friends, especially if you have been out of touch lately. Other people have been trying unsuccessfully to reach you. Respond to all your telephone messages. If a business deal or merger is in the offing, make careful preparations. Go over details thoroughly, especially if a contract needs to be signed. A long-distance trip could be plagued with problems, mostly involving transportation breakdowns. Also be sure to plan your route in sufficient detail.

9. SUNDAY. Good. This is a good day for clearing out drawers, closets, or the garage. Cancers usually find it confusing to have too much clutter around. Get rid of items you are never likely to use that are just taking up valuable space. Spiritual matters may interest you more than usual. This is a favorable time for participating with like-minded people interested in the same subjects that appeal to you. It is important to take practical steps to expand your horizons. Look for ways to add more excitement to your life, excitement that is of your own making. Becoming engrossed in a creative venture is one solution.

10. MONDAY. Stressful. Developments in a love relationship should make you optimistic. If you are thinking of beginning a project, or of trying something new, involve a partner or close friend. They can give you the courage you need to get started. Long-distance travel could lead to a romantic meeting, but be wary of someone who seems too good to be true. You could experience troubles at work as the day progresses. Your authority may be challenged by someone who believes you should treat them as an equal. Aim to be direct about the reality of the situation, even if this necessitates acting against your own nature.

11. TUESDAY. Fair. Career matters are promising at the moment. If you are hoping for a pay raise you will probably get it. In an interview situation, speak openly about money matters and job benefits. There may be extra perks to the job which make it more appealing, but these might not be made obvious right away. Where money matters in general are concerned, be sure to observe protocol. If you have an outstanding loan, now is the time to pay up. Not honoring your agreement could work against you in the future. You are likely to be kept busy and on the go. Do not be surprised if the telephone does not stop ringing; you are in demand.

12. WEDNESDAY. Deceptive. Often over recent months you have not known where you stand with partners and even with friends. This is partly because the nature of your relationships is changing. Such turmoil does not make you very secure. Be wary of involved excuses offered by someone close to you. The problem about lies from the lips of a person you like or love is that you want to believe them. However, you would be foolish to kid yourself. If you think that something peculiar is going on, talk about it. Sooner or later you have to face the music. The longer you postpone the inevitable, the harder it will be.

13. THURSDAY. Changeable. Certain friends and acquaintances are likely to be very good to you. Accept a social invitation; you should have an enjoyable time. However, be sure that you know in advance what expenses might be involved before making a commitment. Otherwise you could be in for a shock. You may also find yourself roped into lending cash to someone or even footing an entire bill for them. You may not really mind because you are a caring person, but you do not want to be taken advantage of. This incident could leave a bad taste in your mouth. Try to be honest and open about your feelings rather than harboring resentment.

14. FRIDAY. Good. There could be some confusion in one of your friendships. This is likely to involve the other person feeling amorous toward you. On one level this is flattering, but on another it is potentially destructive. Your friendship might be at stake if you become involved. You may also wonder what degree of friendship has been there all this time. This is definitely a day for weighing your options carefully. If you are involved in an ongoing relationship, your partner may make a romantic gesture. If you have had your doubts about the affair lately, these should be put to rest, although you may wonder if this is temporary.

15. SATURDAY. Variable. Your day is likely to be extremely busy. Although it is the weekend, you may feel that there is no chance to rest unless you insist on it. This is what you need to do; otherwise you are likely to end up exhausted. You may be putting your health at risk by doing too much. Also try to keep your diet well balanced. Too much of the wrong kinds of foods could be a problem. It is better to concentrate on clearing out toxins from your system rather than adding to them. Ethnic cuisine may be tempting, but do not overindulge. Youngsters will feature in the activities of the day. Keep a watchful, protective eye.

16. SUNDAY. Quiet. If you overdid in any area of life yesterday, this is definitely a day for relaxing, resting, and generally recharging your batteries. Follow your instincts in this respect. If you enjoy meditation, devote extra time to it today. You could experience some useful insights. This is also a time for healing, particularly if recent emotional experiences have been draining. Although you may not feel on top of the world, at least you should find the peace you seek. Without distractions from the outside world you can restore your inner harmony. Listening to light music could be very soothing.

17. MONDAY. Fair. People may get in the way of your plans. One obstacle is needing to spend time being pleasant to certain individuals. The other is having to deal with those who are being challenging and difficult. This does not mean that you will achieve nothing. It is just a matter of performing a balancing act. Partners are the main problem. Your working life should be easier to handle. Providing the channels of communication are clear, you ought to make significant progress. You can rely on colleagues to support you. In addition, more than one lucky break is coming your way.

18. TUESDAY. Easygoing. This is the perfect day for pushing forward with your personal plans. You have ample drive and initiative. If you are anxious to begin a business enterprise, you can use your own skills and talents to lucrative ends. Extra attention to your appearance can pay off in a number of ways. This is a good time to add a new suit to your wardrobe or to try a new hair style. First impressions are very important. If you are going for a job interview, make sure that your appearance is immaculate. Your current desire for action means that you are on the go from dawn till dusk, or later. You should be pleased with your progress.

19. WEDNESDAY. Mixed. Work is intensive and demanding, but you should eventually receive just rewards for your efforts. If you are considering new investment options, be sure to look into several different alternatives. The more thorough your research, the more likely you will find the right one for you. Salespeople could tempt you with special offers which they claim are only available for a limited period of time. These may look good, but do not be overly influenced by the time pressure factor. A love relationship should be very romantic. A candlelit dinner for two could be the prelude to a memorable evening.

20. THURSDAY. Changeable. You may be advised to invest in a proposition which looks hopeful for the future. However, you should not put all of your eggs in one basket. If the stakes are too high, you might be better off avoiding this scheme altogether. Tried-and-tested mutual funds and old-fashioned financial institutions are your best bet. You should receive plenty of encouragement at work. If you are temporarily out of work, a job opportunity could come your way that offers financial rewards truly reflective of what you have to offer. A discussion with a colleague could put you on the right track.

21. FRIDAY. Disquieting. It may seem that other people are treating a certain situation with an inappropriate lack of seriousness. You may also sense a lack of respect for matters which are important to you. Try not to take things too personally. Even if others are not supportive, you can still push ahead with what you believe is best for you. Where money matters are concerned, beware of excessive spending. Your social life may be fun, but costly as well. Get-rich-quick schemes abound at the moment. None is sufficiently sound to jump into. If you take a wild gamble you will probably regret it.

22. SATURDAY. Variable. This is a good weekend to visit other people. Activities which involve your partner should be especially rewarding and enjoyable. If you are single, accept an invitation to a local function. Conditions are excellent for enlarging your circle of friends and acquaintances. This is the ideal way to meet somebody new in the longer term. Work tasks could be a chore. There is so much to be done that routine tasks may spill over into your leisure time. Although partners can be challenging, they can also be the impetus behind your breaking away from the ordinary and reaching a higher level.

23. SUNDAY. Confusing. A colleague could call to discuss a flap about work matters. You may not know what you are expected to do. If you are told to take certain action, you most likely will object, and quite rightly. This is the weekend, and you ought to have the chance to switch off from working life and pursue your own pleasures. While running routine errands you may bump into people whose company you enjoy along the way. Catch up on the latest news and gossip. A visit from someone less than stimulating could be irritating. Find an excuse to send them on their way quickly.

24. MONDAY. Good. If you are struggling to get things done at work, turn to people who you know are reliable. They are willing to help you out of a sticky spot. At home, family or household members could be the extra pair of hands you need when it comes to trying to complete practical tasks or routine matters. If you are seeking new work, use tried-and-tested methods. An application to a traditional institution or family-type business is likely to be most successful. You may have unexpected guests this evening but, unlike yesterday, they will be welcome. Try to take time out to relax and unwind at the end of the day.

25. TUESDAY. Unsettling. There could be squabbles with your partner about domestic or family matters. It would not be wise to try to bring your loved one and your family together at the moment, even if they usually get along well. You may sense a heavy air of disapproval from someone who is usually understanding. If you are unattached, you may bump into a former partner in one of your frequent haunts. The meeting may not be very cordial. Keep a low profile to save embarrassment. If you decide to stay home this evening, your own company is probably the best. This is a good time for short-term financial planning and bill paying.

26. WEDNESDAY. Sensitive. Discussions with family or household members about routine issues should be helpful. This is a favorable time for whirlwind cleaning and other home tasks, especially if you are hosting a Thanksgiving Day party tomorrow. If a parent or child seeks advice, take the time to lend a listening ear. It is important for other people to be able to turn to you, particularly with emotional dilemmas. Your naturally protective Cancer nature allows you to mother even your older friends. Partners are more of a handful; nothing you do seems right to them now. Exactly what is expected of you is not yet clear.

27. THURSDAY. Cautious. A romantic relationship could become intense even though you would be happier for things to remain lighthearted. A lover is about to spring a few surprises on you. Jealousy could be a major problem, although it is not necessarily going to be obvious. You may suddenly feel that you do not really know the other person. Try to remove yourself from an uncomfortable situation. If you are single, you may want to get in touch with someone you find exciting. However, this may also be someone you found to be emotionally damaging to you in the past. Be careful. It might be better to sit tight and put up with a temporary measure of loneliness.

28. FRIDAY. Enjoyable. Romance should be much calmer and loving. A partner may feel bad about recent words or actions and try to make up for it with a pleasant gesture. If you are single, today is much better than yesterday for reaching out to others. Somebody new who you find attractive could appear on the scene. Key places for meeting prospective new partners are music and dance venues. If you are planning to shop for clothing or household articles, take a friend along with you. A second opinion is likely to come in handy. You have more than one reason to feel happy today.

29. SATURDAY. Variable. Focus on routine tasks, but be careful not to wear yourself down with them. There is a tendency to get so involved that you do not move from the same spot. You could get buried under mountains of paperwork if you are not careful. Nevertheless, this is a good time for tackling tiresome tasks such as filling out government forms or filing for insurance reimbursement. If you have recently taken out a new insurance policy, read the details carefully. This is a favorable day for all new beginnings, but a more open attitude is necessary before you can successfully start anything new.

30. SUNDAY. Successful. A social event that you attend may have a rather formal air. You could be introduced to somebody influential, who may be instrumental in helping you find new work or get a better job. Turn to an older friend for help with a tricky practical task that you are struggling to complete. If you find yourself at loose ends, dig out paperwork you have neglected. Conditions are excellent for settling accounts. If you owe money, make an effort to pay it back now; you will feel better for having done so. If someone owes you, tactfully remind them of their obligation.

December 1997

1. MONDAY. Productive. This is an excellent day for activities in conjunction with a partner, close colleague, or good friend. You are likely to make better progress sharing tasks than if you each go it alone. In addition, it is more fun to have someone else involved. Conversations with other people should be very stimulating and get you thinking along new lines. Single Cancer people are likely to be the center of attention. You are especially attractive to members of the opposite sex at the moment. Keep your calendar handy; it is likely to get filled up quickly. The period is auspicious for joining a prestigious club.

2. TUESDAY. Stressful. You have to put a lot of physical effort into current tasks in order to achieve what you want. You could find that your emotions are taxed because you have to negotiate everything you want to do. It is necessary to proceed through the correct channels. If you avoid following protocol, you could end up back where you started. Your approach needs to be more structured than you might like. You want to proceed full speed ahead, without much forethought. However, this goes against your naturally cautious Cancer nature and, while refreshing, may not be good for you. A public revelation about a certain involvement could be embarrassing.

3. WEDNESDAY. Difficult. You may feel like only being around people you know you can trust and confide in, without any judgments being passed. Colleagues tend to be unreliable and chaotic. You do not need other people rocking your boat. You may be hurt by the actions of someone with whom you usually feel comfortable. You could be reading too much into the situation because you are emotionally vulnerable at the moment. Time spent by yourself can be fruitful, giving you a chance to collect your thoughts. You need other people to be compassionate and understanding, but some are bound to be insensitive.

4. THURSDAY. Fair. An exciting business or investment opportunity is likely to arise. It is not in your nature to make snap decisions when the matter in question is important, especially if it involves money. However, because you could feel that this is too good an opportunity to miss, you are apt to do the opposite of what you would usually do. Providing you go over the details thoroughly, this opportunity should turn out in your favor. Seeking the advice of someone with more experience in such matters is a good idea. Counsel from a reliable source can put your mind at ease. This is a fine day for sorting out tax matters and complicated medical bills.

5. FRIDAY. Good. Financial and business issues dominate the day to a large extent. This is a good time for solving problems that have been nagging at you. You may be getting involved in matters which make you feel out of your depth. For this reason it is wise to seek the opinions and advice of people who know more than you do. Work matters ought to proceed without a hitch. Colleagues and higher-ups have a lot of respect for you. If you should need assistance or guidance, it is there for the asking. Do not struggle on alone. You should feel good as far as your health is concerned, but it will be especially important to stay on your regimen in this season of festivities.

6. SATURDAY. Disquieting. You may attempt to run before you can walk where practical matters are concerned. Do not begin anything that you may not be able to finish; it will only frustrate you. Although you could be planning a long trip or exciting venture, you may not be physically up to it right now. If you have any doubts about it, postpone making a decision until another time. Be careful about the choices you make. It is possible that you will commit an error of judgment. This is most pertinent when it comes to meeting new people. Somebody who appears to be arrogant or opinionated may actually not know what is going on.

7. SUNDAY. Pleasant. This is a much better day than yesterday for long-distance travel and also for new ventures. The company of someone you feel at one with should be pleasing. There could be some confusion, however, about what the other person really wants to do. Make sure that you consult together before making firm plans. Involvement in religious and spiritual events should bring you close to other people. If you are romantically unattached, you could meet somebody special under these circumstances, even though you might not expect to do so. Cultural pursuits are also favored. A trip to a museum, art gallery, or theater should be inspiring.

8. MONDAY. Deceptive. You may start the day feeling that you need to get a greater grip on life generally. It can be difficult to do so at work, since this will involve having to direct and encourage other people to get things moving. You are likely to be thwarted because they lack concentration or commitment. Much of the burden is on you to ensure that responsibilities are carried out. You do not have the undivided support of staff and colleagues at your disposal. If you are out of work, this is a good day for an interview. You can create a good impression if you get to talk with the decision maker.

9. TUESDAY. Fair. Today promises to be much more successful where work endeavors are concerned. Staff and colleagues are willing to put in more effort. You should not feel that life is an uphill struggle. An excellent deal could be finalized with a new client, involving signing a contract. Partners may impinge on your professional life more than you like. It might be necessary to devote some time to sorting out personal issues. While you cannot be entirely selfish at work, whatever efforts you are making will be appreciated. Responsibility is a key word at the moment. Others are relying on you.

10. WEDNESDAY. Variable. This is a good day for discussing your hopes and wishes with your loved one. It is important to establish what plans you intend to make, both together and in your separate spheres. The difficulties you may have experienced with a partner yesterday should evaporate now. You are much more able to negotiate on reasonable terms. If you are seeing a former partner, money questions could come up unexpectedly. You may need to get together in order to discuss something that will ultimately benefit you. Be a little suspicious, however. This person's motives are not entirely unselfish by any means.

11. THURSDAY. Mixed. Yesterday the emphasis was on discussion with a partner. Today it is much more on putting into action your mutual plans and wishes. On the job you can achieve a lot by working hand in hand with a competent colleague. What could be a problem in your relationship is another person's need to be in charge. This might seem like something that would be of advantage to you. However, you could sense that the power balance is not right if you are the one doing all the grunt work. You may suspect that you are being manipulated, and you are probably right. It is vital that you discuss exactly what you want.

12. FRIDAY. Changeable. You could easily begin the day feeling flustered and out of sorts. There is probably too much to do at work. Or, if you are temporarily out of work, the pressure to be doing something about it could intensify. However, you may not be feeling either physically or emotionally up to much today. In fact, you may long to stay in bed, or at least at home. A lucky break is likely to reverse your mood. You could receive good news in the mail, or a most welcome phone call letting you know about a stock split or an extra dividend on an investment. Benefits due you may be more than you are anticipating. The achievement of a youngster will make Cancer parents very proud.

13. SATURDAY. Misleading. Today is the reverse of yesterday, with conditions good at first but deteriorating later. Do not become too worried. The advice of someone older and caring could be extremely helpful. If you are confused at the moment, spend time with people who seem to have their lives in order. You should feel safe and secure, rather than inferior or judged negatively by them. One problem as the day progresses is that additional responsibilities are heaped on your shoulders when all you want to do is rest and relax. Tonight's Full Moon can make many Cancers restless and unable to fall asleep.

14. SUNDAY. Demanding. This is one of those days when you cannot seem to get rid of annoying people. There is likely to be a call or visit from somebody hoping to sell you a service. They could make you feel defensive even though their reasons are not justified. What you want most of all is to be left to your own devices. There are times when Cancer people need to climb into a shell and hide away. Because this is one of those days, you would be wise to lock the doors, muffle the telephone, and shut yourself off from outside distractions. A good book is your best companion tonight.

15. MONDAY. Slow. You are raring to go, having had sufficient rest, peace, and quiet yesterday. It may not be easy to carry out your personal plans, however. Professional matters are likely to get in the way. There is a lot of red tape to cut through. What you imagined to be a simple task could turn out to be a major hassle. Nevertheless, you can achieve what you set out to do by making the effort to go through proper channels. Things could take a lot longer than you anticipate. Try to be patient, even if you feel held back on all fronts. Your ruler, the Moon, now in your sign of Cancer gives rise to changeable moods.

16. TUESDAY. Confusing. Other people can be confusing due to their behavior. You may not know if you are coming or going in one particular partnership. The other person could become close-mouthed if you attempt to clarify matters. It may seem like a no-win situation. If you are giving directions or instructions, go into a lot of detail. Otherwise you could discover later that you have been entirely misunderstood. This is not a good day for financial matters. Money that is owed to you could be delayed. The true nature of a business deal may not be clear. Do not make any hasty commitments.

17. WEDNESDAY. Changeable. Financial matters are less confusing than they were yesterday. Nevertheless, you are likely to be faced with a situation you have not anticipated. The terms of a business deal could be turned around. At least you should start to see what is really involved. As the day progresses you should be moving to more stable ground. Business matters require structure if they are to be successful. Traditional sources of funding are much more reliable and fruitful than those you consider to be rather unusual or underhanded. Disruptions to your routine early in the day will finally abate and should not affect your overall output.

18. THURSDAY. Variable. Do not expect to make a quick return on recent investments. This is not a good day for taking risks of any variety. You are apt to be the loser even if you feel that you could be on a winning streak. Effective communication should work wonders in the job. Colleagues are cooperative, although you need to make objectives clear. If you are currently seeking work, this is a favorable day for interviews. You can get by with living by your wits. However, if you embellish what you say with details that are not strictly true, you could end up creating problems where none exist.

19. FRIDAY. Disquieting. Correspondence received today may be rather upsetting. Do not be surprised if you receive a letter containing a threat or bitter comments. Somebody is angry about your personal behavior or that of someone in your company. You may not be at fault at all. However, if you feel that some of the points are justified, attempt to make amends. If this is not the case, seek advice from a levelheaded colleague or friend. Retaliation is not your best bet. The less contact you have, the less likely you are to receive any further communications of this nature. Do not put any promises in writing. Difficulties in a service group make you suspect that not everyone's motives are charitable.

20. SATURDAY. Misleading. There could be disagreements between you and your associates about basic issues. If you are planning to go on a journey, discuss the route and timing well beforehand. Otherwise you may argue once you reach your destination. This is not a particularly good day for trying to contact friends you may have neglected. You could get a frosty reception from them. It may be that you are seen to be intruding, or that you are after something. You know your own motives, but other people are apt to jump to conclusions. Make time to get out for some physical activity to reduce your stress level.

21. SUNDAY. Fair. Today is much better than the past few days for communicating with people. Partners, in particular, should be charming and inspiring. Somebody special cares a great deal about you. It is ideal if you can go out together socially. However, your batteries may start to wear down as the day progresses. This is the point at which you want to go home, although your partner is still in the socials wing. You might have to go your separate ways. You may also need to apply yourself to some outstanding paperwork, such as paying bills or finally sending off holiday greetings.

22. MONDAY. Demanding. Social events centered around your home ought to be fun. There is excitement in the air, and the rapport between family members is likely to be electric. You could have difficulties with an older person, however, perhaps a parent or in-law who does not choose to join in. Do not try to force them. However, you can also have problems if you attempt to leave this person entirely alone. Financial matters require research and concentration. Do not make snap decisions regarding your own money or joint funds. Partners could expect more than you are willing to give, either emotionally or physically. Say no in a tactful manner.

23. TUESDAY. Optimistic. Jokes and general conviviality are flowing. This is an excellent time for a family get-together. If you are in the process of trying to buy a new home or move into an apartment, a deal made today should turn out very much in your favor. You could benefit from a number of hidden extras, such as free appliances or landscaping. If you are job hunting, flex time might be included as an employment incentive. Any financial investment made now is promising. Do not turn down an offer which seems too good to be true; just ask for more detailed information. You could be pleasantly reassured.

24. WEDNESDAY. Variable. One-to-one relationships are especial today. A love partnership has a very romantic aura. Your partner could make a special dream come true for you. One worry at the moment is money. The holiday festivities can be extremely costly. Even if you have spent too much on gifts and your social life, try not to go to the opposite extreme. If you have spent a lot on creating tomorrow's grand event, you may as well enjoy it and tonight as well. This time of Hanukkah and Christmas Eve can be especially wonderful for youngsters. A party may start happily, but there could be a difficult scene later as evening proceeds.

25. THURSDAY. MERRY CHRISTMAS! There could be tension in the air because everyone is hyped up with seasonal cheer. The main thing for you to guard against is a tendency to overindulge. Too much drink and food could leave you feeling out of sorts. The last thing you need is to miss out on the fun. As long as you pay attention to your regimen and moderate your own intake, you should have a very enjoyable time. Be sure to express thanks for the gifts that you receive, even if they are wrong for you or there are a few that do not really suit you. You can always exchange them at a later time. Remember, it is the thought that counts.

26. FRIDAY. Fair. Cancer singles ought to accept a party invitation. It is likely that you will meet someone you really get along with well. If you are already involved in a love relationship, this is an excellent time for discussing mutual plans. If you are entertaining, you can expect to be rushed off your feet trying to get everything done and keep everyone happy. There is a wonderful air of excitement. Your guests are sure to appreciate your efforts and have a good time. Be careful that you do not let slip a secret or confidence, however tempting it may be to do so.

27. SATURDAY. Reassuring. If you have been worrying about career matters, your mind should be put at ease now. A helpful offer could come your way. Practical tasks may seem like a hassle, but you have plenty of help around. Turn to older or more knowledgeable people for advice and practical assistance. This is a good day for writing letters, especially to distant people you have not had much contact with lately. Through one person in particular life may start to open up in fabulous new directions. News received now is likely to be encouraging. There could be an announcement which makes you feel justifiably optimistic about the future.

28. SUNDAY. Good. You may feel quite restless. This is a good time to go out shopping, especially at sales that have already begun. You could find several bargains. There may be excellent deals available on major purchases such as furniture. This is also a time when prosperous business opportunities could arise. You may have to invest quite a bit of money initially, and there is a risk factor involved. However, your stake is likely to pay off over time. Because you are not reckless by nature, you may not feel comfortable about risky ventures. However, if you and several associates are involved, the risks are spread.

29. MONDAY. Difficult. One of your closest relationships is going through a difficult period. Perhaps both of you want entirely different things. You may not know how to broach this issue without causing offense. The usual Cancer tactic is to drop a lot of heavy hints, or else to signify that something is wrong through moodiness. Being offhand with your partner is not going to work because the situation is awkward for both of you. You could simply wind up avoiding each other and the issues you ought to be discussing. Do not put up an emotional brick wall. Even with today's New Moon, which encourages openness and fresh starts, you may feel the relationship is approaching an ending rather than a new beginning.

30. TUESDAY. Deceptive. You are apt to experience increased awkwardness with a partner or close friend until you are both able to speak honestly with each other. At the moment this does not look very likely. You both have things to hide, and neither of you is clear about exactly what you want. This is likely to be an uncomfortable period. Do not give up, however, until you have clarified the issues in your own mind. Unattached Cancers should be wary of getting involved with someone you instinctively have doubts about. Your negative suspicions could be quite accurate, but first try to discover factual evidence.

31. WEDNESDAY. Exciting. It will be difficult for anyone to keep you down today. You have so much energy bubbling inside that you have to get out and be part of all that is going on. Today is excellent for clearing away old baggage so that you are ready to welcome in the New Year. You are coming to the end of a chapter. If a relationship finishes now, it should be on good terms unless the end is very sudden. New opportunities are opening up for you and life looks a lot more interesting. You have plenty to feel optimistic about as your usher in 1998 with the fanfare it deserves.

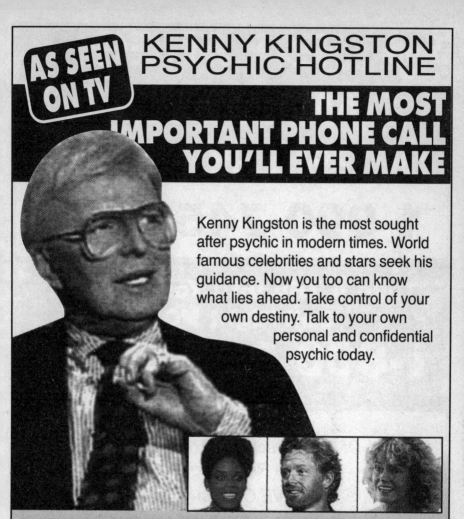

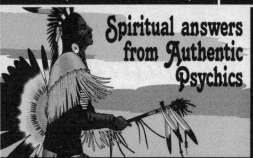

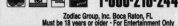